New Playwork

Blackburn
College

New Playwork

Play and Care for Children 4–16
Fourth Edition

Annie Davy & Jane Gallagher

THOMSON

Australia • Canada • Mexico • Singapore • Spain • United Kingdom • United States

THOMSON
™

New Playwork
Annie Davy and Jane Gallagher

Publishing Director	**Commissioning Editor**	**Editorial Assistant**
John Yates	Lib Wright	Tom Rennie
Production Editor	**Manufacturing Manager**	**Marketing Manager**
Sonia Pati	Helen Mason	Natasha Giraudel
Typesetter	**Production Controller**	**Cover Design Controller**
Tek-Art, Croydon	Maeve Healy	Jackie Wrout
Cover Design	**Text Design**	**Printer**
Jackie Wrout	Design Deluxe, Bath, UK	Zrinski d.d., Croatia

Contents

Foreword

One of the principles of playwork says: 'The role of the playworker is to support all children and young people in the creation of a space in which they can play.' Perhaps uniquely, playwork seeks to be of service to the world of the child; to be invited into that world purely to help give it substance and space. The playworker does not have an agenda for children other than knowing that they will, given half a chance, want to play. It is the job of the playworker to co-create with children the environments – physical, social, cultural and emotional – for that simple (and infinitely sophisticated) thing to happen.

I haven't yet met a playworker who doesn't genuinely love their job; although, being an unpretentious lot, they generally just get on with it. Children at play are closest to being themselves than in just about anything else they do. If you can make a living at enabling that, why would you want to do anything else? It's certainly the most fun I ever had at work.

Not that making a living at it is especially easy: playwork still has a long way to go before it is afforded the professional status and value that it deserves. Play in general has been widely overlooked for decades. The policy agenda for children has been, and to a great extent still is, dominated by issues of their protection, education for future employment and diversion from criminality. Fair enough. But all of this misses the simple need of children to be children, which needs the space and opportunity currently denied to very many of them.

The tide may be turning, however. Children's play is beginning to appear more and more in a range of important policies and initiatives for children. There is a growing recognition that integrated children's services, delivering key outcomes through children's centres and extended schools, will need to include opportunities for play, not just care, while significant lottery funding is being used to stimulate strategic growth of free play provision.

Many of these developments are happening because they must. As Lloyd George famously said: 'No community can infringe [the child's right to play] without doing enduring harm to the minds and bodies of its citizens.' Modern living has indeed progressively infringed that right. These policy developments, insofar as they are responding to children's need for more play space and opportunity, are the, as yet incomplete, response to the resulting harm.

The role of the playworker has never been more crucial. The growth in real play opportunities for children that we must hope takes hold will require more and more skilled professionals. This book – now something of a standard for playwork training – is an important resource for that vital development. It is essential reading for anyone working towards a playwork qualification, from NVQs through to foundation degree or diploma level. Always well structured and accessible, this latest edition is even more so.

Enjoy!

Adrian Voce
Director of the Children's Play Council

Preface

This edition of *New Playwork* has been completely revised and rewritten with new material and the latest playwork theory, case studies, activities and photographs. Since the first edition was published 10 years ago, there have been many changes in the lives of children and a rapid growth in services for children beyond schools – mostly in the childcare sector. What has not changed is the importance of play in children's lives. With the development of more childcare, extended schools and children's centres, children are more likely to spend time within formal settings of one kind or another. It is vital that staff working in these settings understand the importance of play. Time and space to play is every child's right and play is essential for children's healthy development and well-being.

A good playworker brings a range of skills, knowledge and understanding to the job. At different times, the playworker needs to be a companion, nurse, builder, artist, storyteller, manager, public relations officer, community worker, bookkeeper, counsellor, all-round games player, referee and more. However, the difference between a playworker and others who work with children is that their primary purpose is to be at the service of children at play. Play is central to all their thinking, planning and work with children – even when undertaking other roles described.

A good play setting is dependent first and foremost on the quality of its staff who can plan and resource the best possible play opportunities for the children. Whether a child goes to an after school club, an adventure playground, a holiday playscheme or another play setting, the opportunities you provide will affect his or her physical and emotional health and well-being, social relationships and disposition to learning. Playworkers offer children opportunities to create their own activities, when they choose and in their own time. They find and create places where children can explore, create, think, feel, discover, learn skills, meet friends, make new friends and take risks in relative safety and with a level of freedom from the constraints of timetables or predetermined outcomes. They provide opportunities for children to explore, through play, their interests whether they are arts, crafts, IT, outdoor play, sports or environmental science in greater depths than they may be able to at home or at school.

Staff working in all areas of children's services are being encouraged to work together across traditional professional barriers. It is important that playworkers are able to explain to others what they are doing and why so that play can be central to children's lives. Therefore, it is essential that playworkers take time for their professional development and to reflect on their practice with others and on their own.

Acknowledgements

We would like to express thanks to the many people who have helped us in various ways during the preparation of this book. First, to the many young people, playworkers, playwork trainers, writers and thinkers (far too many to name individually) who have influenced the content through their conversations with us or through our reading of their published material. Wherever possible, we have pointed readers to the original sources in the 'Further reading' sections at the end of each chapter.

To those who commented on drafts of the whole text or parts of the text (this edition and previous editions), in particular: Di Murray and Jacky Kilvington, Wendy Russell, Harry Shier, Barbara Slatter, Frances Duffy and Helen Wheeler.

To Tom Rennie and Lib Wright (Thomson Learning), Anne Longfield (4children), Anne Webster (Macmillan), the NSPCC Training Project, the Children's Play Information Service and Reading Borough Council playworkers for their help and advice.

To those who contributed examples or case studies: Tracey Collins (PARASOL Project), Sharon Crockett (playworker), Mary Januarius (Information Officer, Kidsactive), Karen King (playworker) and Dolcie Obhiozele (play development officer).

To the children of SS Mary and John School, East Oxford First School and Isis Middle School After School Clubs, PAWS (Drayton) and Blackbird Leys Adventure Playground for recording their thoughts about themselves and their play settings.

Thanks are due to the following for kind permission to use photographs, illustrations, drawings and other copyright material:

Children's drawings – Laura Ashby, Gemma Green, Loren Green, Polly Lowe, Oswah Osborn, Roberto Raskovsky, Nikita Raskovsky and Morgan Dawe.

Illustrations – Val Saunders for her illustrations on pages 37, 67, 85, 87, 95, 100, 108, 144, 151, 153, 162; Karen King on page 150.

Photos – Common Threads Publications Ltd on pages 41, 59 (top), 70, 118, 134 and 143; Jane Gallagher on pages 6, 13, 30, 84, 98, 111, 136, 137, 139 and 140; Kay Gatehouse on front cover, pages 11, 25, 26, 33, 34, 36, 43, 44, 46, 48, 49, 50, 57, 59 (bottom), 61, 63, 76, 80, 81, 82, 91, 102, 105, 116, 119, 121, 123, 146, 159, 172, 182, 190, 194, 200, 206, 208, 232 and 236; Kidsactive/Tilly Odell on pages 11, 19, 97 (top) and 141; Oxford City Council Play Development/Anthony Cunning on page 97 (bottom).

We would like to thank the staff and children of the following play settings for allowing photographs to be taken: Blackbird Leys Adventure Playground, East Oxford Primary School After School Club, SS Mary and John After School Club, Isis School After School Club, Meadow Lane Adventure Playground, Oxford City Council After School Clubs, Tower Playbuses Oxford, Playday in South Parks, Oxford, Thames Valley Adventure Playground, John Watson Playscheme.

Every effort has been made to trace all copyright holders for material, quotations and photos, but if any have been inadvertently overlooked, the publishers will be pleased to make the necessary arrangements at the first opportunity.

Annie Davy and Jane Gallagher

About the book

Who is this book for?

This book is for playworkers: that is, for anyone who works with children between the ages of 4 and 16 years in a setting where play is central to what is offered. You might work in an adventure playground, after school club, hospital or holiday playscheme. Perhaps you work on a playbus, in a play centre, or as childcare worker in your own home. You may work full time, part time or you may be a volunteer. You may be undertaking a playwork training course, S/NVQ or studying for a playwork or related degree.

How to use it

New Playwork is about the values and principles of playwork. It considers the skills and underpinning knowledge required of a playworker. You can use it as a handbook to dip into for ideas and quick reference, or to provide underpinning knowledge for a playwork training course, S/NVQ or other playwork qualification. A quick reference guide is provided on page xvii for those using the book to complete an S/NVQ in Playwork at level 2 or 3.

While the theory throughout is related to practical examples of work with children, we have deliberately steered clear of being prescriptive about specific activities to be undertaken with children of different ages. The focus is on creating an environment and circumstances in which children can play, and on using the children themselves as your starting point in planning for play. Books containing ideas and instructions for activities with different ages – games, art and craft, environmental play, music, drama and cooking – are recommended as further reading. We also encourage you to follow up any area of interest through further reading, reflection and study. There are suggestions for further reading throughout the book and a list of useful contacts can be found in the appendix.

Structure of the book

New Playwork is arranged in two parts. Part One, containing the first three chapters, sets out the framework for playwork – the principles and values, the context for playwork and some of the theoretical perspectives that underpin the work. The chapters in Part Two cover the core work of the playworker from a variety of perspectives, including creating the environment for play, providing play opportunities, being inclusive and developing relationships with children. There are also chapters on additional core competencies required of playworkers around child protection, health and safety, legislation and required paperwork.

Language used

In writing this book, we have tried to avoid jargon. Where it has crept in it is because we have been unable to find a suitable alternative word or phrase. Language changes over time, along with our thinking about what makes good practice in working with children. By thinking about language and being open to challenge and change in the terms we use, we also re-evaluate our working practice. The index should be helpful to help you find particular words or concepts as used throughout the book.

Children and young people

We have used the words 'child' and 'children' throughout the book to mean people aged 4–16, unless otherwise stated. We have tried to keep the different needs of the wide age group in mind throughout.

Play setting

'Play setting' is the term we have used to encompass the whole range of situations and circumstances in which playworkers work. It is not ideal, as it does not convey the wonderful and diverse range of play projects and environments that exist.

Parent/carer

We have used 'parent' to mean the adult or adults responsible for the child within the family or at home, even though this may not be the biological parent. In some cases, we have used 'parent or carer' to emphasise this point.

She and he

We have varied the use of the personal pronouns 'he' and 'she' throughout the book.

Variations in legislation, policy and practice

The playwork standards in the S/NVQs are the same throughout the UK. However, practice will differ to some extent because of the legal and social context in which you work. For example, in Wales, notices have to be in Welsh and English, safety and other legislation differs in Scotland. The law quoted in the book is English law. The principles of good practice are the same, but a playworker moving from one part of the UK to another would be expected to acquire any relevant new knowledge.

A word about standards

As you are working through the activities, you may find that the case studies and descriptions of play settings and expected standards are not what you have to work with on a daily basis or that you are not in a position to do much to change them to begin with. Do not lose heart. This book should be used as a source of ideas for you and your colleagues to work with, towards and beyond.

Features within chapters

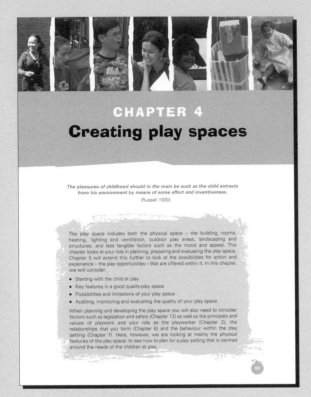

CHAPTER 4
Creating play spaces

The pleasures of childhood should in the main be such as the child extracts from his environment by means of some effort and inventiveness.

(Russell 1930)

The play space includes both the physical space – the building, rooms, heating, lighting and ventilation, outdoor play areas, landscaping and structures; and less tangible factors such as the mood and appeal. This chapter looks at your role in planning, preparing and evaluating the play space. Chapter 5 will extend this further to look at the possibilities for action and experience – the play opportunities – that are offered within it. In this chapter, we will consider:

- Starting with the child at play
- Key features in a good quality-play space
- Possibilities and limitations of your play space
- Auditing, monitoring and evaluating the quality of your play space

When planning and developing the play space you will also need to consider factors such as legislation and safety (Chapter 12) as well as the principles and values of playwork and your role as the playworker (Chapter 2), the relationships that you form (Chapter 6) and the behaviour within the play setting (Chapter 7). Here, however, we are looking at mainly the physical features of the play space; to see how to plan for a play setting that is centred around the needs of the children at play.

Learning objectives Key topics for each chapter are listed at the beginning to help frame your learning.

your senses and your observations of children playing and conversations with children to help you plan the design of your play setting.

ACTIVITY   Appealing to the senses

Plan some interesting ways to enrich the 'sense environment'. This can help you to find out more about the children's likes and dislikes and increase their awareness of and sensitivity towards each other. As a result of your activities and discussion with children about the senses, write down five ways of improving your play environment in its appeal to the senses, such as:

- adding colour to corners used for quiet play or reading by using draped fabrics;
- improving acoustics by using rugs and screens or turning off taped music
- burning essential oils or using incense – or putting lavender oil in the Playdough
- creating a sensory garden, with a textured (but accessible) path of gravel, bark, stones and grass, bells and wind chimes hung up to be moved by the wind or children's fingers and reflective surfaces to play with light
- creating an outdoor music and sounds playscape – with wind chimes and homemade drums and cymbals
- appealing to all the senses by having changing seasonal displays of flowers, leaves, seeds, stones, shells or fruit in the entrance to the play setting.

Possibilities and limitations of your play space

Using a shared space

How to work within a shared space

Your play setting may be a shared space such as part of a school, church hall or community centre or you may work in a purpose-built play centre, adventure playground or other designated play setting. You may have to meet a range of care needs as well as providing play opportunities – for example, providing nutritionally balanced meals for children whose parents are at work or otherwise engaged. Your premises and the kind of service you offer will affect the kind of environment that can or needs to be provided. If you intend to provide meals, you will need a kitchen and somewhere comfortable to eat. If the children are to spend several hours in the facility they will need comfortable spaces to sit, relax, talk, rest and maybe even doze off. Transforming a hall or bare school canteen into an attractive play space is challenging. You can use screens, plants, coloured cloths, rugs, cushions, pictures, tables and movable shelving or other furniture, such as child-sized tables and chairs, to create several different spaces within the larger whole.

If your facility is required to register and meet the national childcare standards, you will need to meet the requirements of your regulating body (such as Ofsted – see Chapter 3). Whatever the challenges, as long as the basic facilities are there (enough space, toilets, washing facilities, kitchen if needed and office space), there are nearly always options and very often solutions if you are prepared to think creatively and give enough time to planning. Sharing premises will require good communication with the other organisations involved. You will need to be clear about the needs of your group and accommodate the

Activities Throughout the book there are activities to assist learning and understanding. In most cases, it is best if you undertake these activities with the support of your co-workers or a senior worker – many require discussion with others.

environment. Others may use more informal opportunities for discussion – such as over a drink or snack. Children's participation in the planning and development of the play space does not necessarily mean always giving them what they want. As a playworker you need to ensure that the play space affords the best possible play opportunities for all children. Sometimes an individual child's wish to destroy other children's dens or models will need to be contained so as not to inhibit the play of others. Alternatively, if children are apathetic and want to do nothing but watch TV or fill the play setting with electronic entertainments, this would present a different kind of challenge to the playworker. The children will need to understand the choices on offer – the possibilities and limitations of the play setting. Limited 'screen time' may form part of what a setting such as an after-school club has to offer. Children attending an after-school club each day may be very unhappy if they are not able to watch a favourite TV programme that forms part of the conversation and culture of the children who go home after school. Contrariwise, something is not right within a play setting where children want to spend all their time in front of a screen ...

CASE STUDY   Patterns and temperaments

Children come with their own personalities, likes and dislikes. Each of the following children from Mudrock Play Centre has a different 'temperament'. You may recognise them as similar to children in your own play setting.

- *Arran* is a stocky boy, very energetic, full of ideas, sometimes hot tempered and impatient. He likes play environments where he can take a lead, plan strategies, make changes. He loves building the fire and 'wide games' that involve teams, strategy and constantly changing landscapes and scenarios using bushes, dens planks and bridges.
- *Jodie* is a tall, pale girl who likes to think deeply about things. She likes space for more structured team games such as football or basketball. She likes to sit on boulders or benches where she will be undisturbed by the hectic going on of others. She prefers one-to-one conversations rather than big group discussions. She is very observant and often very funny in relating what she has noticed about others.
- *Paul* is gentle, easygoing and likes looking after others when he is not daydreaming in the hammock or on the cushions in the book corner. He likes playing with model cars and is quite contented playing on his own or joining in with others, so long as life is comfortable. He likes cooking food.
- *Hafiza* is small for her age, constantly on the go and never sits down for long. She likes skipping, hopping, telling jokes and chattering. She is always surrounded by lots of other children and tends to play in places where they can 'flock' as a group such as at the climbing frame and the craft table.

How would your setting meet the play preferences of Aran, Jodie, Paul and Hafiza? Some play environments such as the beach seem to have almost universal appeal – offering a variety of ways in which children can play. Experienced playworkers learn to recognise that there are universal patterns or which children respond to or bring into their play and that children's individual temperaments influence how they use particular spaces and materials.

Another way of looking at patterns in children's play is by the study of *schemas*. See further reading at the end of the chapter – although most of the research and case studies in this area relates to preschool-aged children.

Case studies Case studies enable you to relate what you have read to actual practice and to develop greater understanding of the subject.

Spotlight on ... Spotlight boxes ask you to consider wider issues around the points being made and how these relate to the play setting in which you work; or they may focus more deeply on one particular aspect or theory. Sometimes the spotlight boxes raise questions to which you are not expected to give full or immediate answers. They may help you to develop 'reflective' practice and to look at your play setting and the way you work in a new light. In some cases, the questions pick up themes that run throughout the book. As you progress through the book and carry out the activities, you will get help in finding solutions to the questions raised.

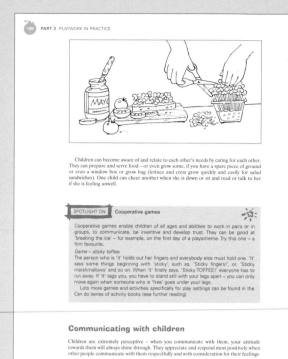

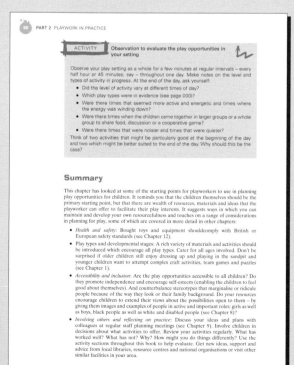

Summaries These provide a summary of the key topics in each chapter to consolidate learning.

Further reading The subject matter within each chapter of *New Playwork* could have made a book on its own. We hope you will explore some of the topics further. You will find up-to-date suggestions for further reading at the end of each chapter.

Appendix: Useful contacts

Some organisations supporting play

4Children (formerly Kids' Clubs Network)
City Reach, 5 Greenwich View Place, London E14 9NN
Tel: 020 7512 2112
Website: www.4children.org.uk
Provides ideas, support and advice on aspects of play and childcare.

Children's Play Council
Tel: 020 7843 6016
Email: cpc@ncb.org.uk
Website: www.ncb.org.uk.cpc
Aims to raise awareness of the importance of play and to stimulate better play opportunities and services.

4Children (formerly Kids' Clubs Network)
City Reach, 5 Greenwich View Place, London E14 9NN
Tel: 020 7512 2112
Website: www.4children.org.uk
Provides ideas, support and advice on aspects of play and childcare.

Children's Play Information Service
National Children's Bureau, 8 Wakley Street, London EC1V 7QE
Tel: 020 7843 6303 Fax: 020 7843 6007
Website: www.ncb.org.uk/library/cpis
Information service for all matters relating to play, playwork and playwork training, including a comprehensive library and resource centre.

Fair Play for Children
35 Lyon Street, Bognor Regis PO21 1YZ
Tel: 01243 869922
Email: fairplay@arunet.co.uk
Website: www.arunet.co.uk/fairplay/home.htm
Fair Play for Children campaigns for children's right to play and provides information, advice and resources for those working with children in a playsetting.

Free Play Network
66 York Road, New Barnet, Hertfordshire EN5 1LJ
Tel/Fax: 020 8440 9276
Website: www.freeplaynetwork.org.uk
Promotes the need for better play opportunities for children.

International Associating for the Child's Right to Play (IPA)
Website: www.ipaworld.org/home.html
International association promoting the child's right to play, with members in over 50 countries.

248

Appendix: Useful contacts A list of important playwork contacts to help extend your learning and open up opportunities can be found in the appendix.

Glossary

Admissions policy printed and published guidelines that a play setting devises to decide who gets priority if the setting is full and there is a waiting list
Adolescence the physical, social, emotional and psychological changes that take place during puberty
Adulteration inappropriate intervention into children's play by an adult for reasons other than facilitating or supporting play
Assertiveness the confidence to express opinions clearly while mindful of the feelings and expectations of others

Behaviour management monitoring and intervention designed to produce positive behaviour
Body language are 'non-verbal communication'
Braille written language for the blind using raised symbols and characters
Bullying frightening, threatening or hurting someone through verbal, physical, emotional, sexual, racist or discriminatory behaviour

Child-centred environment a place where children are respected as individuals with rights and opinions and where their needs are the starting point for planning and provision of services.
Cognition the ability to acquire knowledge by thinking, understanding and solving problems
Confidential information information which must be kept secure and only shared with people who possess the right to access it
Conservation the stage of a child's development when they are no longer dependent on visual and sensory perception and begin to use rational thinking
COSHH Control of Substances Hazardous to Health – regulation of a range of materials which could be harmful – including cleaning materials and some paints and varnish

Disabled the perceived result of an impairment
Discrimination any sort of behaviour that is more or less favourable to a person or group of people based on their group identity, such as their skin colour, religion, gender, etc.

Emotional abuse the malicious withholding of love, attention and stimulation as well as associated physical care from a child
Equal opportunities providing people with the same chances regardless of their background
Ethos the special spirit or attitude of a setting

Hazard something that could cause harm to someone
Hygiene the theory and application of health and cleanliness

Latency period a term used by Freud to describe middle childhood as being a period when strong sexual feelings experienced in preschool years are repressed until puberty
LSCB Local Safeguarding children boards

Medical model of disability the view that a disabled person's impairments can be 'fixed' with medical procedures

Named (key) worker someone who takes special responsibility for the welfare of a newly arrived child and forms a primary relationship with that child on an ongoing professional basis
National childcare standards a list of things that must be in place in every registered childcare setting that inspectors will check when they visit
Nature the element of a child's development influenced by inherited genes
Neglect the denial of a child's right to food, warmth, medical care or other aspects of care including supervision to ensure that they are not exposed to danger
Non-transmittable diseases illnesses and conditions that cannot be passed on from one child to another
Non-verbal communication any communication not conveyed by speaking (often called 'body language')
NSPCC National Society for the Prevention of Cruelty to Children
Nurture the element of a child's development influenced by social and environmental factors

Observation a key playwork skill involving the monitoring (and sometimes recording) of a child's play behaviour or development
Open-access setting play setting where children can come and go independently and can choose to stay as long or short a time as they please

Peer group people with one or more similar factors that draw them together as a group, such as age, interests, or social status
Physical abuse any form of actual injury inflicted (or knowingly not prevented) by a person having care of the child

248

Glossary For easy reference, definitions are provided for key words or technical terms.

Playwork S/NVQs: quick reference guide

PLAYWORK NVQ/SVQ LEVEL 2 *(Mandatory units)*

Unit	Unit part	Chapter
PW1 Contribute to positive relationships in the play setting	**PW1.1** Develop and maintain positive relationships with children and young people	6
	PW1.2 Contribute to positive relationships between children and young people and others in the play setting	6
	PW1.3 Contribute to positive relationships with parents and carers	6
PW2 Support children and young people's play	**PW2.1** Create a range of environments for children and young people's play	4
	PW2.2 Offer a range of play opportunities to children and young people	5
	PW2.3 Support children and young people's rights and choices in play	1, 2, 4, 5, 6, 8
	PW2.4 End play sessions	5
PW3 Contribute to the health and safety of the play environment	**PW3.1** Maintain the health and safety of the play environment's users	12
	PW3.2 Maintain the health, safety and welfare of children and young people during play	12
C35 Deal with accidents and emergencies	**C35.1** Deal with injuries and signs of illness	12
	C35.2 Follow emergency procedures	12
C36 Support the protection of children from abuse	**C36.1** Report signs of possible abuse	
	C36.2 Respond to a child's disclosure of abuse	11
A52 Contribute to the work of your team	**A52.1** Work effectively with your colleagues	10
	A52.2 Improve your own work	9, 10

xvii

PLAYWORK NVQ/SVQ LEVEL 2 *(Mandatory units continued)*

Unit	Unit part	Chapter
	A52.3 Help to improve the work of your organisation	9, 14

PLAYWORK NVQ/SVQ LEVEL 2 *(Optional units)*

Unit	Unit part	Chapter
PW4 Contribute to children and young people's healthy eating and personal hygiene	**PW4.1** Contribute to a healthy eating programme	12
	PW4.2 Contribute to hygiene in the play setting	12
PW5 Escort and supervise children and young people outside the play setting	**PW5.1** Escort children and young people to and from the play setting	13
	PW5.2 Supervise children and young people on trips and outings	13

PLAYWORK NVQ/SVQ LEVEL 3 *(Mandatory units)*

Unit	Unit part	Chapter
PW6 Contribute to an organisational framework that reflects the needs and protects the rights of children and young people	**PW6.1** Investigate and consult on children and young people's rights	1, 2, 6, 8
	PW6.2 Contribute to policies and procedures that reflect children and young people's needs and rights	2, 3, 6, 7, 8
	PW6.3 Promote a diverse and inclusive environment	4, 8
	PW6.4 Contribute to the protection of children and young people from abuse	11
PW7 Develop and maintain a healthy, safe and secure environment for children	**PW7.1** Establish a healthy, safe and secure environment for children	12
	PW7.2 Maintain a healthy, safe and secure environment for children	12
	PW7.3 Implement procedures for accidents, injuries, illnesses and other emergencies	12
PW8 Develop and promote positive relationships	**PW8.1** Develop relationships with children	6
	PW8.2 Communicate with children	6
	PW8.3 Support children in developing relationships	6
	PW8.4 Communicate with adults	6

PLAYWORK NVQ/SVQ LEVEL 3 *(Mandatory units continued)*

Unit	Unit part	Chapter
PW9 Plan for and support self-directed play	**PW9.1** Collect and analyse information on play needs and preferences	1, 2, 4, 5, 6, 8
	PW9.2 Plan and prepare play spaces	4
	PW9.3 Support self-directed play	5
	PW9.4 Help children and young people to manage risk during play	4, 7, 12
PW10 Reflect on and develop practice	**PW10.1** Reflect on practice	9
	PW10.2 Take part in continuing professional development	9, 14

PLAYWORK NVQ/SVQ LEVEL 3 *(Optional units)*

Unit	Unit part	Chapter
PW11 Work with colleagues in a team	**PW11.1** Contribute to the work of your team	10
	PW11.2 Provide support to your colleagues	10
	PW11.3 Respond to conflict in your team	10
PW12 Respond to concerns about possible abuse	**PW12.1** Identify signs of possible abuse	11
	PW12.2 Respond to a child's disclosure of abuse	11
	PW12.3 Follow policies and procedures to report possible abuse	11
PW13 Contribute to children's health and well-being	**PW13.1** Encourage and support a healthy lifestyle	12
	PW13.2 Provide food and drinks	5, 12
PW14 Work with parents and carers	**PW14.1** Establish and develop working relationships with parents and carers	6
	PW14.2 Involve parents and carers in the setting	6
PW15 Administer playwork provision	**PW15.1** Implement access procedures	13
	PW15.2 Record and report key information	13
B226 Develop opportunities in the community	**B226.1** Make people in the community aware of opportunities and benefits	14

PLAYWORK NVQ/SVQ LEVEL 3 *(Optional units continued)*

Unit	Unit part	Chapter
	B226.2 Establish and maintain links with other organisations and individuals	14
B227 Contribute to evaluating, developing and promoting services	**B227.1** Contribute to evaluating service provision	9, 14
	B227.2 Contribute to developing and improving services	9, 14
	B227.3 Contribute to promoting services	14
B228 Organise and supervise travel	**B228.1** Make travel arrangements	13
	B228.2 Supervise travel	13

PART ONE

The playwork framework

CHAPTER 1
Playwork, children's play and child development

Play is the highest expression of human development in childhood, for it alone is the free expression of what is in a child's soul.

(Frederich Froebel, 1782–1852)

Playwork is the provision of environments and opportunities for children's play. The playworker's job is to support and facilitate that play. This chapter looks at the world of children's play and some of the ways in which it contributes to child development. There is a look at historical and more recent theories about children's play and suggestions for using observation and developing your understanding about how children develop to inform the way you support children's play. In this chapter, we will consider:

- What is play?
- Why do children play?
- New theories in playwork: the play cycle
- Play and child development

What is play?

As a playworker, you will recognise play behaviour when you see it – but how does it differ from other kinds of behaviour? Why is it that children play all around the world and that we recognise it as universally important to human development? This has been the subject of many books written from all different kinds of perspective such as education, psychology, biology, sociology etc. and the definition of play continues to be debated, often passionately, by different people working in the playwork sector. The following two definitions are widely used (sometimes with variations) and are quoted in *Best Play – What Play Provision Should do for Children* (NPFA 2000):

> *Play is freely chosen, personally directed, intrinsically motivated behaviour that actively engages the child.*

(This definition draws closely on the work of Bob Hughes and Frank King.)

> *Play can be fun or serious. Through play children explore social, material and imaginary worlds and their relationship with them, elaborating all the while a flexible range of responses to the challenges they encounter. By playing children learn and develop as individuals, and as members of the community.*

Catherine Garvey (1991) suggests the following points as typical characteristics of play:

- Play is pleasurable, enjoyable . . . positively valued by the player.
- Play has no extrinsic goals (i.e. the process of playing is important in itself).
- Play is spontaneous and voluntary . . . freely chosen by the player.
- Play involves some active engagement on the part of the player.
- Play has certain systematic relations to what is not play (i.e. play is linked with lots of other areas of activity: problem solving, creativity, socialisation . . .).

Play can be many things. It can be adventurous, challenging, exciting – scary even. It can be calming and therapeutic. It can be noisy or quiet, fast or slow or a combination of any

'Play is when one person gets together with other people and they have fun. Sometimes you can play on your own with toys or an imaginary friend' (Loren, aged 8)

of these things. Play can be solitary or undertaken in pairs or groups. Play can involve rules and equipment or neither.

Freedom and choice are important concepts to consider when defining play, as are enjoyment and fun – although play can involve tears as well as laughter. Play can help a child to develop and explore aspects of herself and extend her relationships with others and with her environment: she can increase her understanding of the wider world. Play is important in providing children with a means to develop their skills, understanding, self-confidence and self-esteem.

ACTIVITY | Is it play?

Look at the following five scenarios. Discuss with others: in which of them are the children playing and in which of them are they not? Use the characteristics of play suggested by Catherine Garvey (see earlier) to help you decide. Discussion points for the activity are suggested in the text.

Scenario 1: Amena, Joe and Suleika are fixing blankets to bamboo canes to make a den. They are concentrating hard, but finding it very difficult to make their structure stand up on its own. Amena makes a suggestion: 'Get some clothes pegs.' 'Get them yourself,' Joe replies. In spite of some obvious frustration the activity continues for several minutes.

Scenario 2: Pasquale and Louise are sprawled on big cushions on the floor watching TV. They are both engrossed and ignore everything going on around them.

Scenario 3: Alison is bouncing a ball on the ground with a bat. After a few minutes she begins to bounce it against the wall.

Scenario 4: A group of four children are colouring in a picture for a colouring competition. They are concentrating and do not talk, other than to ask for a particular coloured pencil.

Scenario 5: Sebastian and Natasha are having a game of hopscotch. Sebastian: 'You stepped on the line.' Natasha: 'No I didn't.' Sebastian: 'Yes you did.' Natasha: 'No I didn't.' This continues a few times until Natasha says, 'No I didn't and no returns.' Sebastian says, 'Last one to the bench is a slimy toad.' They run to the bench laughing.

See discussion points below.

It is not always simple to define what is play and what is not. The same activity – such as modelling with clay – can be play, if it is freely chosen and involves enjoyable exploration of the modelling materials – or it can be a chore, as in making pots to earn a living. Doing high jumps can be play if it is spontaneous or undertaken by the child for her own reasons – or it can be a competitive sport, where the goal of winning is the most important thing.

Discussion points for activity: Is it play?

Scenario 1:

If you were watching the children in this scenario, you would probably say 'Yes, of course they are playing.' If you look back too at Garvey's characteristics of play, they all seem to fit. Amena, Joe and Suleika are engaged in an activity that we assume is freely chosen. There is a goal or end product – the den. But the end product seems less important than working out how to make the blanket stay up – the process of building. Although there are signs of frustration, the children continue to try. Is this a sign that they value what they are doing? They are involved in problem solving – how to fix up the blankets. They are interacting with each other and Amena is showing creativity in making a suggestion and wanting to try out a new idea.

Scenario 2:

Louise and Pasquale may be enjoying themselves and their activity is presumably freely chosen. There is no specific end product to watching TV, although the purpose of watching might be to gain information, understanding or entertainment. Louise and Pasquale do not seem to be actively involved with each other or their surroundings and therefore one of the characteristics of play is missing. Perhaps you will conclude that watching television is not play, although it may be a recreational or leisure-time activity.

Scenario 3:

Alison's behaviour is also presumably freely chosen and enjoyable. Would she stop if she were not enjoying it or finding value in it? She is actively involved with the bat and the ball, the ground and the wall. She is developing her skills and trying out new ideas by introducing a variation to the activity. The essential ingredients of play are there.

Scenario 4:

The children who are colouring in are presumably doing so of their own choice and may be enjoying themselves – they are concentrating hard. The aim of the activity is specific – to produce the best coloured picture in order to win the competition. (Garvey says play has no extrinsic goals.) Whether this goal is more important to the children than the actual process of colouring will depend on the approach that they take to the activity.

How is play different from other kinds of behaviour?

Scenario 5:

Sebastian and Natasha are obviously enjoying themselves – even when they are disagreeing. They are laughing. They change their behaviour voluntarily when they run off to the bench and they are actively engaged in interacting with each other. They are developing patterns of language use and sharing an understanding of the rules of their game. Sebastian does not 'answer back' when Natasha says 'No returns'. As in scenario 1, you would probably agree that these children are obviously playing, and their behaviour meets all Garvey's (1991) characteristics of play.

Why do children play?

The question 'Why do children play?' has been asked for hundreds, even thousands, of years. Children have a natural impulse to play (termed the 'play drive' (*Spieltrieb*) by Friedrich Schiller in the 18th century). Seemingly a simple act, play has been shown to be a complex phenomenon by countless studies. There are many theories about the *purpose* of children's play, including the following:

- 'Play enables children to learn and practise skills.'
- 'Play develops thinking.'
- 'Play has a therapeutic effect.'
- 'Play is vital for the evolution of the species.'

Although there have been many other theories as to the purpose of play (such as play as a means of 'recapitulating' human evolution or play as simply a means of 'letting off steam' or 'passing time') we will have a brief look at some of the theories that have contributed to our thinking about play in playwork.

Play helps children to learn and practise skills

Over 2000 years ago, Aristotle noted the value of play for children's development. He proposed that children should play in order to practise the skills necessary for 'the serious occupations of later life'. Throughout the ages, children have imitated what adults do. They often use these actions in their play, as a way of understanding their world, and to practise the skills they will need for adult life. Even from a very young age, it seems to be instinctual for babies to copy what they see others do. Through their play, children can develop:

- language, such as jokes and conversations, stories and games using reading and writing
- physical skills, including fine motor skills (such as threading beads) and gross motor skills (such as jumping from one tree stump to another)
- social skills, including debating, sharing, empathising with others, listening and understanding social 'rules'
- emotional competence, understanding and exploring feelings through imaginative play, controlling anger, developing self-awareness and self-esteem through testing boundaries of acceptable risk and challenge
- creative skills, through using the imagination in role play, using the senses, playing with art and craft materials and dancing
- morally, such as being kind, respectful and sensitive to others, helping, having a conscience, avoiding the urge to cheat or bully
- spiritually, including an appreciation of nature, a sense of inner life and a place in the world
- cognitive skills, the ability to think and understand.

| SPOTLIGHT ON | Play types |

As researchers studied how play encourages learning, they noticed that different types of play encouraged different aspects of children's development. Many attempts have been made to classify the different types of play. In 1935 Charlotte Buhler classified play into make-believe games, functional games, construction games and passive play. Piaget categorised play in order of developmental ability: practice play, symbolic (or pretend) play and games with rules. In 1996 Bob Hughes suggested the following play types ('recapitulative play' was added in 2002):

- *Symbolic play* – play where an object may symbolise something else, such as using a piece of string to symbolise a wedding ring. It enables children to exert control over their play, at their own level of understanding.
- *Rough and tumble play* – where the children explore strength and dexterity, without being hurt and where they are obviously enjoying themselves.
- *Socio-dramatic play* – children act out real or potential experiences based on situations they see in their lives.
- *Social play* – where children play together, discovering, exploring and revising social rules.
- *Creative play* – play with a range of materials and tools for its own sake.
- *Communication play* – play in which children use verbal and non-verbal language, such as mime, telling jokes and play acting.
- *Dramatic play* – Children act out events in which they have no direct participation, such as acting out a television programme or a religious festival.
- *Deep play* – play in which children explore risk in order to develop survival skills and conquer fear, such as balancing on a high beam.
- *Exploratory play* – where children find out about the properties of objects and places by manipulation or movement, for example handling, throwing or banging objects.
- *Fantasy play* – play in which the child changes real-life situations into make-believe ones that may be unlikely to occur in their lives, such as fantasising about flying an aeroplane or driving a flashy car.
- *Imaginative play* – play in which the rules of the real world do not apply, such as pretending to be a tree or patting an imaginary dog.
- *Locomotor play* – activities that involve moving about, such as playing tag, chasing others and climbing trees.
- *Mastery play* – play activities that exert control over aspects of the physical environment, including digging holes, making dams, building fires.
- *Object play* – play that develops hand–eye manipulations and movements which bring about a new or wider understanding of the possible uses of everyday objects.
- *Role play* – play that explores straightforward everyday actions, such as sweeping the floor, using a phone or driving a car.
- *Recapitulative play* – play through which children access the play of earlier human evolutionary stages, such as through exploring history, stories, rituals, rhymes, fire and darkness.

When children are playing, they may be engaging in more than one of Hughes' play types. For example, children who are making dams to change the flow of a river are engaged in mastery play and exploratory play, but may also be engaging in deep play if the activity involves an element of risk. Think about why it might be useful to divide play into different types. How could it help you in your job as a playworker?

Play develops thinking

In the early 20th century, new research emerged about the value of play for children's cognitive development – their ability to think, understand and solve problems. Arguably the most famous cognitive theorist, Jean Piaget (1896–1980) put forward the idea that children learn in particular stages and that each stage must be mastered before the next can be attempted. Each stage has types of play associated with it, through which children achieve more complex ways of thinking.

Children's experiences, along with their opportunities to practise skills, help them to develop as individuals. They build on what they have previously learned in order to increase their knowledge and abilities. As each stage is accomplished, they have the potential to add to it by developing skills of an increasing level of complexity. The Russian theorist Lev Vygotsky (1896–1934) wrote of the 'zone of proximal development' (Vygotsky 1980) to describe this area between a child's actual abilities and their potential for development.

Play as therapy

The origins of play as therapy lie in Sigmund Freud's psychoanalytic approach which began in the early 20th century and later developed by others such as D.W. Winnicot and Melanie Klein. Freud believed that play was driven by a child's emotions and feelings and that, by studying their play, the therapist could discover a child's underlying emotional imbalances. The idea that children re-enact conflicts and unpleasant events through play in order to gain some understanding of the event is still the basis of much of the thinking underpinning play therapy today. The therapeutic, or healing, effects of play came to prominence in hospitals during the 1950s, when play was used to help children understand the medical procedures they were undergoing and also to promote their recovery following an illness or operation. Many hospitals today employ 'play specialists'.

Whereas Freud saw play as a means for the therapist to gain an insight into children's emotional problems, other therapists have concluded that play is a therapeutic process *in itself*. The therapist ensures that the atmosphere within the play room is friendly and comfortable. They do not guide or influence the child's play. The idea of such 'non-directive' play therapy is that the child is free to express all her worries, wishes, fears, hopes and distresses through free play and as a result moves towards the natural rebalancing of her emotions.

Play is vital for the evolution of the species

Evidence suggests that the urge to play is instinctive in humans and other mammals. Play enables children to acquire skills and knowledge from their environment, from peers, from family and other adults. Most importantly, play enables children to develop flexible and adaptable responses to changes in the environment and in life circumstances. Such abilities may be essential to survival (such as staying safe, negotiating, standing up for ourselves and making decisions) and adapting to our environment (experimenting, exploring, creating and testing out strategies for overcoming problems). Evidence is growing that from an early age, play helps to activate 'neural pathways' within the child's brain that would otherwise remain unused. Play can therefore help children to use their brains to their full potential.

SPOTLIGHT ON | **Play deprivation**

There is increasing evidence that children who are deprived of opportunities to play suffer from a range of adverse effects such as developing anti-social and violent behaviour, increased physical and mental ill health and likelihood of obesity. There has been increasing public concern that children's freedom to play is being limited by:

- an increase in relatively passive indoor activities such as TV, video and computer games
- an increase in traffic and built-up spaces without sufficient play space
- parents' fears about bullying, stranger danger and 'getting into trouble', which can increase the amount of children's time being programmed with activities through extended schooling and other formal activities.

Lack of play opportunities may mean that children do not develop to their full potential and even 'shut down' some of their capacities for learning. There are factors that are likely to increase children's risk of play deprivation, such as poverty, caring for relatives from a young age or experiencing violence or abuse at home or within the community.

New theories in playwork: the play cycle

Perry Else and Gordon Sturrock (1998) have been instrumental in producing materials that provide new tools and ways of thinking about play and the role of the playworker. They believe that humans are driven to play as part of our basic human development and have developed a way of describing play, called 'the play cycle'. They suggest that play begins inside the child – as a thought or idea or contemplation. This is followed by a 'play cue', a signal that the child wants to play. This signal may be made to a person, or to an object or even to something in the child's imagination. A response to a play cue is termed a 'play return'. A play return comes from the outside world – from another person (or animal) or is experienced from the environment. For example, if the play cue from the child was to roll a hoop to another child, the second child may roll the hoop back, as a play return, to show that she wants to play. Or perhaps the play cue was to kick a ball against a wall. If the 'return' (in this case the ball bouncing off the wall back to the child) is pleasing to the child, then she may continue to play. She may instead change the play or she may decide to ignore the return altogether and do something else. Else and Sturrock suggest that play is defined by a 'play frame'. The 'play frame' is a real or imagined boundary that contains the play; the frame may be the sandbox that the children are playing in, or the 'let's pretend' game they carry with them through the play setting.

Cultural historian Johan Huizinga (1872–1945) also suggested that children designate a real or imagined space in which to play. He said, 'All play moves and has its being within a playground marked off beforehand either materially or ideally, deliberately or as a matter of course' (Huizinga 1971 [1938]). This 'play frame' can be altered by inviting other people or by moving or changing things in some way that varies the response. When the flow of

play ends, the cycle is complete, and another cycle can begin. The important thing about the play cycle is that it is done for its own sake and not some external reward. The role of the playworker in this instance is therefore to recognise and respond to the child's cues. Intervention in children's play which leads or forces it has been called 'adulteration'.

Play and child development

As we have seen, play is not necessarily always about development. Sometimes the purpose of a child's play will be a mystery to us – and may have meaning only to the child or children at play. Unlike other professions that rightly use play as part of their methodology to enhance learning, to provide exercise, to socialise or keep children occupied, playworkers need to develop the trust in the play process for its own sake and support children in their self-directed play.

One of the best ways of learning about children and their play is to watch what they do. Learning to observe children is seen as an important way for you to gain understanding of children's behaviour, their development and their play. Good observation can be a key to discovering their needs within the play setting. Child development is a vast subject and suggestions for further reading are given at the end of this chapter.

Play is important in developing confidence and self-esteem

ACTIVITY   Purpose of play

Watch a child at play for 5–10 minutes. Why do you think they make the choices they make within their play? To learn or practise skills? To learn or practise thinking? For its therapeutic effect? Or for some other purpose?

For centuries people have been fascinated by child development. What makes each child unique? What makes many children of a similar age go through the same phases? Why is it that we think a 5 year old should be ready for school, for reading and writing, a 12 year old to travel across town and a 16 year old to leave home?

Nature/nurture

Children have two biological parents: the two people who provide the sperm and the egg from which the child is conceived. Every child inherits traits from two sets of genes. Their combination will determine the child's physical appearance and may influence many other things about the child. There are different theories about how much the child's character, growth and development are formed by inherited genes (that is, 'nature'), and how much is influenced by things which happen to the child after he has been conceived and born (that is, 'nurture'). A child's development can be affected by:

- nutrition
- the care they receive
- the response they receive from other people after birth and during childhood
- family makeup and circumstances (for example, poverty, wealth, employment)
- the environment in which they live (for example, housing, town, country)
- family culture and religious beliefs
- illness
- other circumstances and experiences of stress (for example, accidents, bereavement, abuse)
- opportunities to mix with other children and adults
- opportunities for education, leisure, play.

By the time a child is 5 years old, and perhaps comes to your play setting for the first time, she will bring with her a range of individual experiences and expectations and will have individual needs for you to discover and help her meet. She will generally have reached over half her adult height and achieved the greatest milestones of development: walking, talking and independent feeding, dressing and hygiene.

Ages and stages

As well as noting the differences in individual children, people studying child development have also identified that all over the world children go through similar stages in a similar order. Before children can read or write they need to be able to recognise shapes, understand symbols and hold and control a writing tool. Before a child can dress himself he must be able to coordinate his hands and fingers well enough to do up buttons or handle zips. Before a child can cross a busy road safely he must be aware of the danger, be able to judge the speed of oncoming cars and know how to be consistent in looking to the right and to the left to see if the road is clear. Each child develops at his or her own rate. No two 6 year olds will be at the same stage in terms of their skills and knowledge and understanding. But it is useful to look at broad stages of what you can expect at different ages, so that you can plan activities that are appropriate. It is no good planning a game with complicated rules for 5 to 6 year olds or one which involves a lot of reading or writing. Equally a 10 year old may object to 'babyish' ring games and lose interest in activities that are not challenging enough.

Knowledge of child development can also help you recognise that a child is nowhere near the stage you might expect for his age. You can then look for the causes of this and, if possible, identify what he needs to enable him to keep up with other children of his age. Remember, children are individuals. Knowledge about stages of development is useful, but it should not stop you from recognising that each child is different and will develop in his own way.

Family and culture

Cultural and family background will have a major influence on many aspects of development. Every culture has different expectations of its children. Every family has different physical, social and economic circumstances.

For example:

The opinion of peers may be more important than the opinion of others

- What is expected of boys and girls in terms of behaviour, dress, future careers?
- What social contacts do they have?
- What resources are available?
- What opportunities are there for education, leisure, work?
- What are the religious beliefs and practices?

Each culture has different adult role models and will provide different opportunities for development. The way the child is perceived by those within and outside her family culture will also have profound effects on her development. Where she is accepted, respected and loved, her sense of identity, confidence and self-worth can blossom. Where she is rejected, humiliated or discriminated against, her possibilities for development will be impaired.

ACTIVITY   **Your own childhood**

1 Think back to your own childhood. What circumstances do you think were a major factor in your own development?

2 Choose a year that you think was particularly important in your development. Draw a line down the middle of a piece of paper:

- What or who helped you to develop positively? Write your answers on one side of the paper.

- What or who had a negative effect on your development? Write your answers on the opposite side of the paper.

Some people or events might have had both a positive and negative effect. If so write down the reasons, for example 'moving house' – negative: felt isolated, lost confidence, missed best friend; positive: enjoyed walking to school, new teacher helped me gain confidence in reading and enjoying books.

Differences in children's development

Every child develops at an individual pace. He or she will develop some skills and understanding easily and face challenges in other areas. Tying shoelaces may be easy for a 5 year old but difficult for his older playmate, who's 7. Some children face additional challenges to the majority of children in their peer group. They may be particularly gifted in a particular area or have impaired sight or hearing or have learning difficulties or muscle control problems. Each child so affected will cope with such challenges in a different way and his or her overall development will be affected accordingly. Find out as much as possible about disabled children within your group, by talking to the child and/or the child's parents or carers and increasing your own knowledge through reading and relevant training. In some cases, the child may seem to have difficulty speaking or communicating, but do not make assumptions about this. Always try communicating directly with the child. Seek guidance, information or advice from other professionals who know and work with the child or other disabled children. Through observation, sensitivity and ongoing communication with those involved, you can plan play opportunities that help the child to be included in the play setting and enable the child to reach her full developmental potential within it.

Within the broad stages of development, children may develop quickly or more slowly. Some have uneven development. They may be intellectually mature for their age, but socially less so; advanced in creativity but emotionally much younger. Disabled children may need support in one area but surpass their peers in another. A child with autism may be gifted at numerical arithmetic; a child who uses a wheelchair may well enjoy physical activity. A profoundly deaf child may enjoy and be very skilled in music, using the senses of sight, touch and rhythm (see also Chapter 8). Whatever her age, and however she compares to what may be considered 'usual', each child needs to be given opportunities to discover and develop her individual skills and talents.

Children – what are they like?

Children aged 4 to 7 – what might they be like?

A 4 year old may be able to tie his own shoelaces or learn this shortly after starting school. As well as gaining in independence in tasks relating to personal care, children in this age group are often learning or developing expertise in a range of other physical skills such as swimming or riding a two-wheeled bicycle. There is often a noticeable growth spurt, sometimes called the '5-to-7 shift', in children's height or weight, although not as noticeable as the growth spurt in puberty. They also begin to lose their milk teeth and develop a new set of back molars. The rapid growth in head size will have slowed down and by the end of this phase brain growth will be almost complete. Fine motor skills are developed for holding and using tools – scissors, pens, sewing needles – for more precise and delicate craft and construction (building, drawing, threading, collage, knotting, modelling).

Children gain increasing hand–eye coordination at this stage and begin to recognise shapes and symbols in the formal ways required for reading and writing. There are major developments in terms of the child's ability to understand concepts related to logic and rational thought. This is the stage of intellectual development that the child psychologist Piaget called the stage of 'conservation'. The child who has reached this stage will be able to use reasoning and no longer relies solely on what his eyes and other senses tell him. For example, he will understand that the mass of a ball of dough does not change when it is rolled into a different shape. A child who has reached the stage of conservation will know that the tall thin glass still holds the same amount of liquid, even though it looks more (the level of liquid is higher up the glass). Most 4 year olds will not be able to understand this. The evidence of their eyes can mislead them – they are not yet able to apply adult-type reasoning to what they have seen.

ACTIVITY   Stages of development

Try this experiment with a 3 year old child, a 5 year old child and an 8 year old child (on separate occasions if this is easiest).

1 Fill three short fat glasses to the same level with water or juice and show them to the child. Does he agree that each glass has the same amount?

2 With the child watching, pour the liquid from one of the glasses into a long thin glass. Ask the child, 'Do all three glasses have the same amount?'

How does age and development affect their answers?

Developing physical and intellectual skills will also enable the child to plan and carry out more complex creative projects from building dens to baking cakes. He will develop the capacity to follow a plan with an end product in mind and be clear about whether and what assistance he requires from an adult. Adult encouragement and a positive attitude towards creative efforts is particularly important. Sadly, without this encouragement, a 7 year old can already believe it when he says 'I can't draw' and will begin to judge his own efforts by the reaction of others. Fantasy and imaginative play may still be strong, but will increasingly be influenced by what is popular in the culture of peer groups with whom the children mix.

Generally, children become less dependent on their parents or long-term carers than in their preschool years. Friends and peer groups take on increasing importance. The

'They have art and sewing that you wouldn't be able to do at home'

'I like cooking mostly . . . painting too and reading books sometimes. I like making cakes out of junk modelling'

'We make up our own plays . . . like a different version – once we did Home Alone 3'

'You make loads and loads of friends'

'Me and my friends playing' (Polly, aged 6)

development of language and social skills will have been influenced by preschool experiences. Some children will already have had a great deal of experience of being in a group, for example in a playgroup or nursery setting, or by mixing with older siblings and their friends. Others will have had no preschool group experience and may take longer to settle in to your play setting. An increasing ability to understand rules will enable children to participate in a greater variety of games. But many 5 year olds will still have only vague notions about fairness and taking turns and may rely a great deal on imitation in this respect. They will learn rules by participating and imitating rather than by having them explained. Many will still enjoy the traditional, preschool circle and singing games or follow my leader, which may be considered babyish by the time the child reaches 8. While children in this age group are increasingly less dependent on their family, they are becoming more aware of how others see them. They are entering a phase when they begin to feel great shame and embarrassment on being shown up in front of friends. How they cope with this will depend partly on the confidence and self-esteem (or lack of it) built up in their preschool years experience. It will also depend on whether the environment encourages them to try out and practise new skills and challenge themselves physically and mentally, without fear of ridicule if they do not succeed immediately.

Play can be very therapeutic in allowing a child to express her feelings about the world as she experiences it and perhaps 'act out' some of her hopes and fears through imaginative play (but be cautious about reading too much into a child's free play, without knowledge and understanding of psychology or play therapy). Boys and girls tend to stick to friendships of their own gender and play becomes increasingly differentiated for boys and girls during these years, although this separation can begin even earlier.

CASE STUDY   **Chain tig – developing through play**

The playworker was watching Gemma and her friends start a game of chain tig. Joanne was chosen to be 'it' and had to try to catch the others. When she 'tigged' another child, the two linked hands and tried to tig more children together. As more and more children were caught, the 'it' became an ever longer chain of children. The playworker noticed that the children were practising many social skills during the game. They agreed on the rules and found a fair way of choosing who would be 'it'. When the chain broke accidentally, they had to negotiate whether this was OK or whether the game had to start from the beginning again. The children worked together as parts of the chain. Older/taller children needed to consider the needs of the younger/shorter children by gauging the pace so that younger children didn't fall over and made sure that they were safe. There were no losers and cooperation was more important than competition to achieve the end of the game.

Physically, children were using their large muscle movements and developing agility and build stamina through running, ducking, stretching and twisting. The game involved lots of aerobic exercise that was contributing to their overall health. The children were also having to use their thinking or cognitive abilities. They needed to understand the rules of the game and to participate in a counting game to decide who would be 'it'. They also needed to work out strategies (problem solving) for how best to catch others – and used language to discuss their strategies – 'go left … circle round … faster … over here'. The children's emotional development was clearly demonstrated through the sense of being an individual but part of the larger group and the expressing of a range of emotions such as excitement, anticipation, fear of being caught and elation at catching or avoiding being caught.

Chain tig (Gemma, aged 6)

Children aged 8 to 11 – what might they be like?

These years are often seen as the period of most stability within childhood. The 8 year old will generally have settled in or become accustomed to school, and will be building on the foundations described in the previous section on 4 to 7 year olds. During these years, children become increasingly able to fend for themselves and to make reasoned judgements. However, they still need to work things out using trial and error and hands-on practical experience with physical play materials rather than using abstract theories or working things out on paper.

CASE STUDY   **Finding the answer through practical experience**

Salima and Naseem are 9 years old. They are playing in the sand. They want to fill a large old-fashioned milk churn with water. They estimate it will take about six trips to the outdoor tap with the yellow bucket to achieve this. In fact, it takes six-and-a-half buckets to fill the churn, so they are very close. They are quite clear that the churn will always take the same amount of water and will not have to estimate next time, although they do not understand about working out the mathematical volume of things on paper. At 5 years old they would not have been able to make this estimation, neither would they have been so sure that the churn would take the same number of buckets to fill it from one day to the next.

'You're not cooped up in one area. There are lots of choices. I like sport, and sometimes art and craft and cooking'

'I think everybody should get together and say "Shall we have more group games and things" 'cos there are some games you can't play with the small amount of people who want to play them'

'N used to bring her saris and we could dress each other up in her saris'

'People should be able to do things on their own if they want to'

'I like being able to talk ... and drawing. Sometimes we can do quiet things ... although sometimes it's not quiet. I like most of all talking to my friend'

'I like juggling' (Oswah, aged 7)

Physically, children will grow steadily in strength and coordination. By the end of this period, many children will be able to cook and use sharp tools independently of an adult. They continue to lose their first teeth and develop the permanent ones. Some may be entering puberty at the end of this period. Children enter puberty at different ages, with girls usually earlier than boys.

Peer groups continue to be very important and most children, given the opportunity, prefer to play with friends outside, or out of adult range, riding bikes or roller skating in the street or making their own way to the local park or adventure playground. Children aged 9 or 10 understand complex rules and realise that they can be subject to change. They can make up their own new rules. This ability to understand rules has been associated with the development of moral reasoning in children. Research suggests that peer groups may have a much greater influence on this aspect of development than parents, teachers or religious leaders. Through play, children sort out sophisticated concepts of fairness, equality, right and wrong. They understand the consequences of breaking rules and begin to identify how their actions affect others or make them feel. A child of this age can begin to be able to put himself into the shoes of another and to realise that other children can also be expected to understand his point of view. At this age, children continue to associate predominantly with members of their own sex. Psychoanalyst Sigmund Freud (1856–1939) referred to middle childhood as an emotional stage, the 'latency period' (Freud 1975 [1905]), in that strong sexual feelings experienced in preschool years are repressed until puberty. Through imaginative play they continue to try out new roles and explore the world around them. Imaginative play is still important, although this may be more personal and private, without the need for any adult involvement. Many hours may be spent by creating imaginative play spaces – whether they are camps or dens, or miniature worlds of model space stations, insect gardens, desert islands or dolls' houses. A child of this age may take up her first hobby, perhaps taking an interest in a particular animal (and she will now be able to take prime responsibility for the care of a pet) or making collections of things, from stamps, stickers or badges to shells, conkers or sweet wrappers. Small toys (the particular type varies with popular fashion) become prized items to collect and swap with great satisfaction. But these can also be a source of resentment and conflict, particularly as some children have parents or carers who are more willing or able to afford them than others.

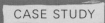

CASE STUDY | **Fossils and dinosaurs**

On returning from a holiday to the beach, 9 year old Stephen brought a bag of shells to the after school club. He was particularly proud of the fossil he had found and talked about the fossil museum he had visited. This captured the imagination of some of the other boys on the scheme and they decided to make their own museum out of cardboard boxes. The prehistoric theme also caught the imagination of some of the younger children – but they went outside and created dinosaur caves and dug in the mud for more fossils, while others made new fossils for the museum out of clay. All sorts of objects were added to the museum over the weeks, from old bones found in gardens to picture postcards from 'real' museums. There was a lot of roaring as dinosaurs invaded the every part of the play space except the book corner, which had to be declared a 'safe zone' by the playworkers to protect those children who were less taken with that particular play theme!

The children's hobbies and interests are a good starting point for art, craft and drama activities. You can also help them to extend their knowledge and interest by providing relevant books. But don't turn the play setting into a classroom. Your aim should be to create play opportunities that are initiated by the children and that they can take in the direction they choose.

The ability to apply creative thinking to problem solving becomes more sophisticated during this period. Confidence and skills development can be encouraged through opportunities for creative achievements. Some children's skill at drawing, construction or use of technology may surpass your own.

Your starting point is the needs and interests of the child

Puberty and adolescence

The term 'puberty' refers to the physical changes that need to occur for a child to become a biologically mature adult. Adolescence refers to the social, emotional and psychological changes that take place over this same time and that will be completed only when the person is recognised as an adult. As with other aspects of development, children will reach puberty at different ages, girls usually maturing before boys of their age group. During puberty, the body produces hormones. In girls, this leads to the development of the ovaries, breasts, pubic and underarm hair and the onset of menstruation (periods). In boys, other hormones lead to growth in the testes and penis, body hair, sperm production and deepening of the voice. These changes are accompanied by an overall 'growth spurt'.

Emotionally, adolescence can be a difficult time, as the rapid changes in hormone levels and bodily changes need time for the emerging adult to adjust to and accept. As children develop at different rates, they may worry if they mature much earlier or later than their friends. They have to deal with new aspects of personal hygiene such as body odour and periods and may become acutely conscious of body hair or spots. Peer groups still play a very important role. Increased physical and financial independence allow more opportunities for potentially negative peer pressure to be exerted to drink alcohol, smoke, take illegal drugs or have sexual intercourse earlier than individual free choice would allow. It is a time when children are often trying to break free from or feel alienated from parents, teachers or other carers, and the less formalised or structured atmosphere of the play setting may enable the playworker to have an important role in giving guidance and support.

'If we've got a problem we can always talk to them [the playworkers]. They're good company'

'Playing on the pulley ... doing parachute games. Gymnastics ... listening to music ... football, face painting ... helping the little kids draw and colour'

'We can look after ourselves more. I know the streets around here'

'Play in balance' (Laura, aged 12)

SPOTLIGHT ON   Concerns about differences in development

Children's development is affected by many things. If you see that a child is obviously a long way behind others of his or her age, you need to think about why this might be. Illness, stress, changes at home such as divorce, bereavement, moving house, bullying, child abuse, pressures from school or home, can all cause delayed or uneven development. A sudden change of behaviour or marked uneven or delayed development should not be ignored. It may be a sign that the child is ill or needs specialist help.

If you are concerned, you can:

- discuss your worries with a senior member of staff
- spend time observing the child to see if there is something within the play setting that is affecting her or whether her play gives any other 'clues'
- talk to the child's parents or carers and see if they can throw any light on things
- contact the child's teachers and see if they share your concerns.

Health visitors, social workers and GPs can give advice on making referrals to other specialist sources of advice. The first step, though, is to discuss the situation with your supervisor or manager.

Young people's thinking and creative capacities really come into their own during this time. They are likely to be full of questions about the world around them, developing skills, and discovering talents that may lead them to future vocations and work or leisure pursuits. They are able to think about problems in an abstract way and work out solutions in their heads without relying solely on direct experience. They may be more aware of environmental and social concerns.

Playwork across a wide range of ages and stages

Few play settings cater for the whole age range of 4 to 16 year olds at the same time. However, where there is a very wide age group, older children will often play an active role in caring for, supervising and encouraging younger children. Many older children will occasionally enter into the play of younger ones (perhaps under the pretext of helping) – dressing up, face painting, constructing bridges or dams in the sandpit.

In a play setting catering for adolescents as well as younger children, their physical and social needs must be considered. Adolescents will require more privacy for matters relating to personal hygiene in washrooms and changing areas and availability of sanitary towels and tampons. There will also need to be comfortable areas in which they can sit and relax and talk or listen to music, perhaps with tea and coffee or other facilities for preparing refreshments (although these should not be accessible to younger children for safety reasons). A play setting catering for a very wide age range needs careful planning and engagement of the children to involve all individuals, so that each child can contribute something at an appropriate level to his or her development.

ACTIVITY   Children's illustrations

1 Look at the illustrations in this section drawn by children of different ages.
  - What can you tell about the child from each drawing?
  - What age do you think the child is and how did you come to this decision?
  - What, if anything, can you tell about the artist's interests and the way he or she perceives the world around him or her?

2 Look at what children said about themselves and their play settings in the quotations in this section. What do they tell you about how these children perceive their own development?

Summary

Children play all over the world and people from all walks of life have studied play and its importance to human development. Playworkers can draw on the thinking and theories of others to help them gain greater understanding, and to provide meaning and depth to their work. As a playworker, you will work with children of different ages. Within each age-band, individual children will be at different stages of development. Observing what children do and talking to them about how they think and feel are two ways of finding out about their development and their play needs. Knowledge and understanding about stages of development and how they relate to different ages can give you a framework in which to place your understanding of the individual children who come to your play setting, and is essential for your professional development as a playworker.

References

Buhler, C. (1935) *From Birth to Maturity*. Routledge.

Else, P. and Sturrock, G. (1998) *The Playground as Therapeutic Space: Playwork as Healing* (known as *The Colorado Paper*). Ludemos.

Freud, S. (1975 [1905]) *Freud Standard Edition 7*. Hogarth Press.

Froebel, F. (1985) *Education of Man*. Augustus M. Kelly.

Garvey, C. (1991) *Play*. Fontana.

Hughes, B. (1996) *A Playworker's Taxonomy of Play Types*. London: PLAYLINK. This publication includes the full text of Bob Hughes play types work. It is available from PlayEducation, 13 Castelhythe, Ely, Cambs CB7 4BU. See also the website: www.playeducation.com.

Huizinga, J. (1971 [1938]) *Homo Ludens: A Study of the Play Element in Culture*. Beacon Press.

NPFA (2000) *Best Play – What Play Provision Should do for Children*. National Playing Fields Association.

Vygotsky, L.S. (1980) *Mind in Society: The Development of Higher Psychological Processes*. Harvard University Press.

Further reading

Brown, F. (ed.) (2003) *Playwork: Theory and Practice*. Open University Press.

Hall, V. and Brennand, H. (2004) *Child Development: Coursework Guide*. Hodder Arnold.

Lindon, J. (2001) *Understanding Children's Play*. Nelson Thornes.

Mooney, C. G. (2000) *Theories of Childhood: An Introduction to Dewey, Montessori, Erikson, Piaget and Vygotsky*. Redleaf Press.

Moyles, J. (1989) *Just Playing – The Role and Status of Play in Early Childhood Education*. OUP.

New theories – useful websites

www.ludemos.co.uk
www.playwales.org.uk

CHAPTER 2
Playwork principles and the role of the playworker

The child has a hundred languages
(and a hundred, hundred, hundred more)
but we steal ninety-nine;
we tell the child
that work and play
reality and fantasy
science and imagination
sky and earth
reason and dream
are things
that do not belong together.

('No way, the hundred is there', poem by Loris Malaguzzi. ©1996 Reggio Children)

Playwork is a growing and developing area of work with increasing opportunities for jobs in a range of children's services. But how does playwork differ from other areas of work with children such as teaching, childcare, youth work, play therapy or social work? A playworker learns to listen and respond to the 'hundred languages of children'. This chapter looks at some of the principles that underpin playwork and how these apply to the role of the playworker. In this chapter, we will consider:

- What is a playworker?
- Assumptions about play, children and childhood
- Finding out about children's play needs
- Principles for responding to the play needs of the children in your setting

What is a playworker?

Most of us did not have 'playworkers' when we were children. We chose where we played, perhaps with a cautionary, 'Don't go too far!' from our parents. Such freedom in our play gave us the chance to explore, make decisions, take risks, set limits and create rules.

Increasingly these days, children do not have such freedom in their play. Children's time is often structured with timetabled activities, extended school and leisure time classes. If they are at home, many will spend the majority of their leisure time sitting down, either playing computer games or watching television. Their parents are often happy to know where their children are and what they are doing, as they might perceive that danger is increasing for children who play in public areas. But children, by nature, are driven to play. If they are not given the chance to play, their behaviour can show signs of irritation, aggressiveness, lack of attention and perhaps withdrawal. If they are physically inactive, they are more likely to suffer ill health and obesity.

Playworkers play a key role in ensuring that the play setting is one where the children want to be. The role of the playworker includes:

- observing, listening to and understanding the play needs of the children
- engaging with children and colleagues in the co-construction and maintenance of the play environment, providing choices in resources and spaces that appeal to a wide range of play types, moods and aesthetic and sensory choices and which are easily continuously adaptable by the children in their play
- ensuring all children who come to the play setting have a right to play and be included in the setting
- being a resource for children in search of new activities and giving encouragement and support to extend and develop activities when requested by the children
- enabling children – as far as possible – to carry out their own ideas, make decisions and carry out plans, at their own pace
- having the self-awareness and professional understanding to be available to join in the children's play when invited – and equally knowing when it's best not to join in or interfere in the play process
- continuously assessing levels of acceptable risk within the play setting, recognising that risk taking is often a vital part of children's play
- ensuring the health and safety standards of the play setting comply with health and safety legislation and that children are not exposed to the unacceptable risk of coming to serious harm
- acting as referee when required, to ensure that the play setting's boundaries of behaviour are negotiated and maintained in order to protect all children's physical and psychological safety and ability to continue to play within the setting.

You may have additional duties, such as:

- administration – keeping records and other written information up to date
- dealing with emergencies
- interviewing and employing playwork staff
- meeting with other people who are associated with the play setting, such as managers, funders, play development workers
- liaising with the children's parents and carers and other agencies with an interest in the children who attend your setting.

| SPOTLIGHT ON | Facilitating play |

The most important role of the playworker is to be at the service of the child at play. A responsive, sensitive adult who does not control children's play can facilitate children's play as a caretaker of the play environment, a protector of the safety of the play space, a bringer of resources, as well as being himself a resource for play. Although this sounds like a simple task, a good playworker knows that it involves a variety of skills and knowledge. Reflection, observation, empathy, caring and self-awareness help playworkers to understand children and the range of needs that must be met to make the best play opportunities possible. Sometimes a range of other needs, such as the need for food, rest, talking about what has gone during the rest of the day, must be met in the play setting before the child is able to engage in play itself.

Assumptions about play, children and childhood

Chapter 3 looks at some of the current legislation, policy and regulation relating to children's services in the United Kingdom today. Every society in the world has a different attitude to children and that will affect the way it is organised. This attitude also changes over time. For example, in 19th-century England, children, on the one hand, were expected to be 'seen but not heard' and, on the other hand, were used as cheap labour in often dangerous industrial activities such as mining or early factories. While this would be unacceptable these days, current policies and attitudes to children often cast them as either weak, vulnerable and in need of protection or as anti-social, disruptive and in need of control. There is often a great variation across different professions working with children in terms of how they see children and their own role. The playwork field has developed principles and values that underpin its work. Central to these values and principles is the idea that children have the right to be recognised as active participants in the creation of their own internal and external reality and experience. Through play, children are able to find out more about who they are and to develop and extend what they are able to do. Playworkers do not see children as 'empty boxes' to be filled with knowledge, or as weak, vulnerable, immature adults to be cosseted and overprotected or as disorderly deviants to be trained and controlled. Playworkers regard children as competent, powerful and autonomous human beings who are active participants from babyhood in developing relationships and interaction with their peers, with adults, with ideas, with objects and with the real and imaginary events of their internal and external worlds.

Chapter 1 looked in more detail at different definitions about play and some of the theories that have been developed about its function and purpose.

Powerful, autonomous child

ACTIVITY   Children's rights

Get a copy of the United Nations Convention on the Rights of the Child (available from HMSO). Consider how you ensure children at your setting are able to act within these rights.

Children's right to play is recognised by the United Nations Convention on the Rights of the Child (Article 31). World leaders, politicians, educationalists and many others agree that play is valuable, even essential to healthy human development. But many things in our adult society can limit or hinder children's opportunities for play. Ideally, every street would have a safe play space, each and every child would be able to meet his or her friends and come and go as she or he pleased, with no roads or other hazards to encounter and overcome. This is not a reality. Parents have become increasingly aware of the dangers of traffic, violence and possible abduction. In many cases, traditional play spaces such as the street are now prohibited to children. Play is seen by many as an unimportant way of letting off steam or passing the time in between real activities such as formal education or work. Play opportunities are shaped by other adult-oriented considerations:

- *Politics, money and town planning*: Towns, cities and roads are built with adult needs in mind and opportunities for play are often overlooked or catered for in a token or inappropriate way: for example, small parks with limited play equipment next to busy roads.

- *Early responsibilities*: Some children need to work from a very young age. They have to care for younger brothers and sisters, or a disabled parent, or they need to work outside the home to contribute to the upkeep of the family.

- *Parents at work, school, leisure-time classes*: Children's time is often structured by the needs of parents' work schedules, school timetables and organised leisure activities such as gym classes, swimming, dancing or music lessons.

- *Consumerism and entertainment*: In our society, where there is a wealth of bought games, toys and equipment, children may have fewer opportunities to develop resourcefulness, to invent or to try out their own ideas. Toy manufacturers rush to produce more attractive and entertaining, or so-called educational, toys. They encourage the children to receive this entertainment or education rather than be active in discovering and exploring the environment in which they live.

- *Television*: The content and timetable of television programmes is also adult determined. Watching TV does not need active participation from the child and often takes up a large proportion of children's free time.

As a playworker, you need to be aware of the conflicting nature of some of these issues. On the one hand, you need to provide a safe play setting with play

How would you find out about this child's play needs?

opportunities that interest and attract the children. But, on the other, you are not there to provide entertainment to be passively absorbed by them or activities that are attractive primarily to parents. You are an advocate and facilitator of the child's right to play. Adults need to take the lead in actively campaigning for and creating play settings. In circumstances that are indifferent or even hostile to the child's right to play, *all* children must have access to play opportunities that expand their horizons and their potential for all-round development.

Finding out about children's play needs

You can learn about children and their needs by asking them directly for their opinions and ideas about the play setting. Observing children at play helps us to know the children's likes and dislikes. This can then inform our choices of play materials and equipment. Some play settings offer children (and their parents and carers) the chance to write ideas and give feedback in a 'suggestions box'. Some play settings are particularly successful at engaging the children to actively participate in the management of the setting, through regular formal and informal meetings and innovative forms of consultation. If children are fully involved, listened to, and their opinions acted on, you are more likely to provide play opportunities that satisfy their needs – and ones that they will enjoy.

SPOTLIGHT ON   **Things to consider when observing children**

If you are observing children outside the workplace, you need to be conscious of the ethical issues involved. For anything other than casual 'child watching' (for example, when you are in the park, at the beach or the supermarket) you need to get appropriate permission. Be prepared to explain what you are doing and why (especially if you are taking notes or want to take photos). Provide reassurance if necessary such as evidence of who you are, your place of work or study and your criminal records bureau clearance:

1 *Make time to observe.* You will need to get agreement from colleagues about when you can observe. It is important that while you are observing you become as unobtrusive as possible. Get your colleagues to agree about when you can leave your usual work and concentrate on observing. Don't feel guilty – observing is important, even if done only for a few minutes at a time.

2 *Decide what you are going to observe and why.* What are the aims of your observation? Are you observing to find out: more about an individual child?; about how a group of children relate to each other?; about a particular activity within a session?; or about how the space is used in order to evaluate and make changes? You may observe more than one of these things at once – but keep your aims simple to begin with.

3 *Decide how to deal with interruptions.* Until children get used to your observing they will be interested in what you are doing and may interrupt with requests for assistance or advice. It may be best to tell the children that you are going to observe before you begin. You can then answer their questions and explain that while you are observing you cannot do anything else and that they should go to another staff member if they need anything until you have finished. Although they may at first change their behaviour if they think or know you are observing them, the more accustomed they become to your observing as a regular activity the less interest they will take.

4 *Decide on a method of observation and recording your observation.* Where will you observe from? How long and how often will you observe for? How will you record your observation? For observations to be most valuable you will need to record what you have observed. This can be done in written form and sometimes with the assistance of a small tape recorder (resources and acoustics permitting!). It takes practice to record written observations as quickly as you need to and it helps if you can develop your own shorthand way of note taking. To save time, have some prepared sheets or pages in a notebook with details to fill in such as aim of observation, date, time and duration (see illustration). Write up your notes more fully when you have time. Some observations are done with the help of checklists, sketches or tick boxes.

5 *Record what you see, not what you think.* Observations need to be as objective as possible. The language you use to record the observation should not be judgemental: 'Tipu drew a single line with a red felt-tip on his piece of paper. He dropped his pen. He walked over and said, "What are you doing?" to R (who was building a den). He did not wait for R's answer but went to the book corner. Picked up a book and put it down. Ran outside to join S, B and P in a game of Unihoc.' This is what you might see. 'Tipu went from one activity to another and did not concentrate on anything and distracted others' is what you might think.

6 *Be aware of confidentiality.* Use initials or first names only when recording observations. Do not write anything you would not want somebody else to read. Keep your observations in a safe place. Be ready to explain why you are observing if asked by parents or visitors.

7 *Reflect on and evaluate what you have observed.* When you have completed your observation, or series of observations, go back to your reasons for observing and ask yourself some questions. See if what you have observed can suggest answers. If you were observing a group activity, for example, you might want to ask: did the activity go as planned? (you will need to know *how* it was planned); how many children joined in?; which children did not?; why might this be? You might want to find out how different children enjoyed the activity. Did all children join in in the same way? Did they seem to be enjoying the activity? How long did each child spend at the activity? Did any child leave the activity before it finished? Why might this be?

Observing children

One of the best ways of learning about children's play and in particular about the play needs and development of children in your play setting is to watch what they do. Most of what child development theorists know and have written about children comes from their direct experience of working with and observing children. This may seem obvious. You know the children in your groups and observe them every working day. But you are also doing a huge range of other things while at work – preparing materials, supervising, sorting out problems, communicating with children and adults, preparing food, joining in play, mediating in disagreements, keeping records. How often do you have the time to stand back and watch what is actually going on over a period of time? Regular observation in your place of work can help you to:

- gain a better understanding of the children in your group: the way they play, their stages of development, interests, behaviour and needs

- identify what leads up to an individual child behaving in a particular way – this is useful if a child is giving cause for concern (for example, not settling into the group, causing disruption, appearing to be bored) as it can give clues as to why the child is behaving in this way

- discover which activities and play opportunities are particularly successful or unsuccessful, with which children, and why this might be so. Observing the play cues of children (see Chapter 1) can also be useful for assessing the play space

- plan and evaluate future activities and play opportunities

- identify what adult behaviour is helpful or unhelpful in encouraging play, including reflecting on your own practice

- discover whether particular times of day in your play setting are likely to cause disruption or stress and think about ways of making changes to alleviate this

- share what you have observed about an individual child or activity or structure of the session with colleagues so that you can plan as a team

- agree where staff can most usefully be deployed.

There may be practical lessons you can learn from your observation. Were there enough materials and equipment? Was there enough, too little, or too much adult response, support or intervention? Were there any health and safety considerations?

There may be other things you can put into practice for the future. Could the play resources be developed to appeal to more or different children or to extend their concentration and enjoyment in it? Which kinds of play seem particularly good at

---

OBSERVATION NOTES

AIM OF OBSERVATION: *To observe single child: Tipu*

Date: *8.8.2005*　　　　Time: *10.35 a.m.*　　　　Place: *Playsetting*

Duration: *2 Minutes*

	ACTIONS	LANGUAGE
10.35	At drawing table	
	T drew red line/dropped pen	
	Walking – den area	T→R "What are you doing?"
	Did not wait for answer	
	Walking – book area	
	Picked up book & put it down	
	Running outside	T→S + B "What are you doing?"
	Joins unihoc game	
10.37		

If you find it difficult to observe and make notes at the same time, practise observing without recording to begin with. If you make time to stand back at regular intervals and practise concentrated observation with a clear aim in mind you can train yourself to notice and remember things more accurately

encouraging different play types (see page 8)? What can you tell about a child from their play cues (or lack of them)? Use what you observed to answer these questions, and, if possible, to increase your knowledge and understanding about the children in your setting, the play process and your self-awareness of your own role as a playworker.

If you cannot get the answers, longer or more frequent observations may be necessary.

As you get more experienced in observing you may find it useful to carry a notepad and pen in your pocket to record quick observations, ideas for changes to be made or issues that need to be raised at a staff meeting. A child's incidental comments or behaviour can be very significant in giving clues to greater understanding. But if you do not record them on the spot, they are often lost in the 'busy-ness' of a session or inaccurately remembered at a later stage.

If you find it difficult to observe and make notes at the same time, practise observing without recording to begin with. If you make time to stand back at regular intervals and practise concentrated observation with a clear aim in mind, you can train yourself to notice and remember things more accurately.

There are many useful ways in which to observe. This book gives observation exercises in many chapters to help you become more aware about particular aspects of your practice. Observing children is a skill that gets easier (and more useful) with practice. There are many types of observation and ways to record observations (see further reading at the end of this section for ideas on this).

Don't forget that children are also constantly observing *you* and each other.

ACTIVITY   Practising observation

1 Observe three or four children, one at a time, who are of the same age group (within the age group of the children you work with). It is helpful to begin observing children outside your work setting, so that you can concentrate on developing your observation skills without being influenced by what you already know about the children or feeling guilty about time taken out of work. You might observe in a park, at a friend's house, in the street, on the beach or in a play setting other than the one in which you work (see Spotlight on 'Things to consider when observing children' with regards to permissions etc.). Spend up to 10 minutes at a time recording what the child says and does. Develop your own

Observing each other

shorthand way of recording/coding what you have seen. (Some of the books listed at the end of this chapter suggest ways of doing this.)

2 Write up your notes.

3 Ask yourself: what was the child doing?; what was his main focus or interest during the observation?; did the child relate to any other children or adults during the observation?; did the observation reveal anything about aspects of the child's play interests or needs?; did you observe the child engaging in any of the 'play types' (see page 8)?

4 Did the observations of different children have anything in common? Can you tell anything about the common interests, play needs or development of children of this age group from your observations?

Principles for responding to the play needs of the children in your setting

Responding to the play needs of the children in your setting and facilitating their play is the core of your job as playworker. Different aspects of this role are explored in greater depths throughout this book, and especially in Chapters 4–8. This section gives a 'taster' of some of the principles that underpin the work.

 SPOTLIGHT ON   The playwork principles

In 2005 Play Wales published the results of a review of the playwork values and assumptions – the principles that underpin playwork and playwork training in the UK. Many major organisations that have an interest in playwork contributed to the review process. After lengthy consultation, the following eight principles were agreed:

1 All children and young people need to play. The impulse to play is innate. Play is a biological, psychological and social necessity and is fundamental to the healthy development and well-being of individuals and communities.

2 Play is a process that is freely chosen, personally directed and intrinsically motivated. That is, children and young people determine and control the content and intent of their play, by following their own instincts, ideas and interests, in their own way for their own reasons.

3 The prime focus and essence of playwork is to support and facilitate the play process and this should inform the development of play policy, strategy, training and education.

4 For playworkers, the play process takes precedence and playworkers act as advocates for play when engaging with adult-led agendas.

5 The role of the playworker is to support all children and young people in the creation of a space in which they can play.

6 The playworker's response to children and young people playing is based on a sound up-to-date knowledge of the play process, and reflective practice.

7 Playworkers recognise their own impact on the play space and also the impact of children and young people's play on the playworker.

8 Playworkers choose an intervention style that enables children and young people to extend their play. All playworker intervention must balance risk with the developmental benefit and well-being of children.

Preparing the play space

Think about how you prepare the play space. How does it look when the children arrive? Children are inspired to play if the environment or activities are exciting, intriguing, adaptable or novel. The same old activities, the same old equipment, and the same old cramped spaces are not conducive to a sense of wonder and an intense drive to play. A variety of choices, a variety of materials, a variety of spaces in which to create play worlds – plus the ability to make choices about how to use the space and materials – will create a play place that children will want to inhabit. Ten cardboard boxes that appeared from nowhere; a rope swing hanging from a tree that wasn't there yesterday; the beginnings of a hole in the ground by a spade; some donated saris, ribbons and shoes – these can create new possibilities for fun and exploration. The play space is not just a physical space, however. As a playworker, you will need to think about it also in terms of how it makes children feel and behave and how it is affected by relationships and behaviour within the play setting. It is also a space in time and the way in which children come and go, and the pressures or freedoms created by the time available within the play setting is also important. More on this in Chapters 4, 5 and 6.

SPOTLIGHT ON   **Boredom and daydreaming**

Children's lives are subject to many of the same stresses of modern life as adults and some that are unique to childhood. Their time is largely filled with programmed activities from school to out-of-school clubs, TV viewing etc. They are expected to constantly progress, to achieve, to 'do well', compete with peers and to earn praise or rewards. Their status and self-esteem may be affected by whether they can get the latest toy or fashion accessory or they may be overloaded with the barrage of communication and information sources from mobile phones to email and the internet that make everyone need to move faster and know more. Adults have choices in how to relax – through hobbies, socialising, health spas, meditation. They can more easily choose when to take a holiday, retire or change jobs. Children have little control over their time and may find few opportunities for 'fallow times', for slowness, daydreaming and simply being bored. What opportunities are there for daydreaming in your play setting? Do you think boredom must be eliminated at all costs?

Safety, challenge and risk

Playworkers have a position of responsibility within the play setting. In order to engage in play, children need to feel secure – that the play setting is a place where they will not be bullied or abused or exposed to unacceptable dangers in terms of the safety of the equipment, for example. Playworkers need to supervise the comings and goings of adults and children and act as guardians of the play space on behalf of the children who use it.

Playworkers should remember also that children play to try out new ideas, to test their own capacities and possibilities as well as the boundaries and limitations or the world around them. An element of challenge is often essential and provides excitement, interest and motivation in play. You can provide resources that give children the chance to decide their own level of challenge. For example, if you provided skipping ropes for the children to play with, what might different children choose to do? One child might put a rope on the ground and jump over it; other children might use some ropes to tie their legs together for a three-legged race. Another child might link some ropes together, tie it to a tree branch and use it as a rope swing.

Some challenging activities will provide an element of risk. As a society, we go out of our way to limit risk and danger in children's lives. But risk helps children to make decisions about how to stay safe in potentially dangerous situations. Much of what we come across in life includes an element of risk, such as crossing roads and playing on high climbing equipment in parks, spending time in or around water – and even cooking on a hot stove or making a bonfire. If we are always making decisions for children, they may end up being unable to make decisions for themselves. If we enable children to learn about risk within the relative safety of the play setting, we boost their confidence and self-esteem and equip them with valuable coping skills for dealing with risk throughout life.

Playworkers need to assess the level of risk involved in an activity – and encourage the children to do the same. The level of risk should not be limitless – that would be irresponsible! But providing a play space where children can make *real* decisions about their own play should be our ultimate goal. More on this in Chapters 4, 5 and 12.

Including everyone

How do you ensure that all children feel welcome to play at your setting? Would accessible doorways and a 'hello' poster in 15 languages be enough? The useful document, *Developing Accessible Play Space: A Good Practice Guide*, suggests that a starting point is to identify the obstacles to play for any child who might wish to access the play space and think about ways to overcome them. Playworkers can do a number of simple things to make sure that any child who comes through the door of your play setting feels immediately at home:

Daydreaming

- go on a training course about how to meet specific needs (this will be even more useful if all staff can attend)
- discuss how to include everyone with the children and staff on a regular basis
- display positive images of children from different cultures and abilities in your setting
- use positive images of children from different cultures and abilities in your publicity leaflets and posters
- think about which activities and equipment can be used to meet all children's specific needs
- keep an eye on meeting diverse needs when you are planning (both short and longer term planning).

If a child with an impairment that you are not familiar with comes to your setting, talk to the child about their likes, dislikes and needs. Talk to their parents or carers, read about it and ask other people. You will be doing your job properly – helping to provide play opportunities for all children. More on this in Chapter 8.

Adults joining in – or interfering?

Adults can play a positive role in children's play. They can help children to acquire new skills, such as using tools. They can get resources which children may not be able to get for themselves. They can act as positive role models, knowing that children learn a lot by imitation. But there are times when it is best for adults to step out of the 'educator' role and let children explore and discover things for themselves. Children often make it known that they would like you to join in their play by giving 'play cues' (see Chapter 1). If they do not, it is often best to leave children to play without adult intervention. If we compare play to a child painting a masterpiece, we would not invite ourselves to join in painting their picture. So, too, would it be invasive to join in a child's play uninvited. As playworkers, you need to trust the play process as one that is vital to the child for her own reasons and the playing child is best placed to determine the content and direction of play. As Johan Huizinga (1970) said: 'Play demands order … the least deviation from it "spoils the game", robs it of its character and makes it worthless.'

As a reflective playworker, you will probably make sure that you are aware of your own emotional issues and responses to what is happening in the play setting. It could be all too easy to use the play setting to work through your own feelings and emotions, but such issues

Adults can play a positive role in children's play

which may arise for you need to be dealt with through personal and professional development and should not intrude into the children's play space (see Chapter 9 for more on reflective practice). Neither should playworkers be tempted to develop the play setting into a classroom or an arena for competitive sports or coaching. Inappropriate intervention in children's play for any of these reasons or other reasons that involve the playworker using her or his position of power as an adult in the play setting for anything other than facilitating children's play is sometimes called 'adulteration' in playwork terms.

CASE STUDY   The role of the playworker

At the adventure playground, Robert and Hafiz are building a large construction using empty oil drums, planks of wood, plastic milk crates and car tyres. They have amassed their building materials from around the playground site and are attempting to balance the third oil drum on top, but are finding it difficult to get up to the height required to achieve this balancing act.

There are four workers. Each would give a different response to this situation:

- *Worker A* sees what is going on. Does nothing. She believes children should be allowed to 'get on with it'. Adults should not interfere in children's play.

- *Worker B* sees what is going on, calls across the playground: 'Oi. Hold on. That's not safe. Let me give you a hand.' Walks over to the children and balances the oil drum in position.

- *Worker C* sees the situation. Walks over to the boys. 'That looks interesting. How many oil drums do you think you can balance on top of each other?' Both boys look at him and say nothing. 'How do you think we can find out?'

- *Worker D* sees the situation. Approaches close to the boys and watches and listens. She discovers that the boys are trying to build a bulldozer. When Robert, teetering on tiptoes and trying to balance a cardboard box looks pleadingly in her direction, she asks: 'Do you think the small stepladder from the store cupboard would help?' As Robert returns with the ladder, she adds: 'There is a pulley in the office that might help in making the bulldozer's lever when you need it. Oh – and have you seen the hard hats in the dressing up box?' As the children get on with their play, the playworker continues on her way.

Which of the responses is most appropriate? Why?

Discussion points for case study: The role of the play worker

The case study shows how adults can respond to children's play in different ways. Worker A believes in a non-intervening approach. Children will learn for themselves. In many cases, this might be true. Alternatively, Hafiz and Robert might have given up in frustration or the oil drum might have fallen on someone's head.

Worker B was vigilant about safety. However, Hafiz and Robert will have learnt nothing about how to build more safely next time or how to take responsibility for their own safety. They will become more dependent on adults.

Worker C was interested in what Robert and Hafiz could learn from the situation about building, number and balance. However, the children's motivation for building was lost. They were unresponsive because the focus of their play had been switched from building a

Play and creativity have always been closely aligned

bulldozer to building a tower and counting numbers of oil drums. The control and the direction of their play was taken over by the adult.

Worker D spent time 'tuning in' to what the focus of the children's play was and waiting for a cue before getting involved. She considered what their needs might be. She made a suggestion and offered resources that would both improve safety and extend the imaginative aspect of their play without taking over control.

Creativity and playfulness

Play and creativity have always been closely aligned. The Next Generation Foundation Report (1999) states:

> *For the creative society, it is playfulness that really matters. Playfulness is a mindset of approach, which applies equally well to children and adults. Playfulness therefore bridges the fundamental gap in the understanding from childhood to adulthood.*

Many play settings recognise the need for resources for a range of creative activities within the play setting – be it arts and craft, music, dance or drama. However, the playwork approach emphasises the creative process that children activate in themselves when they engage with the resources or with each other or with their playworkers in using these materials. Creativity is also involved in a playful approach to a range of other activities that might go on within the play setting – daydreaming, debating and simply pottering about can be part of what goes on when an individual child is 'percolating' a new idea or solving a question or riddle or developing a solution to a problem that has been bothering him. As a playworker, it is important for you to nourish your own sources of creativity so that you will be able to recognise, support and respond to it in the children. More on this in Chapter 9.

SPOTLIGHT ON   **Privacy as well as protection**

Playworkers have a responsibility and legal duty to protect children from abuse. Children will not play freely within the play setting if they do not feel that they are relatively secure and safe from serious harm. Children also often want to play in places where they cannot be observed by others. Some like to make dens and play out their fearful or brave responses to real or imagined dangers. Some like to find somewhere quiet and undisturbed to read or think. For some, it is a rare treat to experience stillness or solitude. Others like to be in relatively wild or unchartered territory where they can explore and discover 'new worlds'. Your play setting may not be able to recreate all these possibilities for all children at the same time – trips and outings to the forest or the beach may be an important part of the additional play experiences you open up to the children. However, human rights and human dignity demand access to privacy as well as protection. What opportunities for privacy are available to young people in your play setting?

It never sleeps, it never blinks,
It never wavers and never winks
It's way up high and watching.

Every night and every day,
It keeps its vigil watching children play
It's supposed to keep us safe.

Sometimes it's like we're on Big Brother,
But it's watching you and no other,
The camera on the wall.

Is the camera really working?
Or is it just up there lurking,
To stop us from misbehaving.
Should I feel glad, or maybe sad?
That people think we would be that bad
That they need to relentlessly watch us?

(Poem by Gemma, aged 13)

Summary

This chapter follows on from Chapter 1 in broadly covering the current definitions, principles and approach of playwork. It has provided an overview of the role of the playworker and stressed the need for reflective practice and for playworkers to develop skills in observation in order to know how best to facilitate and serve the playing child.

References

Huizinga, J. (1970) *Homo Ludens*. Paladin.
Malaguzzi, L. (1196) 'No way, the hundred is there'. Translated by L. Gandini. From the Catalogue of the Exhibit *The Hundred Languages of Children*, p.3. ©1996 Infant-toddler Centers and Preschools, Instituzione of the Municipality of Reggio Emilia. Published by Reggio Children, Via Bligny, 1/a-42100 Reggio Emilia, Italy. info@reggiochildren.it
Next Generation Foundation (1999) *Report*. www.ngf.org.uk.
Play Wales (2005) *Report*. www.playwales.org.co.uk.

Further reading

Bonel, P. and Lindon, J. (2000) *Playwork – A Guide to Good Practice*. Stanley Thornes.
Hughes, B. (2001) *Evolutionary Playwork and Reflective Analytic Practice*. Routledge.
Newstead, S. *A Busker's Guide to Playwork*. Common Threads (email info@commonthreads.co.uk).
NPFA (2000) *Best Play – What Play Provision Should do for Children*. National Playing Fields Association.
Play Wales (2000) *The First Claim ... A Framework for Playwork Quality Assessment*. www.playwales.org.co.uk.

Material from Websites

Developing Accessible Play Space: A Good Practice Guide. Office of the Deputy Prime Minister, 2003. Can be found on the website: www.odpm.gov.uk or call 0870 1226 236 for a copy.

The Next Generation Foundation website: www.ngf.org.uk.

Books with useful sections on observing children

Bartholomew, L. and Bruce, T. (1993) *Getting to Know You – A Guide to Record Keeping in Early Childhood Education and Care*. Hodder & Stoughton.

Brown, F. (1989) *Working with Children: A Playwork Training Pack*. Leeds Metropolitan University Play Research Unit.

Lindon, J. and Lindon, L. (1993) *Caring for the Under-8s*. Thomson Learning.

Moyles, J. (1989) *Just Playing?* OUP.

CHAPTER 3
Playwork settings, policy and legislation

We find play present everywhere as a well-defined quality of action which is different from 'ordinary' life.
(Johan Huizinga, 1872–1945)

Playworkers work in many different types of setting. This chapter gives some examples of different kinds of settings and sets out some of the current legislation and frameworks that affect how they operate. In this chapter, we will consider:

- What is a play setting?
- Aims and objectives
- Legislation and quality standards
- Every Child Matters: the role of local authorities in planning local services for children

What is a play setting?

Children use a wide range of settings outside school and home. Each setting will have particular aims and serve the needs of different groups of children, parents and the community. In a play setting, children's play will be a central part of what happens there and the staff should have knowledge and understanding of a playwork approach to working with children.

You may work in an after school club, a play centre, a holiday play scheme, a playbus, an adventure playground, as a childminder in your own home or another kind of play setting altogether.

Playwork and childcare

Many playwork settings also provide a childcare service to parents. Sometimes these are called 'playcare' settings. In these settings, there is always a contract between the child's parent or carer that the child will be looked after until she or he is collected at the end of the session. The purpose of such a setting might be to provide a range of things including security, a healthy meal, personal and social advice and support and so on. Playworkers in this kind of setting might be particularly challenged in having to fulfil the role of carer, or substitute parent, as well as supporting children to develop their own play and feel relaxed enough to 'hang out' in a space that they can make their own. The role of the playworker is explored in more depths in Chapter 2.

'It depends what you actually want to do. If you want to play outside you can play outside. If you want to make something particular you can make it'

'It's fun. It keeps you off the streets. Stops you getting into trouble. I just like it here'

'You're never bored here. Never'

'Some people are not allowed home on their own – like me – and there wouldn't be anyone to look after them if they went home on their own and there wasn't an after school club'

'You get to see your friends when you don't see them at other times. Friends that don't live near me'

'It's good in the summer because you can get out – but it's good in the winter because it's warm too'

The following examples describe some playwork settings. If you are relatively new to playwork, they will enable you to build a picture of the kind of settings in which playworkers work. It is useful for all playworkers to visit a range of play settings and read about practice in other settings as part of their ongoing professional development.

ACTIVITY	Survey of play settings

Conduct a small survey within your local or neighbouring area. Find out from your local authority what provision for play is made for school-aged children within this area. There will probably be both supervised settings (holiday playschemes, after school clubs, playbuses) and unsupervised settings (parks, recreation grounds). If possible, arrange to visit or volunteer to help in one or two different kinds of supervised play setting. If your area has few such facilities, you may need to look at another area. It is useful if you can visit play settings in contrasting areas such as an inner city area and a rural one.

The adventure playground

The adventure playground has a large Portakabin placed on a fenced-in piece of what was once wasteland. It backs on to a large housing estate.

Outside there are several large and small structures, built from old telegraph poles, railway sleepers and various other pieces of reclaimed material such as tyres, oil drums and plastic tubing. The structures are always changing under the influence of new ideas thought up and carried out by the children and playworkers. Sometimes there are large rope swings or aerial runways. At other times, a tree house or a skateboarding ramp is the main focus of structural activity. The playworker ensures that safety standards are maintained.

There is a large sandpit, big enough for six large 12 year olds to stand or sit in and create forts or fountains (with water from the outside tap) or bury each other in up to the neck. There is a small vegetable garden, some bushes and trees and the focal point of the outside area is a large open fireplace with logs in a circle around it for seats. Children and workers gather here to keep warm in winter, to have barbeques in summer, to chat, to brew a cup of tea or make some pumpkin soup at Hallowe'en. The adventure playground borders on a sports field that is used by some of the children and workers for more structured team games.

Adventure playground

The building is not used much unless it rains. There are toilets, a small kitchen and office space. There is a big store cupboard with arts and crafts materials, sports equipment, musical instruments, tools of all kinds and some games. There is a comfortable corner with soft chairs and a settee and an inviting display of books. The walls are covered with pictures, posters and graffiti, created or chosen by the children.

The adventure playground is open every day after school until 6 pm. It is open from 10 am until 4 pm at weekends and all day in the holidays.

Children come and go as they please throughout the opening times. There are always staff there to welcome them and to ensure that the playground remains a safe, as well as an adventurous, place to be.

Many exciting things go on through the different seasons. Festivals are celebrated. Friendships are made and broken. Tears and fears are shared as well as joy and laughter. Most of all it is a place that belongs to the children. Here is a space where they can decide what to do. They create their own challenges and get help and support, if they need it, to put them into action.

SPOTLIGHT ON   Adventure play

Adventure playgrounds usually have 'supporting children's free play' as their main purpose. They began in the 1940s and were originally known as 'junk playgrounds'. They are usually 'open access' meaning that children come and go as they please on a drop-in basis and much, if not all, of the play takes place outdoors. They exist mainly in big towns and cities. If you do not work in an adventure playground, try to arrange to visit one – either in your local area if there is one or find one nearby by contacting one of the national organisations that promote adventure playgrounds (see appendix).

When you visit, think about the following:

- What can children gain from this kind of play setting that might not be offered by other types of play setting?

- What possibilities for 'adventure' are offered by the play setting in which you work?

The after school club

The after school club is based in a community hall in the centre of a medium sized town. It is open every weekday from 3 pm until 7 pm. The children, aged from 5 to 12 years, are collected from three local schools by the playworkers. There is one large hall, toilets and a kitchen. They have use of a small hardcore area that can be used for ball games and suchlike outside and a park down the road that is often used by groups of children from the club, accompanied by playworkers.

The playworkers aim to offer a 'home-from-home' atmosphere, with the extra benefits of having a large group of same-age children to play with. The room has to be set up daily as other groups use it at other times.

As the décor is drab, the playworkers cover the walls each day with large pieces of coloured fabric stapled to pieces of display board on the walls. These cloths provide a backdrop for children's artwork. Sometimes they are used to set the scene for a particular theme around which the play opportunities for the week are based: shades of blue and green materials when the theme is water; mirrored fabrics from India when the festival of Diwali is being celebrated.

They have several movable screens and pieces of furniture – some of which double as pieces of storage equipment for art materials and games. With these they divide the large room into more welcoming small areas – a relaxing area with books and beanbags, a 'messy' area for art and craft and water play, table space for board games. There are three large trunks (with air holes in lids) that contain a variety of imaginative play materials – dressing-up clothes, blankets, cloths, hats and props, picnic and teasets, dolls, musical instruments and puppets. The children take these trunks, which are mounted on castors, to particular areas of the room in which they wish to build their houses and hidey-holes or create their cafés, islands, doctor's surgeries or theatrical productions.

The after school club offers a cooked meal to all children and caters for a variety of dietary needs – there is always a vegetarian option, which is particularly important as there is a large local Hindu population whose children attend the club. There is a television in a small side room and the children negotiate a limited amount of viewing time with each other and the staff. The children remain at the after school club until collected by their parents.

The playbus

The mobile play project is based on the outskirts of a large town. It has an office space, a large storage unit and parking for its two double-decker playbuses. One of these buses goes out to rural areas where the children lack access to other play opportunities. This bus also visits travellers' park-up sites in and around the town. The other bus goes to areas of the town that lack playgroup or other play facilities: a large housing estate and an area of the town with a lot of temporary accommodation where children and families have little or no play space during the day.

Playworkers on both buses run a variety of play sessions geared to different age groups. During term times they might run an under-5s session in the morning and a youth group for 10 to 14 year olds in the early evening. They also have holiday sessions for 5 to 9 year olds. The kinds of session they offer will be largely decided by the groups they are working with. Where the bus goes changes over time, depending on where a need for additional play resources is identified.

Both buses are brightly decorated on the outside with pictures designed by children. Inside, the downstairs areas are converted to provide a comfortable seating area with children's books and an information stand with welfare rights advice and health and community information aimed at parents and older children. There is a 'Portaloo' with

Playbus

running water in the washbasin. There are pull-out tables for games, puzzles and construction activities.

Upstairs there is a small kitchen area. Most of the upstairs is often used for messy and creative play opportunities of all kinds from potato printing and sandplay to woodcuts and glass painting. Sometimes the whole upper deck is filled with a variety of soft play equipment, for more energetic activity sessions. At other times the area is used to create an imaginative play area – a cave, a Bedouin tent, a spaceship, a Chinese restaurant . . . The under-5 sessions are for children together with their parents or carers. Sessions for older children are usually drop-in sessions where children come and go as they please. The bus tries to park close to the homes of the children it serves, preferably with no major roads to cross.

SPOTLIGHT ON Different spaces

Playbus workers have to be adept at working within a very small space. Playworkers in other play settings may need to break up a large echoing hall into smaller, inviting and comfortable play spaces. Some settings have access to plenty of outdoor space, whereas others may be much more limited. Playworkers need to develop skills in making the most of what is available, which might include using local parks, school grounds and other community resources. Often the most difficult spaces to work with are those that are shared (for example, within a school or community centre) where things have to be 'packed away' each day. Wherever possible, the place space should belong to the children and they should have the maximum opportunities to develop and adapt it in the way that suits their play. The play environment is considered in more detail in Chapter 4.

The holiday playscheme

Two classrooms and the school hall of a village school are used to accommodate 30 children from surrounding villages and four playworkers.

The scheme runs from 10 am to 4 pm on weekdays for two weeks in the summer holidays. The playscheme aims to offer a 'holiday' for children and a break for parents. The focus is on group activities, including several daytrips – to the seaside, the zoo, a theme park and so on.

Each day starts with cooperative games in the hall, using soft balls or a parachute. Then there is a choice of art-and-craft activities, board games or team sports outside on the sports field or indoors in the hall. There are limited opportunities for free play: a Playdough table, a book corner, face painting, a climbing frame outside.

Children bring a packed lunch. Most children are brought and collected by their parents, but the playscheme organisers have teamed up with a community transport scheme to enable children who

Holiday playscheme

are in isolated areas without transport to attend. This transport scheme also enables several children who are wheelchair users to attend. The playscheme staff ensure that all the activities are accessible to all children in the scheme.

The extended school

The large primary school is in the centre of a housing estate. Over recent years, with help from different sources of new funding, the local community, working with the school governors, have developed a dedicated play centre – two rooms with separate toilets and kitchen attached to the school.

Children can come here out of school hours between 8.00 in the morning and 6.00 in the evening every day of the year apart from weekends, a week at Christmas and bank holidays. This space is dedicated to the children who use it and they are constantly engaged in deciding how it should be developed. There is access to the school playing fields where a wide range of sports and ball games are organised. The play centre does not provide full cooked meals, although the school's meal service provides a cooked breakfast in term time. Staff at the play centre supplement the children's packed lunches in the holidays with healthy snacks such as soup in the winter and barbeques in the summer.

The playworkers work with a range of other professionals who work with children on the site – for example, the school nurse and health visitor who have an office and clinic room onsite. They also liaise with the teaching assistants who run the homework club in the neighbouring IT suite, as many of the children go there for help with their homework before or after coming to the play centre. The children who come to the play centre are also able to come and go to other activities offered after school, such as drama club, sports sessions and music lessons. Because there are so many other activities organised onsite, the playworkers see their role as providing a space that is not structured and that can respond flexibly to the children's individual needs to chat, listen to music, mess about on their skateboards or simply read or daydream.

ACTIVITY   Survey of children's play

1 Conduct a small survey among a group of children aged 4–8, 8–12 or 12–16 in your local area and ask them:
   - Where they spend most time playing.
   - Where they would like to spend most time playing, if there were no restrictions or limitations. (*Note*: It is probably best if you arrange to carry out this survey by making contact with a school in the area and getting permission to carry out your survey within the school.)
2 Does the provision meet the needs and interests expressed by the children?

ACTIVITY   Creating a home-from-home atmosphere

Make a list of the things you do in your play setting to develop a homely environment. Each child's experience and idea of what makes home will be different. Talk to the children in your setting about what they think would make the setting more 'homely' and whether there is anything they could do to make the environment a good place to relax in.

Any setting can become a play setting

The children's centre

Like the extended school, the children's centre houses a range of services for children. There are lots of opportunities for parents too – with family planning and maternity classes, a job seekers' club, adult education classes, family centre drop-ins and year-round childcare service for children from 6 months old to 12 years old. Playworkers from the out-of-school scheme collect children from three local primary schools. The centre is managed by a national voluntary organisation and a committee, which has representation from all the statutory agencies as well as several parents. There is a strong focus on parent participation and parents often volunteer to work in the out-of-school play setting and several have trained as playworkers there.

During term time in school hours, the rooms used for the out-of-school centre are used by play therapists to support children referred by other agencies who are considered vulnerable and need of additional support.

Aims and objectives

Many settings, such as the after school club and the children's centre described earlier, are providing childcare as well as play opportunities. Each setting is different and aims to meet particular needs for a particular purpose. Sometimes, the purpose is written down formally in a vision statement or as aims and objectives. Because play is an important part of what is provided, these settings employ playworkers to staff them.

SPOTLIGHT ON   *Best Play's* 'Playwork objectives'

The booklet *Best Play* (see further reading at the end of the chapter) sets out the following seven key objectives for playwork settings:

Objective 1: The provision extends the choice and control that children have over their play, the freedom they enjoy and the satisfaction they gain from it.

Objective 2: The provision recognises the child's need to test boundaries and responds positively to that need.

Objective 3: The provision manages the balance between the need to offer risk and the need to keep children safe from harm.

Objective 4: The provision maximises the range of play opportunities.

Objective 5: The provision fosters independence and self-esteem.

Objective 6: The provision fosters children's respect for others and offers opportunities for social interaction.

Objective 7: The provision fosters the child's well-being, healthy growth and development, knowledge and understanding, creativity and capacity to learn.

Are there any written aims and objectives for the setting you work in? How many are about providing opportunities for children's freely chosen play? Are there any objectives that are related to other things such as childcare or education?

Legislation and quality standards

Play opportunities should always be provided within the current legislative framework relevant to children's rights, health and safety and well-being. The legal aspects of your work are raised in relevant chapters throughout this book but the following section relates specifically to registration of out-of-school play and childcare settings in England. Standards and regulation and inspection arrangements vary across England, Scotland, Wales and Northern Ireland and it is recommended that readers gain the guidance documents from the organisations listed under further reading at the end of the chapter.

National standards and regulations

The Children Act 1989 provides a regulatory framework for all childcare provision for children aged under 8 years, including after school clubs and holiday playschemes. The requirement to register covers all settings that provide play and childcare for children under 8, for a period or total of periods of more than two hours in any one day, where the care takes place on non-domestic premises on more than five days a year. Settings that only offer provision to children over 8 years old can gain official recognition for the quality of what they offer by undertaking a recognised quality assurance scheme. This will also enable parents to claim tax credits to offset the cost of fees.

The Children Act 1989 set out minimum standards for floor space, staff ratios, staff qualifications and other aspects affecting the quality of childcare. The Care Standards Act 2000 (Part VI) revised the standards and from September 2001 transferred the responsibility for the registration and inspection duties from local authorities to the Office for Standards in Education (Ofsted).

The 14 national standards are the basis on which your play setting will be inspected. They cover:

1 *Suitable person.* Adults providing daycare, looking after children or having unsupervised access to them must be suitable to do so.

2 *Organisation.* The provider must meet required adult-to-child ratios and organise space and resources to meet the children's needs effectively.

3 *Care and learning.* Providers must meet children's individual care needs and promote their welfare. They must plan and provide a broad range of activities to develop children's emotional, physical, social and intellectual capabilities.

4 *Physical environment.* The premises must be safe, secure and suitable for their purpose. They must provide adequate space in an appropriate location, be welcoming to children and have the necessary facilities for a range of activities that promote their development.

5 *Equipment.* Furniture, equipment and toys provided must be appropriate for their purpose and help to create an accessible and stimulating environment. They must be of suitable design and condition, well maintained and conform to safety standards.

6 *Safety.* The provider must take positive steps to promote safety within the setting and on outings and ensure proper precautions are taken to prevent accidents.

7 *Health.* The provider must promote the good health of children, take positive steps to prevent the spread of infection and take appropriate measures when children are ill.

8 *Food and drink.* Children must be provided with regular drinks and food in adequate quantities for their needs. Food and drink must be properly prepared, nutritious and comply with dietary and religious requirements.

9 *Equal opportunities.* The provider and staff must actively promote equality of opportunity and anti-discriminatory practice for all children.

10 *Special needs* (including special educational needs and disabilities). The provider must be aware that some children may have special needs and ensure that appropriate action is taken when such a child is identified or admitted to the provision. Steps must be taken to promote the welfare and development of the child within the setting in consultation with the parents.

11 *Behaviour management.* Adults looking after children in the provision must be able to manage a wide range of children's behaviour in a way that promotes their welfare and development.

12 *Working in partnership with parents and carers.* The provider and staff must work in partnership with parents to meet the needs of the children, both individually and as a group. Information must be shared.

13 *Child protection.* The provider must comply with local child protection procedures approved by the area child protection committee and ensure that all adults working and looking after children in the provision are able to put the procedures into practice.

14 *Documentation.* Records, policies and procedures that are required for the efficient and safe management of the provision, or to promote the welfare, care and learning of children must be maintained. Records about individual children must be shared with the child's parent.

Shortly after an inspection, the setting will be given an inspection report that will give an inspection grade from the following:

Grade 1: Outstanding

Grade 2: Good

Grade 3: Satisfactory

Grade 4: Inadequate.

A Grade 4 means that your setting will be given limited time to make changes or, in rare cases, closed with immediate effect.

Inspectors will also be looking at how your play setting meets the five outcomes for children in Every Child Matters (see below).

What would this child say to the inspection officer?

ACTIVITY Registered?

Does your play setting have to be registered and inspected? What is the name of the body responsible for registration and inspection? If your setting is not registered, do you understand the legal reasons why your setting is exempt? If the answer is yes – when was the last inspection? Read the last inspection report for your setting. What was highlighted as strengths or weaknesses? Were there any action points?

Other relevant legislation

There are many other laws affecting individuals and organisations that can have a bearing on playwork. Chapter 8 looks at legislation affecting unlawful discrimination. Other legislation mostly relates to management responsibilities in a play setting and establishing its legal status as an organisation or an employer.

Every Child Matters: the role of local authorities in planning local services for children

Every Child Matters, the government's vision for children's services, was published in September 2003. It proposed reshaping children's services to help achieve the following outcomes for children during their childhood and in later life:

- be healthy
- stay safe
- enjoy and achieve
- make a positive contribution
- achieve economic well-being.

The Children Act 2004 makes local authorities responsible for setting up the arrangements to ensure that different agencies working with children cooperate. Such services include primary care trusts, youth offending teams, the police, children's services, education and social services and also play and leisure organisations and voluntary sector and community groups. They will usually do this through means of establishing a children's trust.

The provision of adequate play and recreation opportunities forms part of the government's requirements, inspection and review of local authorities and children's trusts. The legislation also makes for new arrangements for safeguarding children (see Chapter 11).

Legislation is designed to protect the welfare of children

Local authorities also need to plan and coordinate a workforce development strategy that will ensure that all qualifications for people working with children, including playwork, have a 'common core' of knowledge and skills covering:

- effective communication and engagement with children, young people and families
- child and young person development
- safeguarding and promoting the welfare of the child
- supporting transitions
- multi-agency working
- sharing information.

Local authority children's services departments can provide information on the range of services available and also training opportunities for playworkers within their local area.

SPOTLIGHT ON   Play and quality assurance

Using a quality assurance scheme can help support you and your colleagues think about the way in which you work and how you can improve the services you offer. A quality assurance scheme can guide you, with the support of external mentoring, through a self-assessment process about different aspects of quality in your provision.

Whether you are a child, parent, playworker or inspector you will have your own idea about what makes for 'good quality' within a setting. Your opinions will be affected by your own experiences and likes and dislikes as well as your professional understanding of what makes for 'good practice'. Quality assurance schemes aim to develop agreed standards that we can all sign up to. They will cover a range of areas such as health and safety, effective communication, behaviour and so on. Because most schemes cover a range of settings, the central role of play within the play setting and the unique role of the playworker in supporting children at play and the values and principles underpinning playwork may not always be covered as comprehensively as the standards about care. Look out for the schemes that have been developed by the playwork sector – see further reading at the end of the chapter.

How would you judge the quality of this play opportunity?

Summary

This chapter has given an overview of the kinds of settings where you might work as a playworker and some of the current policies and regulations that will impact on the work you do. It stresses the importance of developing clear aims and objectives and working with others to increase your understanding of minimum standards and the meaning of quality within a play setting. These ideas are developed further in other chapters of the book.

Reference

Huizinga, J. (1970) *Homo Ludens*. Paladin.

Further reading

NPFA (2000) *Best Play – What Play Provision Should do for Children*. National Playing Fields Association.

National policies

Every Child Matters: http://www.everychildmatters.gov.uk.
http://www.childpolicy.org.uk – links policy information on children's services across the four nations of England, Scotland, Wales and Northern Ireland.

Regulation and inspection

England

http://www.ofsted.gov.uk or contact your local authority or children's information service for guidance.

Scotland

Scottish Commission for the Regulation of Care: www.carecommission.com.
  Her Majesty's Inspector of Schools, Scotland (HMIS)
  Tel: 0131 244 8293
  www.scotland.gov.uk/hmie

Wales

National Assembly for Wales, Care Standards Inspectors for Wales www.csiw.wales.gov.uk.
  Her Majesty's Inspectorate For Education and Training in Wales is called ESTYN
  Tel: 02920 446446
  www.estyn.gov.uk

Northern Ireland

Oak House, Limetree Avenue, Millennium Park, Naas, Co. Kildare
  Tel: +353 (0)45 880400
  www.hse.ie
Department of Education Northern Ireland (schools)
  Tel: 01247 279279
  www.deni.gov.uk

Quality assurance

www.surestart.gov.uk/ensuringquality/investorsinchildren/endorsedqualityassuranceschemes.

Play Wales (2001) *The First Claim … A Framework For Playwork Quality Assessment*, available from www.playwales.org.co.uk

Quality in Play – a playwork-based nationally endorsed quality assurance scheme available from: London Play, Units F6 and F7, 89–93 Fonthill Road, London N4 3JH. Tel: 020 7272 2464

PART TWO

Playwork in practice

CHAPTER 4
Creating play spaces

The pleasures of childhood should in the main be such as the child extracts from his environment by means of some effort and inventiveness.

(Bertrand Russell, 1872–1970)

The play space includes both the physical space – the building, rooms, heating, lighting and ventilation, outdoor play areas, landscaping and structures; and less tangible factors such as the mood and appeal. This chapter looks at your role in planning, preparing and evaluating the play space. Chapter 5 will extend this further to look at the possibilities for action and experience – the play opportunities – that are offered within it. In this chapter, we will consider:

- Starting with the child at play
- Key features in a good quality play space
- Possibilities and limitations of your play space
- Auditing, monitoring and evaluating the quality of your play space

When planning and developing the play space you will also need to consider factors such as legislation and safety (Chapter 12) as well as the principles and values of playwork and your role as the playworker (Chapter 2), the relationships that you form (Chapter 6) and the behaviour within the play setting (Chapter 7). Here, however, we are looking at mainly the physical features of the play space: to see how to plan for a play setting that is centred around the needs of the children at play.

Starting with the child at play

A child's eye view

How do you find out about how different children experience the play space and what are the key features of their preferred play places? You could simply ask them to tell you, but you are likely to get deeper insights and more information by asking them to take you on a journey around their play spaces (see activity 'Where do you like to play?') or by simply watching and listening to children at play. You will be able to use what you learn to plan the play space.

Our surroundings are important to us. Buildings, parks, wild places such as woods and beaches – each will have a different impact on how we feel and want to behave. It follows then that the nature of your play setting will affect the way the children feel and want to behave. Your starting point should be the children's experience of the play space and the opportunities for play that are contained within it. Individual children will have different preferences according to their age, personality and temperament.

ACTIVITY | **Where do you like to play?**

Look back at the survey you were asked to carry out in the activity 'Survey of children's play' in Chapter 3. What did the children in the age range say about where they liked to play? If possible, ask a couple of children of different ages to take you on a journey around some of their favourite play spaces and tell you what they like about them. Ask open-ended questions such as: What do you like to do here? How does it make you feel to be here? What is it about this place that makes it interesting or fun? Which places don't you like? Why? If you are doing this outside of the play setting, you will need to explain what you are doing and get permission from the parents or carers first (see Chapter 2, page 27).

SPOTLIGHT ON | **How does this place make you feel?**

When thinking about the play space in your role as a playworker, it is useful for you to be aware of your own preferences. How do different kinds of spaces affect you now? For example, how does it make you feel to be:

- in a room with a fire on a wet winter's day?
- in a large institution such as a hospital or government office?
- in a dark forest?
- on the top of a high tower?
- at the seashore on a summer's day?

Think back to your own childhood, to times and places you remember as times of happy play:

- Where did the play take place?
- Were you alone or with others?
- Was there an adult present?

Think about one particular favourite play space. What did it feel like? What were the sounds, sights, smells and textures? Ask others to recall their experiences to you or read autobiographical accounts of childhood play. You should be aware of the possibly powerful nature of reflecting on your own feelings about places to play that can be both pleasant and/or unpleasant depending on your personal experiences. Be sensitive to the fact that individuals all react very differently. One person's snug secure hidey-hole might be another person's claustrophobic nightmare.

When adults talk about their childhood play experiences there will often be common features – such as strong memories of outdoor play and places away from adults or where there was an element of excitement. However, not all adults can recall happy play memories and the playworkers' attitude to the play space may be shaped partly by past experience.

Children need to feel that they belong to and have rights within their play environment. They should be involved in the decisions about what happens there and be able to get what they need without adult help whenever possible. Older children, with greater experience and maturity, will be able to consider the wider needs and limitations of the play setting. They can be consulted more formally about what resources should be provided and what activities are offered. A younger child's choices and decisions will relate to his own needs and the way he wants to play within the possibilities open to him. A child-centred environment for play will enable the children to initiate and take their play in many directions at a pace they feel comfortable with.

Do the children in your play setting know what play materials are available to them at any time? If the answer is no, there may be good reasons:

- Some materials may be too expensive or in short supply to allow unlimited access.
- Other materials are potentially too dangerous to allow unsupervised use by the children, particularly by younger children if you have a wide age range.

In either case, however, there is no reason why the children should not know of the existence of all play materials and equipment. Only then can they know to ask when they need something. Limited or inaccessible storage space or the fact that children may 'spoil' equipment should not be reasons to limit access. Enabling the children to feel that the play setting belongs to them is part of your role as a playworker. Your aim should be to encourage children's independence and sense of responsibility towards the play setting. Some play settings hold children's meetings to help plan activities or make changes to the

Wide open spaces invite playfulness

environment. Others may use more informal opportunities for discussion – such as over a drink or snack. Children's participation in the planning and development of the play space does not necessarily mean always giving them what they want. As a playworker you need to ensure that the play space affords the best possible play opportunities for all children.

Sometimes an individual child's wish to destroy other children's dens or models will need to be contained so as not to inhibit the play of others. Alternatively, if children are apathetic and want to do nothing but watch TV or fill the play setting with electronic entertainments, this would present a different kind of challenge to the playworker. The children will need to understand the choices on offer – the possibilities and limitations of the play setting. Limited 'screen time' may form part of what a setting such as an after school club has to offer. Children attending an after school club each day may be very unhappy if they are not able to watch a favourite TV programme that forms part of the conversation and culture of the children who go home after school. On the other hand, something is not right within a play setting where children want to spend all their time in front of a screen.

CASE STUDY   Patterns and temperaments

Children come with their own personalities, likes and dislikes. Each of the following children from Mudrock Play Centre has a different 'temperament'. You may recognise them as similar to children in your own play setting.

- *Arran* is a stocky boy, very energetic, full of ideas, sometimes hot tempered and impatient. He likes play environments where he can take a lead, plan strategies, make changes. He loves building the fire and 'wide games' that involve teams, strategy and constantly changing landscapes and scenarios using bushes, dens planks and bridges.

- *Jodie* is a tall, pale girl who likes to think deeply about things. She likes space for more structured team games such as football or basketball. She likes to sit on boulders or benches where she will be undisturbed by the hectic going-on of others. She prefers one-to-one conversations rather than big group discussions. She is very observant and often very funny in relating what she has noticed about others.

- *Paul* is gentle, easygoing and likes looking after others when he is not daydreaming in the hammock or on the cushions in the book corner. He likes playing with model cars and is quite contented playing on his own or joining in with others, so long as life is comfortable. He likes cooking food.

- *Hafiza* is small for her age, constantly on the go and never sits down for long. She likes skipping, hopping, telling jokes and chattering. She is always surrounded by lots of other children and tends to play in places where they can 'flock' as a group such as at the climbing frame and the craft table.

How would your setting meet the play preferences of Arran, Jodie, Paul and Hafiza? Some play environments such as the beach seem to have almost universal appeal – offering a variety of ways in which children can play. Experienced playworkers learn to recognise that there are universal patterns or which children respond to or bring into their play and that children's individual temperaments influence how they use particular spaces and materials.

Another way of looking at patterns in children's play is by the study of *schemas*. See further reading at the end of the chapter – although most of the research and case studies in this area relates to preschool-aged children.

Key features in a good quality play space

The features that make up a good play space are those that enable the best possible opportunities for play. It is important when considering this section to read Chapter 2 about the values and principles of playwork and the role of the playworker and to have some understanding of what is meant by play and also about child development (see Chapter 1). The ways in which children may use these different spaces and how you can plan for and respond to play opportunities within them is explored in more detail in Chapter 5. Health and safety, relationships, child protection and behaviour are also explored elsewhere in the book. This section focuses on physical features of the play space. Ideally, the play setting should enable children to engage the full range of play types (see Chapter 1) in ways and at times that are set by their own needs, ideas, mood and temperament.

These are some of the features that may make a play space attractive:

- wide open spaces with room to run and have a long view
- enclosed spaces with possibilities for privacy and not feeling 'watched' every minute
- places that encourage sociable activity – such as circles of seats or a camp fire
- places where the children feel safe from bullying or other kinds of abuse
- a space where daydreaming is supported (hammocks are good for this)
- places with movable 'loose parts' (see Chapter 5)
- possibilities for getting up high, for movement, challenge
- possibilities for testing boundaries and learning about risks (see Chapter 12)
- places that appeal to the senses in terms of texture, colour and sound
- contact with natural features such as trees, bushes, rocks, sand and the elements of earth, water, fire and air
- contact with living creatures – insects and animals.

Play spaces enable children to be themselves

What makes this play space attractive to children?

Principles and values

The underpinning values of the play setting contribute greatly to the environment in terms of mood, appeal and the possibilities for play and development for all children through the ways in which:

- children are involved in planning and decision making – do they feel the play setting is truly theirs and that they can change it according to their own ideas and for their own reasons?
- relationships between people are developed and maintained so that they feel safe and secure enough to develop their play
- individual children are recognised for their unique abilities and valued for what they bring to the play setting
- the play environment relates to the wider world and enables children to develop a sense of identity and a sense of their place within it.

Equal opportunities

Some children have needs that can be more challenging for playworkers to meet if all children are to benefit from play facilities. In planning the play environment, physical access (ramps, toilets, handles, location of resources) needs to be considered for wheelchair users or others with mobility impairments. In the case of sensory impairment, the environment may be particularly important in enabling the child to make sense of the world. Textured surfaces will be much more interesting than complicated patterns or colours to a child who cannot see.

Boys and girls are also quick to pick up any bias as to what kinds of play are 'suitable' or 'acceptable' for their gender. In planning the play space you need to ensure that children of both sexes have opportunities to engage in different kinds of play and that parts of the play space (dressing up and role play or ball play area) are not always dominated by children of only one gender.

Gateway to the wider world

Through play, children develop connections and deepen their understanding about themselves, their own and other cultures, the world in which they live and their place within it. Children from all cultures need to have their own family culture acknowledged and you can introduce positive images of different cultures into the play environment and the activities available.

This may seem quite ambitious, but will definitely be easier and come alive more if you can enlist the help and support of people with firsthand, daily experience of other cultures. Start with the interests and backgrounds of children in your setting.

 ACTIVITY   Celebrating diversity in the wider world

Think about the resources in your setting. How many of them come from other countries or reflect positive images of the wider world? Imagine you are a visitor from China or the Republic of Ireland (or another country of choice) and collect together a range of play materials that could be used to enrich the play setting. Engage the children in this process. Here are some ideas:

- collect books, posters, magazine articles with positive images of the country in question, its people and their lives
- find out about their major national festivals – how are they celebrated?
- prepare and eat national recipes food, using appropriate cooking and eating implements
- borrow or make national costumes for dressing up or drama
- read stories from other places
- try out culturally specific games and art and craft activities
- listen to music from the country in question
- look at the way other people write – for example, Chinese pictograms, ancient Egyptian hieroglyphics
- listen to other languages and accents – on story tapes from the library if you do not have the real-life examples in your setting or your community.

Another way of supporting play and a developing sense of identity is to enable children to take photos within the play setting and draw themselves and their families (be sure you have paints and paper that can reproduce a variety of skin, hair and eye tones). Older children could interview each other about their lives and their families. In one play setting the children became so enthusiastic about this – using tape recorders and microphones – that they regularly made 'This is your life' – or 'This is my life' – type stories and programmes. As a playworker you need to be sensitive in your support and responses to this kind of play. The emphasis should be on celebrating diversity: everyone has something to offer.

Outdoor play, the elements and contact with the natural world

Children's access to outdoor play in many communities is increasingly restricted due to traffic, dense housing and parental concerns about safety. Many children are also leading increasingly less active lives – with much of their play confined to indoors or sitting in front

The natural world draws children in to deep and prolonged play

of a screen. In order for children to develop their sense of identity and their place within their community and the wider world, they need opportunities to explore and become increasingly independent. This begins early when a baby begins to crawl and explore previously inaccessible places – no longer dependent on being carried or pushed in a buggy. As the child gets older, her opportunities to roam further away from the familiar increase and she needs to be supported to understand the risks, push the boundaries and extend her independence without being exposed to unacceptable risk of harm. Sadly, many of our public spaces are not very welcoming or accessible to children and this is where play settings have a particularly important part to play.

You only have to watch a child at play in the woods or on the beach or with pets or making mud pies in the backyard to observe the way that the natural world draws children in to deep and prolonged play that engages them at many levels. Access to the natural elements, to trees, water and sand seem to have a profound effect at an emotional and spiritual level – being in turns calming, stimulating and on occasions 'awesome', inviting children to literally 'wallow' in their play.

The design and development of your play space will hopefully contain lots of possibilities for access to all the elements – an outdoor tap, for example, is essential. Many adventure playgrounds have a 'fire pit', which enables children to learn about safe lighting and care for open fires, to watch the flames, to sit around it telling jokes and stories, to cook potatoes, sausages and chapattis. If you cannot have an open fire, you may be able to have a barbeque occasionally or use candles (supervised, of course) when the appropriate occasion arises. There is more on using the elements for play opportunities in Chapter 5.

SPOTLIGHT ON   'Loose parts'

> *In any environment, both the degree of inventiveness and creativity, and the possibility of discovery are directly proportional to the number and kind of variables in it.*
>
> (Nicholson 1971)

Why is it that sometimes when we give a child a brand new toy, they seem to get more pleasure out of transforming the box? Why is it that brand-new fixed equipment play parks are sometimes ignored by children in favour of the neglected garage site or deserted builders' yard? Materials that can be used and transformed by children – that they can change, unpick, break down and build back up again are essential in any play space. Natural materials such as mud, sand, water, cut grass and fallen leaves provide excellent examples of 'loose parts'. You can also resource your play setting with a range of huge cardboard boxes, tubes, milk crates, car tyres, sheets, tarpaulins, hosepipes, guttering, buckets and barrels, steps, spools, ropes, pulleys, etc. Health and safety and storage arrangements will need careful consideration, but the primary aim is to enable the children to use the resources and features of the play setting to transform it into the kind of spaces they want and need for their play.

Using the senses

Your memories of childhood play and the descriptions of other people's memories will conjure up impressions relating to your senses – sights, sounds, smells, textures – as well as social and emotional experiences. It is through the senses that a baby first awakens to the world: through sight, sound, touch, taste, smell and movement she gains information that leads to an understanding of the environment in which she finds herself. This awakening through the senses continues throughout childhood and later life. Children of all ages will enjoy activities and play opportunities that appeal to their senses.

Walk into any play setting and squat or sit so that you are the same height of the children using the facility. Ask yourself what the setting has to offer to each of your senses. Take hearing, for example: what noises are being made by the children and adults present? Laughing, shouting, excited screaming or contented babble? Is taped music played continuously in the background? What kind of music? At what volume? Does the room echo disconcertingly? Can children get away from unwanted sound? Ask similar relevant questions relating to touch, sight, smell, taste.

ACTIVITY | Sensory walks

Introduce sensory walks to help discover more about how children experience the play setting with their senses and to find out more about likes and dislikes and what encourages play:

1 Everybody walks around the play setting discovering things that they like or don't like in terms of touch, smell, sound. (With younger children, it is probably better to choose just one or two senses at a time.)

2 Everybody finds a partner. One person wears a blindfold and the other person leads the blindfolded partner on a 'sense walk': asking them to listen to, touch, smell the things they have discovered for themselves. Can they guess what each thing is? Do they share the same likes and dislikes?

The materials used in the design and resources of your play setting will have an impact on how appealing the children find them to their senses. A metal climbing frame has a different 'feel' to wooden one, a plastic or nylon tent feels entirely different to be in than a canvas or cotton one. There are endless possibilities for the use of different fabrics to transform areas of the play space – from sackcloth to rich velvets or pieces decorated with mirrors and embroidery. Use them for discovery and comparison, particularly if you can get hold of pieces of fabric from around the world. What is it made from? How does it feel? What does it smell like? Is it brightly coloured or pastel? You can use fabric for sewing, for dressing up, for wrapping round furniture, draping round walls, numerous art and craft activities or for creating hidey-holes and many other things.

The senses, then, can be a starting point when looking at how children experience the play environment. Use

Why might children find this activity appealing?

your senses and your observations of children playing and conversations with children to help you plan the design of your play setting.

ACTIVITY   Appealing to the senses

Plan some interesting ways to enrich the 'sense environment'. This can help you to find out more about the children's likes and dislikes and increase their awareness of and sensitivity towards each other. As a result of your activities and discussion with children about the senses, write down five ways of improving your play environment in its appeal to the senses, such as:

- adding colour to corners used for quiet play or reading by using draped fabrics
- improving acoustics by using rugs and screens or turning off taped music
- burning essential oils or using incense – or putting lavender oil in the Playdough
- creating a sensory garden, with a textured (but accessible) path of gravel, bark, stones and grass, bells and wind chimes hung up to be moved by the wind or children's fingers and reflective surfaces to play with light
- creating an outdoor music and sounds playscape – with wind chimes and homemade drums and cymbals
- appealing to all the senses by having changing seasonal displays of flowers, leaves, seeds, stones, shells or fruit in the entrance to the play setting.

Possibilities and limitations of your play space

Using a shared space

Your play setting may be a shared space such as part of a school, church hall or community centre or you may work in a purpose-built play centre, adventure playground or other designated play setting. You may have to meet a range of care needs as well as providing play opportunities – for example, providing nutritionally balanced meals for children whose parents are at work or otherwise engaged. Your premises and the kind of service you offer will affect the kind of environment that can or needs to be provided. If you intend to provide meals, you will need a kitchen and somewhere comfortable to eat. If the children are to spend several hours in the facility they will need comfortable spaces to sit, relax, talk, rest and maybe even doze off. Transforming a hall or bare school canteen into an attractive play space is challenging. You can use screens, plants, coloured cloths, rugs, cushions, pictures, tables and movable shelving or other furniture, such as child-sized tables and chairs, to create several different spaces within the larger whole.

If your facility is required to register and meet the national childcare standards, you will need to meet the requirements of your regulating body (such as Ofsted – see Chapter 3). Whatever the challenges, as long as the basic facilities are there (enough space, toilets, washing facilities, kitchen if needed and office space), there are nearly always options and very often solutions if you are prepared to think creatively and give enough time to planning. Sharing premises will require good communication with the other organisations involved. You will need to be clear about the needs of your group and accommodate the needs of others. For example, you may need to take down displays every day. It will be helpful if a representative of your play setting is the 'link person' with a representative of any other organisation which uses the same premises. He or she can make time to discuss shared interests and concerns. In particular, your play facility will need to negotiate adequate storage space and how various spaces can be used. Can any equipment be shared? Encourage the children to keep their belongings tidy in the cloakroom or other designated area. Some children may need reminding to take all their belongings home, including bags, artwork and clothing.

ACTIVITY | Sharing a play space with other organisations

Look at your own play setting. Consider the following list of issues that can cause difficulties for playworkers in creating an environment:

- Can you leave most of your play materials in place or do you need to recreate your play environment every session?
- Do you have enough suitable furniture and equipment?
- Can you provide for outdoor play?
- Are you able to display the children's choice of artwork or photos?
- Do you have enough storage space?

What are the greatest challenges in planning and preparing the play space at your setting? Discuss your findings with your colleagues. Are there any areas you can think of in which you could make improvements?

Creating a sense of identity for the play setting within a shared space

If you share a building you can nurture your group's own sense of identity by giving it an interesting name, displaying children's artwork and having a noticeboard with posters, newsletter, photos or publicity material. The children of one after school club we visited had each made their own distinctive name badge out of beads and metallic paint. These were worn when the club met and left on the noticeboard in between times, making a very attractive display. The children of the same club also had their own self-made cushions, each decorated with the individual's name and made from a wide variety of fabric scraps. They were large enough to sit on at story times or just to relax. Each child had also decoratively painted his or her own cheap enamel mug for use while in the club. In this way, children's creative contributions can also be used to develop the identity of the play setting as a whole. Even if you have to take down displays each night you can support the children's pride in their creative achievements, and in their play setting, by making them part of the same thing. Try fabric painting on large sheets, for example, which can be folded and put away. Use chalkboards or other wipe- or wash-down surfaces for creating screens or encouraging graffiti art. Look at the idea on page 66 for a quick wall display or room divide that can be easily folded up and put away at the end of the day. Use large sheets of thick paper or card. The children can choose how they will use them: a collage on a particular theme, for example. The pieces are held together with ticker tags through holes punched in the corners. You can use individual pieces of artwork or create a group mural with different children completing sections of one picture.

A foldaway screen display (drawn by Polly, aged 6, Roberto, aged 7, and Nikita, aged 8)

Making the most of limited outdoor space

Children should be able to play out of doors as well as in. Sadly, the time spent in your play setting may be the only opportunity some children get to do this. If you do not have interesting, safe and easily accessible outdoor play space as part of your play setting, you will have to be creative. How can you make the best use of the space you have got? Can the children grow things in pots? Can you use paint to cheer up stretches of concrete or tarmac? Build up a stock of materials (milk crates, planks, tyres, hoops, skipping ropes) with which the children can transform and use the space they do have. Look around your local community for any nearby parks or other open spaces that you might be able to use or visit on a regular basis. If you live in a city or town there might be some wilderness or conservation areas for you to explore. In rural areas there may be a friendly landowner with a coppice or piece of woodland that you could use.

Auditing, monitoring and evaluating the quality of your play space

It is important for you to be able to reflect on, analyse and evaluate your play space: how is it being used, and when and where it should be changed in order to continue to meet the needs of the children who use it. Here are some of the questions you might ask:

- How well is the play setting used – is the demand for use of the play space by local children increasing or decreasing?
- Do the kinds of play and activity that happen here reflect playwork values and principles (see Chapter 2)?
- Can children engage in the full range of play types (see Chapter 1, page 8)?
- What do children say about the play setting?

There is a range of tools you can use to do this, such as checklists, surveys, observations or using a playwork-based quality assurance scheme.

ACTIVITY   Observing your play space in use

1 Draw or sketch a plan of your play setting – indoors and out (see example sketch).
2 Label each area A, B, C, D, E etc.
3 Every 15 minutes for one session, scan the indoor and outdoor area and mark how many children are using each area.
4 Add any additional information, such as children walking between areas.

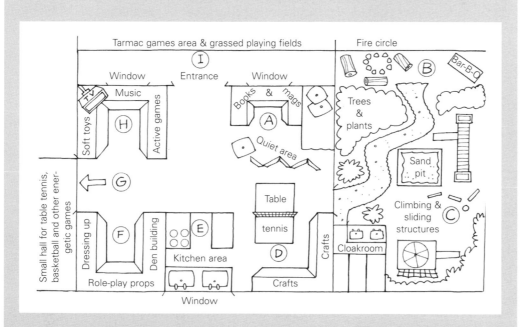

5 After the session ask yourself:

- Are any areas hardly used or not used at all?
- How can I change little used areas so that they are better used or more attractive to children who currently don't use them?

Talk to the children about your findings. Have they any ideas?

You can also use this observation exercise to discover something about adult involvement in your play setting. For this, you will need to mark the number of adults present in particular areas as well as numbers of children. Are some areas used by children only if adults are present? Why might this be? You can also find out about whether some areas are used more by older children or more by girls or boys.

The activity 'Observing your play space in use' provides you with one tool for undertaking this on a regular basis. It is a very useful form of observation, so keep your plan of the play setting and a copy of the blank observation sheet. You can use the format of this observation to find out many things about how the play environment is used and by whom – for example, if you wanted to monitor whether boys and girls are getting equal access to different play opportunities.

Summary

Making flexible and creative use of space is just as important if your play setting has sole use or shares use of your building. There should be spaces in which children can be noisy as well as spaces in which to be quiet; spaces in which to be active – run, jump, climb, play ball – and spaces in which to be still. There should be opportunities for creativity, even if it is sometimes messy and places that lend themselves to sociable play and interaction as well as places that afford privacy when desired (hidey-holes and dens). Use equipment that is versatile and easily moved. Overall, the play environment should foster the child's inborn motivation to play and develop, to be curious and to explore. Your role as a playworker is to be constantly aware of how the play space is being used, its possibilities and limitations and how you can work with the children to extend the possibilities it offers for play.

References

Russell, B. (1930) *The Conquest of Happiness*. Allen & Unwin.

Nicholson, S. (1971) 'How not to cheat children: the theory of loose parts'. *Landscape Architecture* October, cited in Hughes (1996) below.

Further reading

Bruce, T. and Meggitt, C. (1996) *Child Care and Education* (section on schemas). Hodder & Stoughton.

Davy, G. and Voors, B. (1983) *Lifeways – Working with Family Questions* (chapter on the temperaments by Ann Druitt). Hawthorn Press.

Hughes, B. (1996) *Play Environments: A Question of Quality* available from www.playeducation.com.

Kids/Kidsactive publications on adventure playgrounds and inclusive play. (See appendix at the end of this book.)

Melville, S. (2004) *Places for Play*. Playlink. Available from www.freeplaynetwork.org.uk.

Titman, W. (1994) *Special Places, Special People*. WWF/Learning Through Landscapes. (LTL also produces other publications particularly geared at people working in schools, www.ltl.org.uk.)

CHAPTER 5
Opportunities for play

Children love their seashell toys,
and with them they learn about the ocean,
because a little piece of ocean
inside the child, and inside the toy
knows the whole ocean.

(Rumi, trans. Barks 1991)

Chapter 4 looked at how the play environment or play space affects opportunities for play. This chapter focuses on the opportunities themselves. The starting point is always the children's interests, together with resources and materials available and the way in which you and other playworkers respond to them and use them for your planning and reflection. Some play settings use a programme of activities. Others use a play-based quality assurance scheme to audit and evaluate the quality of the environment and play opportunities they offer. This chapter looks at factors such as timing, resources and the kinds of materials and activities that are used in play settings with all age ranges. It is important to remember not to impose a rigid structure or programme within the play setting, as this will not enable children to initiate and develop their own play. In this chapter, we will consider:

- Beginnings
- Planning ahead
- The role of the playworker
- Meeting changing needs and the needs of different age groups
- Structure, time and rhythm
- Materials, resources and equipment
- Food is more than eating
- Developing resourcefulness: a playworker's toolkit
- Endings

Beginnings

Beginnings are important, as they can set the tone for what is to come. The first day at a play setting for a child, the first day of a holiday playscheme, the beginning of the day, the start of a new activity – each beginning presents new possibilities for play. The energy, enthusiasm and ideas you bring can set the tone for what is to follow.

There are many ways to begin and in deciding on how you start each session you need to consider the children and where they are coming from. Do they know each other? Are they likely to be tired, shy or restless or needing to be energetic? What will the play setting look and feel like to them when they arrive?

Consider the two case studies that follow and the different approaches to children coming into the play setting. The case study 'Playing after school' shows how one playworker met the different needs of the children in her group. There were some more structured activities (or materials for particular types of play) for those who wanted them, but the freedom and space for others to withdraw into their own world of play and set their own pace for joining in. The case study 'Steven's play journey' describes the journey of an individual child from the 'craft table' through an imaginative play trail through the different play opportunities offered in an adventure playground. The wealth of resources and sensitive playworkers available to Steven helped him to take his play in new directions.

CASE STUDY   Playing after school

At one after school club, the playworker put considerable time and effort into planning each session. She would ensure that each session had organised activities that the children liked to do: cooking, making things to take home and outdoor games. Nevertheless, four of the children (aged between 5 and 9) would always bring their own teddies, dolls, dolls' clothes, feeding bottles and carry cases. They

On a play journey

would use a small side room that had a door that could be closed for privacy and create their own world of play. It had upright chairs with throw-over covers, which provided perfect screens for hiding. The tables had wheels and every object in that room was used in their play. Sometimes they would put the dolls to sleep so that they could join the other children for a drink and a biscuit or to participate in an activity and then go directly back to their own play. These children came directly from school and the kinds of spontaneous, child-centred play that they wanted to engage in were not possible at school: it could be seen as childish or babyish, the kinds of things you do in a playgroup. (Dolcie Obhiozele, Play Development Officer, Oxford City Council)

CASE STUDY   Steven's play journey at the adventure playground

Steven is 6, fair haired, with a freckled, round face. He wears blue jeans with green monster patches emblazoned all over. He has a moderate learning difficulty and he can be an extremely demanding child, with a very short attention span, who needs to be constantly amused. Steven has an engaging manner and attaches himself to the playworker who will help him do what he wants to do. Steven usually wants to make masks. Today is no exception. We go over to the arts and crafts corner, find silver paper and white card, green pens, scissors and sticky tape. Steven draws a face, with eyes, nose, ears and big green horns. We cut out the mask, attach string to the ears so it fits over his head. Arms and legs also require adornment, so we make bracelets out of silver card to go round his wrists and over his ankles. All togged out, Steven surveys himself in the mirror and sets off, roaring fiercely at those he encounters. The green monster is eager for an adventure today. He finds it in the jungle. Slashing the undergrowth he goes deeper and deeper into the jungle, on the lookout for tigers and dragons. Stray branches slow his progress, the way ahead is unclear. But wait … help is at hand. Another explorer of uncharted territory, Jonathan, is on the scene. He offers us his own hand-drawn map, to help us find our way. Urging us to keep the map and warning us 'Be careful!' he waves us off into the bush. Before long, we encounter Jonathan, our trusty map bearer, once again. Together, we press on, successfully avoiding being eaten by tigers and dragons. At last we reach our destination – the castle. At the castle (a slide and climbing structure to the less imaginative), we are joined by other children who are playing a game with a tennis ball. Children take turns to roll the ball down from the top of the slide to the child sitting at the bottom, who then runs up the slide with the ball. Several turns and the game exhausts itself. Time for something new …

There's a little old man who lives in a house. The house is made of three big foam rings, stacked one on top of the other, red, green and blue. It has a removable black roof. Inside is the little old man, with moustache and beard – he's 8, going on 88. At first, Steven is definitely not welcome. But the little old man relents and lets him in. Once in, there appears to be no way out except by burrowing a tunnel through the wall of the house. And then more unwelcome guests arrive. They clamber onto the roof and are unceremoniously kicked off by the residents. A new game! How long can the guests stay on the roof before they are kicked off and the house collapses? (Kidsactive 1992/93: Adventure play – a child's experience, annual review.)

ACTIVITY   Observing play journeys

1 If Steven (in the Case study 'Steven's play journey') came to your play setting, with his green monster patches and wish to make a mask, what possibilities would there be for him to achieve his wish and take the lead in the way he wanted to develop his play?

2 Think of an example you have observed within your own play setting where a child was able to develop his choice of play at his own pace and in his own way. Observe and follow the play journey of one or two of the children in your play setting through an entire session if possible. What does this tell you about that particular child and her interests? How far was this child able to initiate her own play? What play types were used? Were there any limiting factors (lack of resources, health and safety restraints, intervention from other children or adults)? How could you alter or adapt the play setting to enable this child to develop her play further?

Planning ahead

Checklists

You can use a checklist of questions to ask yourself to plan for a single session or for preparing for the week ahead. Try it first when planning a single activity with a group of children. You can refer to it if an activity did not go well, to help you decide why.

Children

How many children are you planning for? What are their ages? Do you know their interests, language, cultural backgrounds? Have you considered the needs of all children, including disabled children? Will your activity (or programme) cater for the whole age range or have you provided alternatives to suit different stages of development and abilities? The children who come to your play setting are the starting point. In a holiday playscheme, at the start of the year or in a new play setting, you won't know them or their interests – how will you engage them in initiating and planning what happens from the start?

Play types, choice and extension

Is there potential for variety, choice, stimulation and fun? What are the opportunities within the activity/programme for children to explore different types of play? How flexible is the activity? Will the children be able to use the materials to develop related activities if they want to extend or change direction?

Materials and equipment

What materials and equipment will the children need? Make a detailed list. Do you have enough materials? How much will they cost? Do the materials and equipment comply with health and safety regulations? Will the children need to wear protective clothing?

Identity and inclusion

Will all the children have the opportunity to participate regardless of gender, race, ability, religion? How will you encourage this? Will the children be able to try out other identities in their play?

The role of the playworkers

What will your own involvement be? Play opportunities are child led, even if you might be introducing new materials and equipment. Beware of making the play setting into a classroom. Remember the children's response to the materials and space you set up might be very different from what you anticipate. This is part of the joy of playwork.

What will you do if an activity flops (children get hurt, do not engage, become abusive, are not interested or find it too difficult)?

Will extra supervision be needed to carry out particular activities?

Do you need special parental consent or approval?

How will you make use of special skills within your team or do you wish to bring in other adults from outside?

CASE STUDY   Using the checklist to plan a water slide

The weather is hot and the children have been wanting to play with water – they have doused their heads under the outside tap, squirted each other with empty washing-up liquid bottles refilled with water and constantly wish they were at the swimming pool. After some discussion with the children, one playworker suggests they might create a water slide. The playwork team use the planning checklist to ensure they have the equipment they need and agree roles and responsibilities. They let the children know what's happening and remind them to bring swimming costumes or a towel and change of clothes. They ensure that there are spare towels available and use a roll of sturdy builder's plastic stretched up the grassy bank in the centre of the outside play area. They involve the children in testing out the best method of making the slide work. How long should the plastic be? How much water should be used and how should it be released on the slide? In the rush of initial enthusiasm, several children are hurt as they hurtle down the slide without waiting for the person before them to get off – bumping knees against heads. The playworkers put a stop to the play so that health and safety rules can be negotiated and the effectiveness of the slide reviewed. Initially, playworkers have to act as referees until the children take on this role for themselves. Gradually the children introduce ever more effective ways of using the slide – they switch from using the hose (ground gets too soggy) to using buckets. A little soap is added for lubrication to make it faster.

Using a programme of activities

A programme of activities which is displayed on a noticeboard or given to children to take home can make some children feel more secure. Many children (and their parents) like to know in advance what activities will be on offer in their play setting. You can use a programme of activities to plan a whole season in an after school club, a week-long playscheme or a one-off special playday. It can help you to:

- work more effectively together with your colleagues
- share ideas about what you wish to offer and how it is to be organised and supervised
- be sure you have the right resources and equipment for the activities that are planned
- plan trips and outings
- audit your play setting to ensure that children are able to get involved in the full range of play types.

	Monday	Tuesday	Wednesday	Thursday	Friday
FREE PLAY OPPORTUNITIES FOR ALL CHILDREN THROUGHOUT THE DAY EVERY DAY ACROSS THE WHOLE PLAY SETTING					
Morning					
Special activity	Mask making – visiting community artist and storyteller	Creating a beach – building the new sandpit	Trip to seaside	What's in a box? – bring boxes of all shapes and sizes	End-of-week feast – bring food to share, cooking in fire, barbeque
Play types supported	Symbolic play; dramatic play	Symbolic play; object play; exploratory play	Rough and tumble play; locomotor play; deep play	Symbolic play; creative play; object play	Social play; communication play
Afternoon					
Special activity	'High drama' – stories and video making	Den building – using willow and hazel		Let's go fly a kite – bring a kite or make your own	Music jam – bring instruments and favourite CDs
Play types supported	Imaginative play; fantasy play	Recapitulative play; fantasy play		Exploratory play; mastery play	Social play; object play

This is a programme used by playworkers in their planning. It covers only a very small part of the play opportunities that will be provided because the play environment and materials are used by the children for ongoing play activities such as den building, daydreaming, climbing, swinging, playing with water and games of all kinds. This programme helps the playworkers plan for additional or 'special' activities that require extra resources or advance planning. Here, they have suggested the predominant play types they anticipate will be supported during each activity. This is for their planning purposes only – not for general display. At the end of the week, they will review this programme and see whether what happened related to what they had anticipated. It may be that the playworkers find that they did not anticipate correctly at all. In this week for example, the children might get so involved in building the sandpit that they do not get round to the den building and that it is during the boxes and kite flying that the playworkers observe children most engrossed in fantasy and imaginative play. The programme gives the playwork team a 'hook' for their discussions, planning and reflections on their work. The playwork sector is developing a range of other tools for planning and evaluating its work. See particularly the Play Wales website for *The First Claim* (see further reading, Hughes 2001), the playwork matrix and the Playwork Quality Assurance scheme produced by London Play.

SPOTLIGHT ON   Activities versus play opportunities?

You may think that play is incompatible with any kind of structured programme. But a programme of activities within a play setting can be very useful in helping you and your co-workers to plan together. A programme does not in itself ensure the provision of good-quality play opportunities. If planned and carried out too rigidly it could hinder children's play – particularly when many children already spend much of their time in structured activities. Key elements in good programme planning include providing children with choices and involving children in the planning. The programme and the way in which you use it should be flexible, responding to the children's ideas and enthusiasm. Used in this way, a programme of activities can help create varied and stimulating play opportunities.

Other factors to consider in your planning include: the age range and preferences of children, the time available, premises, storage space, opening hours and resources as well as skills and preferences of staff. Remember, spontaneity is an important element of play. Be flexible. You may have to adapt even the best laid plans. A week's programme may have to be altered because Monday's activity is so successful the children want to continue and extend it for the rest of the week or because it snows and children want to play snowballs all day. It is a good idea to have some contingency activities up your sleeve. These could be games that can be played with no equipment and might be suitable for confined spaces – when the coach breaks down on a trip for example (see for example *Whatever the Weather* from the CAN DO series of activity books – see further reading at the end of this chapter). It is also good to have ideas for 'wind-down' games and activities for the end of the session or the end of the day, when children are feeling very tired or excited or ready to go home.

Themes

It may be helpful to choose a theme around which to plan activities. All or some activities can be linked to a theme lasting a day, a week or the whole summer or school term. A theme can extend children's knowledge and interest in the world around them. Stories, games, art and craft activities, outings and cooking can all be chosen around a theme such as 'water', 'animals' or 'galaxies'.

There are many ways in which playworkers think about play opportunities. As play in playwork is child led, voluntary, flexible and often spontaneous, it is useful for playworkers to have tools or 'maps' to place their ideas on and enable them to reflect on what they do. (See further reading.)

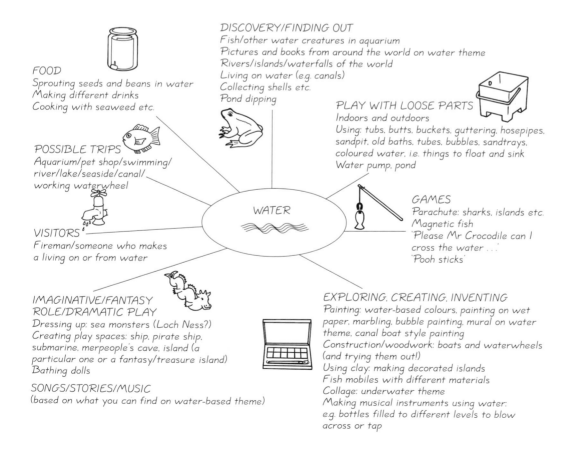

FOOD
Sprouting seeds and beans in water
Making different drinks
Cooking with seaweed etc.

DISCOVERY/FINDING OUT
Fish/other water creatures in aquarium
Pictures and books from around the world on water theme
Rivers/islands/waterfalls of the world
Living on water (e.g. canals)
Collecting shells etc.
Pond dipping

PLAY WITH LOOSE PARTS
Indoors and outdoors
Using: tubs, butts, buckets, guttering, hosepipes, sandpit, old baths, tubes, bubbles, sandtrays, coloured water, i.e. things to float and sink
Water pump, pond

POSSIBLE TRIPS
Aquarium/pet shop/swimming/
river/lake/seaside/canal/
working waterwheel

VISITORS
Fireman/someone who makes
a living on or from water

WATER

GAMES
Parachute: sharks, islands etc.
Magnetic fish
'Please Mr Crocodile can I cross the water …'
'Pooh sticks'

IMAGINATIVE/FANTASY
ROLE/DRAMATIC PLAY
Dressing up: sea monsters (Loch Ness?)
Creating play spaces: ship, pirate ship, submarine, merpeople's cave, island (a particular one or a fantasy/treasure island)
Bathing dolls

SONGS/STORIES/MUSIC
(based on what you can find on water-based theme)

EXPLORING, CREATING, INVENTING
Painting: water-based colours, painting on wet paper, marbling, bubble painting, mural on water theme, canal boat style painting
Construction/woodwork: boats and waterwheels (and trying them out!)
Using clay: making decorated islands
Fish mobiles with different materials
Collage: underwater theme
Making musical instruments using water: e.g. bottles filled to different levels to blow across or tap

The role of the playworker

Your role in planning and facilitating opportunities for play within the play setting may include:

- providing choices in materials, equipment, ideas, space
- enabling children – as far as possible – to carry out their own ideas, make decisions and carry out plans
- being aware of and responding to children's play cues and joining in when asked
- acting as referee when required to ensure that the play setting's boundaries of behaviour are observed, especially with regard to ensuring reasonable health and safety and protecting children from physical and psychological harm
- being aware that the play opportunities are set within the limits of opening times and resources and balancing this with the importance of the children having the freedom to set their own pace and take play in the direction they choose
- implementing health and safety legislation and guidelines for materials and equipment used
- giving encouragement and support to extend and develop play opportunities as appropriate
- ensuring all children have equality of opportunity and equal access to the play opportunities, resources and activities
- being prepared to do what you are asking the children to do – they may need a role model before trying a new activity.

Meeting changing needs and the needs of different age groups

You may already be clear about what works and what doesn't for the children in your play setting, and their range of interests, likes and dislikes. But children change and develop, new children will come and no play setting should be static in the opportunities it provides for play.

Here are some ways you can refresh your ideas:

- actively involve the children in ongoing planning
- share ideas with other playworkers
- use the numerous activity ideas books now available (see further reading at end of this section)
- attend training courses.

Play settings take a range of age groups and even where there is a narrow band of age ranges, children will be at different stages of development and have different

Younger and older children can learn from each other

levels of skills and interests. As a playworker you can plan to ensure that there is a range of materials and equipment to meet differing developmental needs – for example some children may be able to use sharp tools or to develop more complex rules within their play. Your skill as a playworker is to recognise and support children who want to take their play into realms of greater complexity and possibly risk management. Beware of making assumptions about children and don't insist children stick to the opportunities planned for a particular age group. Older children will enjoy and participate in those planned for younger ones and, health and safety considerations permitting, younger children may well be able to engage in activities developed by older ones.

CASE STUDY   Puppet-making across the age range

At Rington Kids' Club, the children had taken a great interest in playing with and making their own puppets. Rob, the playworker, researched a range of puppet-making activities that he thought would be suitable for different age ranges.

5 to 7 year olds

Making a variety of simple puppets: paper bag, paper plate, sock puppets, using junk materials, glue, sewing. Using puppets in imaginative play, storytelling, talking to each other.

8 to 10 year olds

Making more complicated puppets: papier mâché or clay heads, puppets on sticks and puppets with strings. Making cardboard box puppet theatres. Inventing and writing scripts for puppet shows. Performing shows to each other (and parents?) including 'selling tickets' and serving biscuits/squash refreshments.

11 and over

Making a variety of still more complicated puppets: marionettes, life-size puppets, plaster moulds, shadow puppets, etc. Building a puppet theatre (including scenery and lighting). Creating a show to be put on to the local community as a fundraising event (including designing tickets and posters, budgeting, selling tickets, preparing and serving refreshments). Making a video of the show to replay to the whole club.

   Rob provided a wide range of materials within the play setting and some books on puppetry. In the event, the most satisfying activity was the free play that all age groups took part in with all kinds of puppet. They spent a lot of time exploring a variety of materials and adding suggestions of their own. Often the simplest materials (for example, paper bags) worked best – even for the older age groups. There was particular interest in some of the books that showed puppetry from different cultures – including the use of shadow puppets. Some of the youngest children had the best suggestions about putting on the puppet show and developing a story line, while the older children took on the business of the 'public performance' – making posters, selling tickets and videoing the show.

Structure, time and rhythm

Playwork settings usually have opening and closing times. Within those two markers a variety of things happen. Some places will have mealtimes, story times and maybe a programme of activities that will be more or less structured. But as we have seen throughout this book, play is not about structured activities and a programme of activities should not be allowed to turn into a timetable.

Rhythm, by way of contrast, is a natural part of the development of all living organisms. Babies need to develop rhythms of sleeping, eating and activity to survive in the world and repeated interruption or distortion leads to disorientation and breakdown of normal functioning. You can help children gain a sense of security and confidence by incorporating familiar rhythms into the way the play setting functions. There should be times to be active, times to be quiet, times for sitting together and talking, planning and sharing food. You can develop a sense of rhythm by paying attention to the pacing of the session or an individual activity: that it has a beginning, a middle and an end, and that time is allowed for clearing away. The week can also have its own rhythm, with opportunities for different types of activity on different days of the week and the rhythm of the year may be incorporated through seasonal activities, the celebrations of birthdays or festivals of different faiths and cultures. Rhythm can have endless variations and the children in the setting should be able to initiate and develop it. Some children will want a faster more complicated rhythm, others will prefer a simpler, slower pattern. You as playworker can keep the beat: ensuring that individual needs are met, but that one child's or small group's rhythm is not allowed to dominate or obliterate another's.

Materials, resources and equipment

There are many good publications containing ideas and instructions for different types of activity to do with children in the play setting. The further reading at the end of this chapter offers just a very small sample of the ones we have found useful. Some focus on a particular theme or type of activity (games, craft or music) in far more depth than can be done here. Here we look at a range of activities and play materials that might be included in your programme of activities. It should not be seen as a complete list of ideas: it is for you and the children you work with to decide which are appropriate for your needs.

Games

- *Games that need no equipment* (indoor and outdoor) – guessing games, circle games, quizzes, hiding games, traditional children's games, singing games, chasing games, co-operative games, mime games such as charades or 'Give Us a Clue'.
- *Board games* – snakes and ladders, draughts, Ludo, chess, Monopoly, cows and leopards, chequers, Lotto, Trivial Pursuit.
- *Other games* – card games, jacks, Mencala, Twister, Jenga, Connect 4; games with pen and paper such as noughts and crosses; table-top games such as table tennis, Karrom, bar football, pool.
- *More active games* (indoor and outdoor) – games using balls and bats, footballs (ordinary outdoor and sponge indoor), skittles, bowls, boules, hopscotch and team games such as rounders, cricket, football and Unihoc.

Sporting activities are often of great interest to children and can be a valuable part of what a play setting has to offer. In a setting where providing opportunities for play is the main aim, the focus should not be on competition. Many games encourage cooperative play, building relationships and developing trust as well as being great fun. They include parachute games, trust games and games where the players invent or change the rules (see further reading).

Small-scale toys and construction

Toys such as jigsaws, cars, boats, trains, farm and zoo animals, commercial construction and small play equipment such as Lego, Duplo, Mobilo and Meccano also provide opportunities to play. Your play setting can provide opportunities for children to move through different activities, without losing continuity in their play. They should be able to get the materials they need without losing momentum. Play with toys can stimulate ideas for other play activities.

CASE STUDY | Toys as a starting point

The children had been spending a lot of time playing with a box of trucks, cars and trains. One day we showed them a book about tunnels and bridges and suggested they might like to make some constructions to use with the cars. A mixed group of boys and girls went enthusiastically to the craft area where there were a lot of flattened cardboard boxes, paint, glue, tape and other bits and pieces. The children did not refer to the book again but eagerly began trying out their own ideas. They divided themselves into groups – three boys aged between 6 and 10 years and two girls, both aged 8. One 5 year old boy began to experiment on his own, but was soon joined by an older child who asked if he could help. I was able to relish observing cooperative play in all its glory. Each group demonstrated its ability to be creative, developing their social skills by listening and discussing their ideas. The three boys, Jo, Paul and Dominic, made a long rectangular tunnel with road signs and traffic lights. Erin and Emma made a triangular construction. They used mosaic pieces of Sparkle Art as cats' eyes on their road. Ian and Richard made a drawbridge kind of construction using string to pull up a sort of 'car chute' or slide. Very little adult input was necessary or required. I was reminded of how rich is the variety of children's play and how a simple activity can give opportunities for all-round development and fun. The different constructions produced were quite simply brilliant and were used for several weeks in a variety of ways by all the children at PAWS in their play. (Karen King, playworker at PAWS after school care scheme)

Toys and construction for large-scale active play

Equipment that can encourage active play is limited only by space available, cost, safety and your imagination. Remember the theory of 'loose parts' (see Chapter 4, page 62) and provide boxes of all shapes and sizes, barrels, tubes, climbing frames, planks, tyres, slides and chutes, seesaws, rocking boats, trampolines, skipping ropes and materials for making dens, ramps, jumps, tunnels and hidey-holes. Large wheeled toys are often very popular – rollerskates, bikes, scooters, skateboards, go-karts and trucks. Soft play equipment made of large cut-out shapes of covered foam can offer wonderful possibilities for play. A soft play area or room is often particularly attractive to younger children and to children with mobility difficulties or sensory impairment, as it can open up new ways of moving and sensory experience. Commercially produced soft play equipment is expensive, but even one or two pieces can be a great addition to your range of play equipment. Think also about using soft mats and cushions that can be homemade (but be aware of fire regulations in relation to soft furnishings). An adventure playground will have more elaborate construction materials for building structures for climbing on, swinging off, sliding down or playing in. (See Chapter 12 for safety considerations.)

Environmental play

Environmental play

Environmental play can take place in cities as well as rural areas. Nature trails, treasure hunts, collecting things, observing wildlife – ants and woodlice, as well as rabbits and pigeons – can provide good starting points for further exploration and games. They can lead to art, craft and drama activities, as well as special themes and projects. As with all play opportunities, children will approach environmental play with different cultural and social experience and expectations. Sensitivity is required in encouraging some children to get their hands dirty (in digging or planting in soil, for example) or approaching or handling insects or other animals. The following case study contains ideas for environmental play.

CASE STUDY   Play in the woods

We aim to give city children the opportunity to experience how the woodlands can be used in a fun and practical way. Every day is different depending on the individual children and their interests. However, it would be true to say that each day has a similar rhythm and pattern. Here is a typical day in camp. After collecting the children we lead them through the forest, stopping only to collect ferns (for den building) and for each of the children to select themselves a walking stick. The children choose strong, straight pieces of hazel and at the same time learn something about woodland management and coppicing. We lead the children into camp blindfolded – after all, it is a secret camp deep in the woodlands! The blindfolds make them more conscious of sounds, smells and textures. They remove their blindfolds once they are all round the campfire. Some children sit around the fire and use penknives to whittle their walking sticks with a variety of patterns and markings. (There are sharp tools all around camp and it is vital that the children learn to use all of them safely in order for them to participate in the camp's activities.)

A group of children immediately get involved in making charcoal and artist's charcoal. They work in pairs, splitting the logs with large axes and sawing them to length using old-fashioned double-handed saws. These pieces they pack tightly into an oil drum. The artist's charcoal is made by cutting willow withies and wedging them into a tin to be included in the oil drum. The children carry fire from the main campfire and get a fire blazing at the top of the oil drum before placing the hinged lid and turning the whole drum over to burn for up to eight hours.

Another group of children are using the shaving horses and pole lathes. With supervision and guidance they go through the whole process from sawing the log from the tree to splitting the green wood into usable sections. Using double-handled draw knives they make a section of the wood round and place it on the pole lathe. Then using a variety of chisels they turn the wood into a paper knife, a candle stick, a stool leg ... One child makes a tombstone cross for her guinea pig, which died that morning.

Other children are involved in living den building. These are mostly dome-shaped 'benders', decorated with ferns, heather and sheep's wool. Others are making wood sculptures and totem poles. At the end of the day there is also a 'spider's web' of forest life and the beginnings of a forest 'tunnel' using willow and hazel. For some of the children who come, just being in the woodland is enough and they spend all day poking and feeding the fire or gazing at the sky though the woodland canopy as they swing in the several hammocks we have slung between the trees.

We end each day round the fire toasting marshmallows, sharing stories and swapping ideas. The children are happy, exhausted and very dirty. Over the years we have also experimented with cooking in underground ovens, making paper from pulped-down bark and woodland plants and flowers, making rope ladders to climb trees and tree houses. (Sharon Crockett, playworker on Project Sparrowhawk, an annual environmental playscheme run for 8 to 14 year olds by Oxford City Council)

Many areas now have forest schools and if you are close to one you may be able to share woodland. Contact your local authority.

Using natural materials

A lot can be made of natural materials in creating play opportunities. Sand, water, mud, fircones, stones, shells and pebbles have dozens of possibilities, from simple tactile, sensory experiences of digging in sand, pouring water, sorting shells, to the elaborate construction of miniature fantasy worlds, complex scientific or technological experiments (making a watermill) or cultivating your own garden, allotment or windowboxes.

Recycling

Environmental awareness can also be encouraged through using recycled materials for play. Scraps of fabric or paper, carpet, wool, corks, cardboard, plastic, cotton reels, old blankets, tyres and timber that are considered junk by others can be transformed into dens,

Using natural materials

games and creative art and craft projects with a little creative thought and action from children and their playworkers.

Stories, books and drama

Stories and books provide a starting point for many kinds of play. A book corner with an attractive display of books reflecting different themes, cultures and lifestyles and covering a wide range of subjects and with comfortable seating can also be attractive for children wishing to relax or rest away from the more energetic activities. Stories and books can be the inspiration for imaginative play, drama, dance and music.

These activities can be encouraged by providing other materials: face paints, dressing-up clothes, play wigs, mirrors, puppets and additional props near or around the book corner.

For younger children, imaginative play can also be fostered through a home corner with small tables, chairs, pretend cooking equipment, dolls, prams and telephones. This can be varied by setting up a shop, café or fantasy play spaces such as a space station or treasure island, using whatever interest and materials you have available. All such activities provide good opportunities to promote positive images of different cultures and of disabled children in different roles that counter negative stereotypes.

Music

For music, remember the range of instruments available from other countries that are now available: African skin drums, Chinese bars, Indian bells, maracas, as well as triangles, tambourines, recorders, whistles, cymbals and even a piano if available. Homemade percussion instruments can use beans, rice, containers of all kinds, wool spools, bottles, teaspoons, combs, papers, plastic or cardboard tubing, hubcaps, string and much more at little or no cost. Simply experimenting with different sounds can be fun in itself or you can help the children to create their own band or orchestra to accompany a drama, story or game. A tapeplayer and range of styles of recorded music is also useful for dancing, listening and relaxation or stimulating and accompanying imaginative play. The children can also record their own stories and music.

Woodwork

For woodwork, you need a workbench and safe devices for clamping as well as a range of timber offcuts in different shapes and sizes. Use real (not toy) tools and make sure they are properly used, stored, maintained and supervised by a playworker who knows how to use them. Blunt, ineffective or broken tools can lead to frustration and improper use, which is a safety hazard.

Modelling

For modelling materials consider using various types of modelling and potter's

Making music outdoors

clay – both red and gray. Unless you have access to a kiln for firing, the end product will not be very satisfactory as it will crumble and break easily. If children want to make, paint and keep model figures or dishes, you can use clay with nylon fibres which enable it to harden without firing. Alternative modelling materials include Playdough, saltdough, Plasticine, wax, pastry and Fimo.

ACTIVITY   Planning ahead with children

1 Ask the children in your play setting to think of a theme or subject that they would like to use to plan the next week's activities.

2 Using large sheets of paper and coloured pens and crayons, encourage them to write down as many different games, activities (perhaps including visits, outings or inviting visitors) and types of play as they can that relate in some way to their chosen theme.

3 Make a theme chart or collate the children's ideas and drawings into a collage. Involve your colleagues in deciding which of the ideas are feasible.

SPOTLIGHT ON   Homework clubs and study support

Many childcare settings now include a place for children to do homework and an adult to help them. If your play setting provides childcare after school it may be that the children will be unable to relax and play until they have had a chance to complete their homework. Remember that the play setting is not a classroom but that play and playwork do contribute to children's opportunities to learn and explore. A play setting can offer the flexibility to enable a child to make scientific discoveries, develop practical skills, apply mathematical thinking, learn about other people and create works of art in a way that suits his or her own particular style of learning.

Food is more than eating

Food plays a large part in our lives other than providing nutrition. Meals or snack times can be ideal opportunities for social interaction in the play setting. The time spent sharing a meal can be a time to get to know one another, share information about likes and dislikes or customs and habits or plan what to do in the next week, day or half-hour. What children are used to eating will be influenced by family and cultural background. Dietary requirements need to be observed (such as offering vegetarian, kosher, halal or non-dairy alternatives). Children can share information about what they eat at home, and preparing and offering snacks that originate from a range of different cultures can be fun and an interesting way to introduce children to aspects of a culture other than their own.

Enhance the play environment with displays of fruits and vegetables from different countries, which children can touch and taste. Try a tasting session where children taste different foods without looking at them and guess what they are. Have a quiz or use reference books to help children to discover where these fruits and vegetables are grown.

Collect pictures of positive images of families of different cultures at mealtimes. The children could draw or paint their favourite foods. Have an international food celebration and serve dishes (perhaps prepared by parents/carers at home) from around the world, or compile an international recipe book for use within the play setting or to be reproduced for sale to parents, carers and others – the children could illustrate it.

Whether you can cook with children and what you can cook will depend on your play setting's facilities. On one adventure playground we know, children cooked blackberry jam on an open fire with berries they had picked from their periphery hedge. They also regularly baked potatoes in the hot ashes. Even if you don't have a fire or a kitchen, you can involve the children in cold food preparation: fruit salad, other salads, sandwiches and sweets (as an occasional treat). Children of all ages enjoy cooking. It offers endless possibilities for learning skills, independence and lots of fun. Children's imaginative play often revolves around food and they can make pretend food from clay or saltdough baked hard in the oven and painted as props for a café, shop, picnic or tea party. Before cooking with children, talk to them about good hygiene practices and the reasons for them and ensure you can provide supervision before the children use a kitchen or a fire outside.

ACTIVITY   Appealing food?

Providing food in the play setting can provide a social focus as well as an opportunity for exploration and discovery with a whole range of senses:

1 Try tasting different foods with a blindfold on: food from different countries and cultures, sweet, sour, salty.

2 What effect does sight have on taste? Try adding unusual colour to foods to make: green orange juice, blue baked beans, purple rice and peas, for example. Think about different ways we make food look appetising. Try out different garnishes. (*Note:* Some food colourings can cause allergic reactions in some children. You could use natural edible colours such as beetroot juice.)

3 Does sound affect taste? Try eating in silence, eating with music, eating while chatting.

4 Touch and taste. Try eating the same food with fingers and with cutlery or chopsticks. Does food taste different if served from china/wooden/metal/plastic bowls, cups or serving dishes?

Developing resourcefulness: a playworker's toolkit

Each one of us has our sources of support and inspiration. For you, this might come from a friend, a colleague, a teacher, a book, an experience of nature or a piece of music, your family or your work. More often forgotten is the wellspring of resourcefulness that each of has within ourselves.

On one playwork course, the students were asked to bring with them something that was important to them in their work: their 'essential tool'. The first student to present their essential tool to the group said: 'I bring with me first and foremost my imagination and sense of humour.' It was so obvious. Everyone revised their presentations of the very practical tools they had brought – tools that were practical but perhaps not essential.

One essential item in our own playworker's toolkit is a bundle of different coloured muslin cloths of all shapes and sizes. They are very lightweight and can be folded into a small bag or basket, but when spread out they cover a very wide area. They can be used in endless activities with a wide age range:

- for dressing up – cloaks, belts, hats, scarves, saris, belts and more
- spread over tables and chairs to form tents, houses and dens
- knotted into simple puppets or dolls
- as blankets, tablecloths and curtains (when the sun is too hot or bright)
- as colourful and quick backdrops to displays of artwork, puppet shows or drama
- knotted into tight rings to be used in a variety of throwing and catching games or for juggling practice.

Another major consideration in developing your toolkit will be cost. A playworker's tool kit need not be costly. Use recycled materials where possible. (See the CAN DO series of activity books in further reading at the end of this chapter.)

Using lightweight cloths to create varied play opportunities

 ACTIVITY   Your own personal playworker's toolkit and resource file

1 Develop your own playworker's toolkit. You can write a list or draw pictures or diagrams.

   You could assemble ideas and practical items in a special toolbox. Things you might want to include:

   ● personal qualities and skills

   ● your sources of support and inspiration

   ● essential pieces of equipment that you would bring with you if you were going to work with a group of children where there were no material resources on site – a ball?, paper and crayons?, a pack of cards?, a ball of string?, your favourite book of cooperative games?, balloons?, face paints?

   Include only items that you could easily carry with you. Think about how many different play opportunities you could create with each item.

2 Develop a resource file either for yourself or with colleagues for your play setting. Use a large loose-leaf folder, so that you can continuously add and update information. Divide it into sections, which might include:

   ● games of all kinds

   ● art and craft activities (with instructions)

   ● essential materials and good sources of materials

   ● fillers – five-minute activities to use as contingency plans, at the end of a session, or while waiting for a bus

   ● useful contacts

   ● tried-and-tested ideas for local visits and trips.

   Are there other sections that might be useful to your particular play setting?

   Your resource file could include photographs, comments, notes and evaluation of particular activities.

Developing your resourcefulness is important. Playwork, like life itself, is often a serious and exhausting business. You need resilience to cope with physical and mental demands made in your work. You have huge responsibilities and perhaps insufficient funds, support and recognition of what your role entails. You may have to cope with the practical and business sides of running a play facility: shopping, budgeting, meetings, planning, liaising with others, dealing with the concerns and complaints of the users. Yet you cannot afford to lose sight of the intrinsic value of play itself, for the children, for yourselves and for human development and society at large. You need to look at ways of gaining support and constantly rejuvenating your ability to look at things afresh, to play and to celebrate your work.

Resourcefulness is a skill that you can develop. You need to evaluate, change and build on your toolkit in the light of your own experience and the shared experience of others. Many playworkers become adept at begging and borrowing ideas, skills, expertise, transport, materials, (offcuts, scraps, end of lines, advertising give aways) from a range of sources. Get to know:

● local traders and businesses

● resource centres, schools and community groups

- parents and children
- other playworkers.

Endings

Endings are also important. Depending on how you end a play session, a child could go home feeling happy, fulfilled and confident or they could go home feeling angry or upset. When you are planning the play activities and opportunities, think about how you will bring them to an end. Where possible, let children finish their play in their own time. You may want to make them aware of what other play opportunities are available. At the end of the session, complete any relevant records. Some ideas for ensuring smooth endings at the end of the day/session:

- Allow plenty of time for finishing off the session. It is often a good idea to let the children know when they will have to finish. For example, you might tell them when there are 10 minutes left.

- Involve the children in tidying up and allow plenty of time for this. Try not to make tidying a chore or a behaviour issue! This may be a good time to get feedback from the children and plan future activities together. You will also need to judge whether it is appropriate to disrupt play in order to clear up in time. There are occasions when children are so deeply engaged in their play that it may be better to let them have the extra 10 minutes playing and tidy up yourself after the children have gone.

- Many play settings end with a quiet 'together time'. This might be circle games, a story or a chat for those who want to be involved.

- Try not to let a child go home with negative feelings, such as anger, sadness or frustration. Endeavour to sort out any conflict or anxieties before home time.

- When you are saying goodbye to a child, you may want to ease the transition with a comment about what you observed went well for the child or by looking forward to the opportunities that might be developed tomorrow.

- In an open-access or drop-in session, it may be equally important to note when a child is leaving and acknowledge that you value their presence by saying something like: 'Nice to see you Kurosh. Hope you will drop in again soon.'

Winding down

ACTIVITY   Observation to evaluate the play opportunities in your setting

Observe your play setting as a whole for a few minutes at regular intervals – every half hour or 45 minutes, say – throughout one day. Make notes on the level and types of activity in progress. At the end of the day, ask yourself:

- Did the level of activity vary at different times of day?
- Which play types were in evidence (see page 8)?
- Were there times that seemed more active and energetic and times where the energy was winding down?
- Were there times when the children came together in larger groups or a whole group to share food, discussion or a cooperative game?
- Were there times that were noisier and times that were quieter?

Think of two activities that might be particularly good at the beginning of the day and two which might be better suited to the end of the day. Why should this be the case?

Summary

This chapter has looked at some of the starting points for playworkers to use in planning play opportunities for children. It reminds you that the children themselves should be the primary starting point, but that there are a wealth of resources, materials and ideas that the playworker can offer to facilitate their play interests. It suggests ways in which you can maintain and develop your own resourcefulness and touches on a range of considerations in planning for play, some of which are covered in more detail in other chapters:

- *Health and safety*: Bought toys and equipment should comply with British or European safety standards (see Chapter 12).
- *Play types and developmental stages*: A rich variety of materials and activities should be introduced which encourage all play types. Cater for all ages involved. Don't be surprised if older children still enjoy dressing up and playing in the sandpit and younger children want to attempt complex craft activities, team games and puzzles (see Chapter 1).
- *Accessibility and inclusion*: Are the play opportunities accessible to all children? Do they promote independence and encourage self-esteem (enabling the children to feel good about themselves). And counterbalance stereotypes that marginalise or ridicule people because of the way they look or their family background. Do your resources encourage children to extend their views about the possibilities open to them – by giving them images and examples of people in active and important roles: girls as well as boys, black people as well as white and disabled people (see Chapter 8)?
- *Involving others and reflecting on practice*: Discuss your ideas and plans with colleagues at regular staff planning meetings (see Chapter 10). Involve children in decisions about what activities to offer. Review your activities regularly. What has worked well? What has not? Why? How might you do things differently? Use the activity sections throughout this book to help evaluate. Get new ideas, support and advice from local libraries, resource centres and national organisations or visit other similar facilities in your area.

- *Keeping records*: Records of activities and equipment available are particularly important for new staff and in places where there may be a high turnover of staff (e.g. some summer playschemes). They are useful when for one reason or another the planned programme of activities cannot go ahead. A diary, logbook or scrapbook (involving the children) with pictures and photographs can record activities that have been successful. This can also be useful for publicity for your play setting and as evidence for your personal portfolio if you are working towards an NVQ in playwork (more on paperwork in Chapter 13).

References

Hughes, B. (2002) *A Playworker's Taxonomy of Play Types*. PLAYLINK. This publication is available from PlayEducation, 13 Castelhythe, Ely, Cambs CB7 4BU. See also the website: www.playeducation.com.

Rumi (1991) *Shouldering the Lion*. (trans. Coleman Barks). Threshold Books.

Further reading

CAN DO series of play activity books with a difference – published by Thomson Learning and edited by Annie Davy (2002):

- *Eco Ventures* – Hannah Sugar, KCN, Thomson Learning.
- *Serious Fun – Games for 4–9s* – Phill Burton, Dynamix, Thomson Learning.
- *Serious Fun – Games for 10–14s* – Phill Burton, Dynamix, Thomson Learning.
- *Whatever the Weather* – Jane Gallagher, Thomson Learning.
- *Cool Creations* – Mary Allanson, KCN, Thomson Learning.
- *Sticks and Stones* – Sharon Crockett, Thomson Learning.

Lear, R. (1996) *Play Helps: Toys and Activities for Children with Special Needs*. Butterworth-Heinemann.

Shephard, C. and Stormont, B. (2004) *Jabulani*. Hawthorn Press. Lovely ideas for making music (with a CD).

West, S. (1991) *Open Sez Me – The Magic of Pleasant Discoveries*. Open-Sez-Me Books. (Four books with a range of clear, illustrated ideas for multicultural activities and play ideas for winter, spring, summer and autumn.)

Quality assurance and playwork principles

Conway, M., Hughes, B. and Sturrock, G. (2004) *The Playwork Matrix*. From phase one of the 2004 consultation on playwork principles: www.playwales.org.uk.

Hughes, B. (2001) *The First Claim – A Framework for Playwork Quality Assessment*. PlayWales. www.playwales.org.uk.

London Play (2001) *Quality in Play*. Nationally accredited playwork Quality Assurance Scheme (0207 272 6759)

CHAPTER 6
Relationships with children and parents

Grown ups never understand anything for themselves, and it is tiresome for children to be always and forever explaining things to them.

(A. Saint-Exupéry, *The Little Prince*)

Developing and maintaining good relationships with children is a theme that runs throughout this book. It assumes a basic understanding of child development (see Chapter 1) and relates to many of the underpinning values and principles of playwork (see Chapter 2). This chapter focuses on how you can form good relationships with children. There is also a focus on good communication, and how to get the best out of your relationships with parents and carers at the play setting. In this chapter, we will consider:

- Welcoming new children
- Building and maintaining relationships with children
- Communicating with children
- Good relationships with parents and carers

Welcoming new children

Going to any new place can be daunting. Most people, children and adults, need support in adjusting to a new situation. When a new child visits or comes to the play setting for the first time, ask yourself: 'Who is this child? What brings her to the play setting? How can we help her to feel welcomed and at ease? What does she bring with her in the way of interests, skills, past experiences, values, beliefs and expectations?' Try to think about how she might be thinking.

ACTIVITY　　New situations

1 Think about new situations that you have faced in the past, for example:
   - the first day of a new job or course;
   - going to a social gathering where you did not know most of the people present;
   - a holiday in another place.
2 Write down:
   - things that made you feel uncomfortable;
   - things that put you at your ease.
3 Think about the last two or three children who were new to your play setting. How do you think they felt? What did you, your colleagues and the other children do to make them feel comfortable?

The activity 'New situations' asks you to think about how you felt when facing new situations in the past. It may be that you felt shy, staying on the sidelines to observe the codes of conduct and the nature of interaction between other people. Perhaps you asked yourself, 'What is expected of me in this situation? How do I fit in?'

Things that made you feel uncomfortable might have included:

- being overloaded with information you didn't have time to take in
- being excluded or ignored
- other people making false assumptions about why you were there
- being expected to join in activities or take on tasks that you had not been prepared for or were unwilling to do

How do you welcome new children at your setting?

- getting conflicting information from different people.

  Things that helped you feel more comfortable may have included:

- having clear and accurate information in advance about what the situation would involve
- knowing why you are there
- a friendly and welcoming reception from others
- a safe place to put your belongings
- individual attention from someone who supported you through the situation, making introductions and explaining anything you didn't understand
- other people understanding your reason for being there
- having time to adjust at your own pace without being pressurised to conform or perform before you were ready.

A named worker

In some settings new children are given a particular named worker (sometimes called a *key worker*) – someone who will take special responsibility for the welfare of that child and help him to settle in. This worker is someone who can also exchange information with the parent about the child's adjustment to the play setting or his behaviour and progress within it. Often the child will choose the adult with whom he wishes to form a particular bond – to share information or concerns with, to ask for help or advice or simply to join in with play and other activities. Even if there is a named worker policy in your setting, there should be flexibility between the staff to offer the child the freedom to make such choices.

Setting the scene

There are many things you can do to help enable a new child to feel comfortable in the play setting. Each child may need a different approach, depending on the type of play setting and the child's individual needs and circumstances:

1. Offer a smile and greeting.
2. Introduce yourself and others in the play setting.
3. Find out the name of the child (the full legal name will go on the records, but you also need to know the name by which the child wants to be known – shortened name or a nickname).
4. Make sure you can pronounce the child's name correctly. If it is an unfamiliar name to you, practise it and ask the child if you have got it right. If you do not do this, it can make a child feel unimportant or singled out as odd.
5. Explain any routines – where to hang coats, where the toilets are, what refreshments are available and when. Show where the ground rules are displayed and run through them briefly.
6. Introduce the child to others. Encourage other children to involve the new child in their play and to show her the ropes. This will be particularly important if the new child does not know any other children in the play setting.
7. Young children may find it easier to settle if they can make their first visits with their parents. Try to make this possible for as long as is needed by the child and is possible for parents.

8 Give plenty of time for the child (and parents if they accompany the child) to ask questions. You may need to arrange a time for them to visit when this will be possible. Give parents and children information (verbal and written if appropriate), including factual information (about opening times, typical pattern of a session, fees) and information about policies relating to attendance, behaviour and equal opportunities. Try to give the information as answers to questions, rather than overloading them with information which will not be taken in.

9 Provide a play environment that offers interesting and stimulating opportunities for play. Let the child know about the play opportunities and choices on offer.

10 Respect each child as individual and unique. Show that she is valued in the play setting for the qualities, skills and attributes she brings with her – of herself and of her family, culture and past experience.

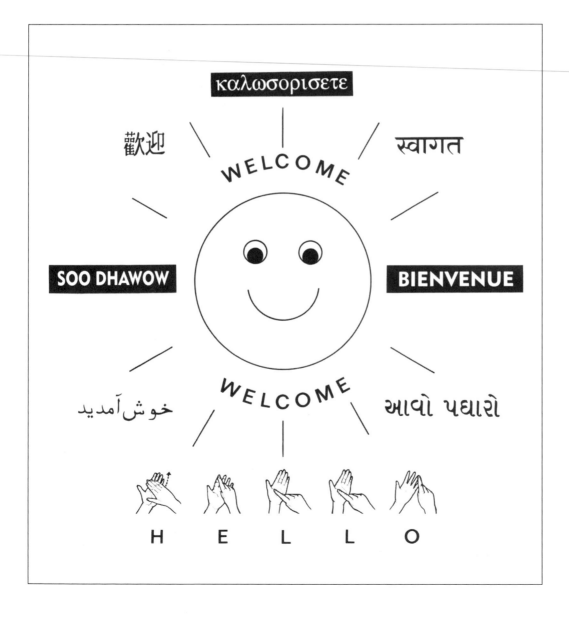

ACTIVITY   Welcoming new children

Consider the following situations:

1 François is 6. He has very recently come to England with his parents who are attending a three-year course of study. He visits your playcare setting with his mother, who wants him to start next week. He speaks very few words of English. His mother speaks fluent English. He looks anxious, holds his mother's hand and hides behind her back.

2 Yulan is 13. She comes to your open-access play setting one Saturday with her friend Amanda, who has been coming for several months. Yulan settles in quickly in a game of 'Twister' with a group of other girls. When you go to talk to her, she appears to withdraw. You offer her an information leaflet and emergency contact form, but she refuses, saying, 'I don't know if I'll be able to come again.'

3 Christopher is 9. You have been asked by the duty social worker to collect him from school along with your usual children for the after school club. Christopher's mother has been admitted to hospital as an emergency. Christopher has been informed by the social worker and his teacher. The social worker will visit during the session and his grandmother will pick him up.

What might you do to help each child settle into your play setting? Which of the suggestions given in the section 'Setting the scene' would be appropriate and why? What else could you do?

Getting to know you

The way in which a child settles into the play setting will depend partly on his age, temperament, stage of development and previous experience. Some children have had more experience than others of adjusting to new settings and circumstances. However, a child who has undergone considerable changes in play and care settings might find it just as difficult or more difficult to settle than a child who attends a play setting for the first time. He may be insecure and vulnerable because of the many changes he has faced. An older child may come alone to visit the setting. You will need equal sensitivity to recognise and meet what the older child or adolescent needs to help her settle. She may want just to observe for a while and to find her own way into making social contacts and getting involved in activities. Or she may appreciate your involvement and help in making introductions. Offer her the same information and time to ask questions or share concerns as you would a younger child and his parents.

In an open-access setting, a child may come with friends, loiter around the edges of the play setting for a while and come back for longer the next day. He may initially shy away from any prolonged contact with adults. In this case, give him a welcome greeting. Let him know you are available if he wants to know anything. Give him basic verbal information together with any written information and registration form to take away. Leave him to determine for himself the pace at which he wants to make contact and join in. Get to know as much as you can about the child as soon as possible, ideally before he comes to the play setting. This does not mean prying: ask only questions that have direct relevance to your being able to meet his needs. Such information includes:

- language(s) spoken
- dietary requirements

- medical conditions that might require medication or emergency treatment
- family and emergency contacts
- particular hobbies or interests
- where relevant, who will collect the child from the play setting.

 **ACTIVITY** **You're welcome**

1 Make a list of all the things you do to help welcome new children into your play setting.
2 See if you can add at least two new things to try.

Confidentiality

Some children and parents will be very forthcoming about other aspects of their lives: income, divorce, medical or other problems in the family. Such information must be kept confidential. Share with colleagues only information that is essential for them to care adequately for the child within the play setting, or information that leads to concerns about the safety or well-being of the child (see Chapter 11). Never share personal information about one child with another child or his parents.

Meeting individual needs

All children have particular needs that need to be met before they can make the most of the play opportunities in your setting. A child may need support with mobility, communication, personal hygiene, feeding or gaining confidence. She may require special adaptations or equipment to enable her to play or carry out tasks relating to personal independence. If you provide food, make sure you can provide for any dietary requirements of individual children. If a child does not speak fluent English and you do not have a worker who speaks her 'mother tongue', you will need to consider ways to help her communicate with you and you to communicate with her. You might use signs, gestures and picture symbols, and/or learn some basic words in her language. Take time to help her if she wants to learn English words. Encourage other children to join in. Your contacts with other agencies (see Chapter 14) will be valuable sources of help and advice in meeting individual children's needs.

Be proactive in finding out how you can meet individual needs. By doing so, you will help to ensure that the children feel comfortable, happy and valued. You could find out their needs by:

- asking the children and the parents directly
- having a suggestion box and feedback sessions
- having children's representatives at your committee meetings
- observing the children at play
- being approachable and letting the children know they can come to you with any issue at all.

Building and maintaining relationships with children

It takes time to develop trusting and confident relationships. You need to get to know the children. They need to get to know you. The way in which you communicate is very important. There are many ways to work towards building and maintaining good relationships in the play setting.

Establishing trust

A good starting point for establishing trust is to look at your own thoughts and beliefs. How much do you trust and respect children? Do you believe that, given the chance, they will play positively, help others, act responsibly and speak truthfully? Or is it your belief that children will be disobedient and naughty the moment an adult's back is turned? Your attitude affects your relationship with children, so take a close look. Children respect adults who trust them to behave positively, and in turn, are likely to return the trust.

Other ways to promote trust include the following.

Valuing children's decisions

We show children further trust when they have the freedom to make their own decisions in their play. They can also help to decide what activities and equipment they should have at the play setting – after all, they are the experts when it comes to play.

Meaning what you say

Children will learn to trust you if you follow through what you say. For example, if you say, 'I'll just finish talking to this parent, and then I will get the tent out of the cupboard for you,' then try to carry out your promise. If you finish talking to the parent and then decide that setting the tent up would be too time consuming, you will have a very disappointed child, who will be very reluctant to trust you again in future.

Telling the truth

If children can rely on you to tell them the truth about things, they will feel respected and valued and are more likely to come to you for advice and information when they need it in future. If you make things up, the child is likely to find out at some later point and be confused and disillusioned with what you say. They are also likely to lose their trust in you. (There is more on this subject under 'Answering children's questions' further on in this chapter.)

Helping children to trust their own feelings

A child, in tears after a fall, may be told by an adult, 'Silly thing, there's no need to cry about a little fall!' This teaches the child to doubt her own emotional judgements. If the adult instead says, 'Are you upset because you fell over? Where does it hurt? Shall we get a plaster for you?' it shows the child that her feelings are valued and taken seriously.

Being consistent

In order for a child to learn to trust you and feel confident in the play setting, you need to be consistent. Try not to treat children in different ways according to your mood: smiling one day, distracted the next, with humour the third day and with sternness on the fourth. Of course, different circumstances and events will affect the way you react on particular days, but be clear about the reasons for this and explain them to the children. If you don't do this, they may wrongly blame themselves for your behaviour or lose confidence in you. There should also be consistency between staff, particularly in behaviour management (more on behaviour in Chapter 7).

Relationships of trust

Developing self-reliance and self-esteem

A child's self-esteem will be affected by the respect received from other children and adults towards his language, culture, skin colour, family, appearance, particular skills, abilities, achievements, beliefs and needs. With older children, dress codes and sexuality or sexual orientation may also be important factors. Using resources, activities and images that reflect diversity in all these areas are important parts of enabling all children to develop both self-esteem and respect for others. Also look for books and posters that show people from different parts of the world, of both genders, with all kinds of skin tones and dress codes and disabled people in a variety of positive circumstances and roles.

Encourage children to recognise their own and other children's individual talents and achievements by highlighting and praising them. Give praise for social skills as well: 'I think it was great the way you made Kumran feel welcome today Tariq' or 'It's good to have someone like you Alice to cheer us up with your jokes.'

Group activity to focus on listening and cooperation

ACTIVITY Promoting self-esteem

1 Look at two or three of the play activities you are planning for the coming week. Consider the resources you will be using and ask yourself whether each promotes self-esteem and values diversity or whether it promotes stereotypes and a limited world view.

2 Notice how often you praise children's positive qualities, talents, skills, behaviour and achievements. Try to count how many times you do this naturally in one session. You could take turns with another colleague to observe this in each other. Compare this with the number of times you rebuke, control or limit a child or groups of children.

As children develop confidence and self-esteem, they also develop self-reliance. They learn to trust their own skills and judgements – about their ability to care for themselves, to assess the risks and safety of a situation, to take responsibility and care for their environment. Plan activities that present a challenge but that are achievable with the minimum of assistance. Where possible, make resources available and accessible to children.

Making their own decisions can help children to develop self-reliance. Being able to initiate and develop their play in their own way and for their own reasons is therefore of central importance in the play setting. They could also be involved in decisions about the rules, the range of resources, the food on offer, trips out and the design and décor of the play setting.

Children's ideas and feedback

Valuing children's ideas and advice about the running of the play setting is linked to much of what we have already discussed in this chapter – building children's self-esteem, self-reliance, trust and confidence. It is an absolute must if you want to create an equal, two-way relationship. If a playworker is not interested in the views of children, you might rightly question whether he or she is in the right job.

Article 12 of the United Nations Convention on the Rights of the Child states that children have the right to give their views when adults are making decisions that affect them and to have their opinions taken into account. Some adults find it difficult to 'give up control' of a situation. But that is one of the beauties of playwork – children can expect to be fully respected as individuals, with valuable actions, opinions and ideas that they demonstrate through their play and their interactions with playworkers. These ideas are then fed into the decision-making process of the play setting, ensuring that the setting is constantly evolving and meeting the specific play needs of every child.

To gain children's trust in the feedback process, we must endeavour to put their ideas into practice. Children can quickly see through a tokenistic or superficial approach to involving them. How children feel when they see their own ideas in practice is written all over their faces.

Sense of achievement

Helping children to develop relationships with others

As we develop our relationships with children, so too can we help them to develop their own relationships with other children and adults. In a playwork setting, children should always be allowed to choose their own relationships – and never forced to play with others against their will. There may be times when you might ask a child or children to play with someone who is new or who is feeling left out. If you are sensitive in your choice of child to ask, it is likely that within a few minutes, they will be playing together like old friends. Even if a lasting friendship does not form, the new child will have gained confidence from the companionship.

All relationships are strengthened by going through a variety of experiences together, such as:

- sharing moments of hilarity and joy
- arguing, debating and coming to a decision together
- helping each other through difficult situations.

It is the thought processes and decision making that are important here – and, again, it is the playworker's job to stand back and let children develop their own skills for dealing with other people. Adults tend to jump in too often and too quickly! Trust the child's ability to work out things for himself. Give children the freedom to develop their own strategies for dealing with disagreements (provided they do not unduly interfere with the play opportunities of others). If they have seen positive role models, whom they like and respect, they are more likely to follow that example. They may, however, have some negative role models in their lives that they copy at times and so you need to be on hand to support the interaction, if necessary. Again, it is about your sensitivity and your ability to judge a situation – this comes from common sense, experience, deep respect for children and developing your own professional self-awareness about the impact of your actions on play and relationships. It is not about forcing children to get on well with others – it is about helping them to *enjoy* getting on with others.

 ACTIVITY   Cooperation

Read the section on 'Observing children' in Chapter 2.

1 Plan and set up two play opportunities that you think will encourage cooperation of many different skills and talents – one for a group of 6 to 7 year olds, and one for a group of 12 to 13 year olds.

2 Observe each group of children as they get involved in the play opportunity.

3 Afterwards, consider whether all children who wanted to could contribute and whether their contributions were recognised by others. Were there any gender differences?

4 Would you do anything differently next time?

Encourage children to share their skills and use them to support each other in the play setting. Provide opportunities for them to discover their own talents and to discover and value those in others. A child who cannot run fast or has little confidence to climb or skip might be exceptionally good at using woodwork tools or organising a team game. A child with a speech impairment may excel at art or construction or have a good imagination.

Children can become aware of and relate to one another's needs by caring for each other. They can prepare and serve food – or even grow some, if you have a spare piece of ground or even a window box or grow bag (lettuce and cress grow quickly and easily for salad sandwiches). One child can cheer another when she is down or sit and read or talk to her if she is feeling unwell.

SPOTLIGHT ON   Cooperative games

Cooperative games enable children of all ages and abilities to work in pairs or in groups, to communicate, be inventive and develop trust. They can be good at 'breaking the ice' – for example, on the first day of a playscheme. Try this one – a firm favourite.

Game – sticky toffee
The person who is 'it' holds out her fingers and everybody else must hold one. 'It' says some things beginning with 'sticky', such as, 'Sticky fingers!', or, 'Sticky marshmallows' and so on. When 'it' finally says, 'Sticky TOFFEE!' everyone has to run away. If 'it' tags you, you have to stand still with your legs apart you can only move again when someone who is 'free' goes under your legs.

Lots more games and activities specifically for play settings can be found in the Can do series of activity books (see further reading).

Communicating with children

Children are extremely perceptive – when you communicate with them, your attitude towards them will always shine through. They appreciate and respond most positively when other people communicate with them respectfully and with consideration for their feelings.

Many of the skills of effective communication are the same whether you are dealing with children or with other adults. Some are referred to in Chapter 10. The main difference in communicating with children is that you need to apply your knowledge and understanding of child development. Most children will not have the range of vocabulary that you have, so you may have to choose your words carefully and check that they are understood. Children will also have various levels of understanding of rules, expected behaviour and particular concepts, such as safety and fairness. They may have shorter concentration spans and memories. You may have to communicate the same information many times before it is taken in.

Listening

Listen actively by looking at the child and by trying to find out what the child is trying to communicate. Don't interrupt, interpret or judge what is being said. Do give the child your full attention or let the child know when this will be possible. For example: Child: 'My sister's gone to Italy.' Don't fob her off or jump to conclusions with 'How lovely' or 'Lucky thing.' The child is telling you this piece of news because it is important to her. It may not seem lovely or lucky to her. Try something like, 'Just let me finish pouring this paint and I'd like to hear all about it.' Your body language is as important as any words you speak in letting the child know you are listening. Look interested – make eye contact, nod and smile. Don't fidget, look at your watch, out of the window or walk away. Beware of putting false interpretation on to cultural differences in the way people use and interpret body language. For example, direct eye contact in some African and Asian cultures is a sign of insolence, not respect or listening.

Body language

Non-verbal communication often says more than the words you say. Eye contact, as already mentioned, is one of the main ways to show someone that you respect someone and are interested in what they have to say. (But try not to stare – it can make a person feel uncomfortable or self-conscious.) Other aspects of body language that can aid (or hamper) communication are as follows.

Body position

If you are interested, your are more likely to turn towards the person you are talking to. Turning away can show disinterest or boredom. Folding your arms is often a defensive position and can be seen as aggressive. Arms at your sides or in your lap is an 'open' position and reflects that you are relaxed and friendly.

Personal space

Respect a child's personal space. Getting too close can be a sign of aggression or unwanted intimacy. Sometimes a cuddle is appropriate and at other times, it is inappropriate. Watch a child's body language to help you gauge their feelings.

Mirroring

If you are sitting having a discussion with a child, mirroring, or copying, some of their gestures shows that you are listening and that you empathise with what they have to say. For example, if the child leans forward, you might do the same. You can observe this happening quite naturally in a comfortable conversation. It does not need to be contrived.

ACTIVITY   How would you communicate?

Discuss with another playworker how you would get involved if you were faced with the following situations at work. It is helpful if you can actually practise what you would say and how you would intervene (if at all). Where possible, ask others (your co-workers or playwork trainees) to role play the parts of the children so that you can try out direct responses to one or two of these situations:

1   Osse and Tamari are 8 and 9 respectively. They have discovered several piles of leaves swept up by the caretaker the night before. They are throwing them at each other and laughing. Osse takes a dive into the middle of one of the piles. Tamari covers him with leaves. Three other children join in and are about to scatter the leaves in the other piles.

2   Lara, aged 11, has spent a long time painting a picture of herself and friends playing in your play setting. The playworker would like to put it on the wall or in the scrapbook that is kept in the play setting to record special events. Suddenly, Lara starts flicking bright red paint over the whole page.

3   Lucy, Gemma and Alexandra are 7. They have built a cardboard box train. They go to the playworker, who is helping two other children make some papier mâché, and ask if he will come and be the engine driver and take them to the seaside.

Answering children's questions

As a trusted adult, you will be asked questions about important issues. Questions about sex, death, religion, illness and politics may be difficult to answer for many reasons:

- You recognise that there are many social taboos around the subject.
- You are uncertain how to explain a complex issue to a very young child.
- There are many different answers depending on what you believe.
- You don't have enough information to answer the question.

Choosing together

- You think the parent should answer such questions.
- You don't want to be accused of indoctrinating the child.

Whatever your reasons for finding the question difficult, the child has a right to an honest answer. If you cannot answer in an appropriate way immediately, explain why. You can ask for time, 'That is a very interesting question and deserves a proper answer which I do not have the time to give today. I will talk to you about this tomorrow/on . . .' Then make sure that you do – having got the appropriate information or having shared ideas with colleagues about the most appropriate ways to answer the question. There are always several ways to answer a question honestly. Give answers in language that will be understood by the child. You can say, 'People believe different things about this. I think. . . but others think . . .' It is useful to practise giving answers to questions about subjects that we find awkward to deal with – and to consider how the answer should be phrased differently to children of different ages and stages of development.

ACTIVITY Answering difficult questions

Get a friend or colleague to play the part of a child asking questions that you might find it difficult to answer. Here are two ideas to get you started:

1 Shamira, 6 years old, and just learning to read, brings a newspaper over from the craft table. 'What is HIV?' she asks. Fourteen-year-old Brendan is standing close by and says, 'My sister says you can get AIDS from kissing. Is that true?'

2 8 year old Maria says: 'My grandma died. My mum says she's gone to heaven. Betty says there's no such thing as heaven. Where do you think my grandma is now?'

Discuss what was easy/hard about answering these questions. Share ideas about other ways you could have answered. Think about questions you have found difficult to answer in the past. Ask others about questions they find difficult.

Recognising and dealing with feelings

Part of emotional development is about recognising and dealing with feelings. A baby expresses feelings of hunger, tiredness, cold, anger, frustration or boredom by crying. A 2 year old can throw a tantrum – lying on the floor, drumming feet, screaming and even holding his breath – for the same reasons. As a child develops increasingly complex and sophisticated means of communicating her feelings (particularly through the development of language), she has less need to resort to such extreme measures to let her feelings be known.

In a play setting, young children may still have a limited vocabulary to express their feelings and limited understanding of their causes. In the following case study, the emotions Rita is experiencing may be anger, frustration or simply hunger – but probably not the hate she is expressing. She cannot relate the various causes of her emotions to each other or to how she is feeling at present. She may also be frightened at the strength of her emotional outburst and be unable to find a way out of it. In such cases, it will be important for the child to have your understanding, support and reassurance. You may need to hold her for your own or her safety – or just give her a reassuring hug. Wait for her to calm down before helping her to sort out what happened and why.

CASE STUDY   Dealing with strong emotions

One day, Rita, a 6 year old girl, was late for school, had no time for breakfast, was told off by her teacher and had an argument with her best friend at lunchtime. The final straw was being told she couldn't have a second biscuit on arrival at the after school club, because the playworker had just eaten the last one. She flies at the playworker, hitting and punching and screaming 'I hate you, I hate you.'

Play settings can provide opportunities for children to express and explore some of their feelings in a safe and accepting environment. Through play, they can learn to recognise and name different emotions and practise ways of dealing with them. Many children learn to suppress their feelings and 'put on a brave face' or to 'pull themselves together', which may make it difficult for them to identify or express their feelings.

Be wary of interpreting a child's expressed thoughts, feelings and play. Remember each child has learned different ways of dealing with feelings, which may not be the same as your own. From the time we learn to talk, we may learn that outward displays of emotion (crying, shouting, laughter) are not generally accepted in everyday or public situations. By the same token, we may be brought up in a situation where open displays of emotion are encouraged. Cultural and social backgrounds shape our attitude towards emotions and acceptable ways of expressing them.

Developing assertiveness

Assertiveness is about having the confidence to explain your feelings and expectations clearly, while acknowledging and respecting the feelings and expectations of others. With children, be prepared to negotiate, and if possible find a win–win rather than a win–lose solution. For example, you might say: 'I understand that you expected us to go to the park today and that you are feeling very disappointed. It was not possible for me to take you because I had to have an emergency meeting with the social worker. If the weather is OK I will take you to the park tomorrow.' Make sure you can keep your promises!

Try to communicate in ways that will not provoke a defensive response. Avoid judging a child by her behaviour or being certain that you can provide the superior solutions. Don't use phrases such as 'you always' or 'why can't you ever', 'you are', 'the best way to'. These phrases label and judge the child and undermine self-esteem. They do not constructively criticise behaviour, help the child to change or invite her to contribute her own views. Try phrases which begin: 'It hurts when you' or 'I felt it was unfair when you' or 'Have you thought about'. Encourage children to participate in finding solutions to problems. Provide options and try to be flexible without being passive and over-compliant yourself.

Meeting the communication needs of every child

If your play setting is working towards meeting the requirements of the Disability Discrimination Act and including everyone (see Chapter 8), then you will probably have already made provision for facilitating play for children with communication needs. It is important to remember that communication and interaction do not have to involve the use of language and speech.

If a child with a communication impairment comes to your setting, discuss his particular needs with the child and his parents initially. They can help you to understand the child's individual communication needs and may be able to teach you what works best for the child. For example, if a child with Asperger Syndrome comes to the setting, he may prefer communicating with gestures or he may require more time to respond to questions or he may find too many questions confusing. By finding out his requirements, you will increase your ability to communicate with the child – and his ability to communicate with you – and you will show him that you fully respect his right to be at the play setting. You might discuss a child's communication needs with your manager. You or your manager might also talk to the child's school, in order to find out how best to provide for the child.

Be positive: a child who can use sign language or speak more than one language has a very valuable communication skill to share with others in the play setting. Any perceived 'difficulty' may be your and the other children's inability to understand her. What is required will depend on the reason for the communication impairment. Speech therapy and non-verbal languages (such as British Sign Language, Makaton and Signalong) can provide a hearing-impaired child with vital opportunities for expressing herself. Other aids to communication use signs and symbols (such as Braille). There is steady growth in computer and other technological developments to assist people who have particular communication needs.

Ask the child or her parents for advice in making your play setting a place where she feels comfortable and capable of understanding and being understood. Review your approach as the child gets older – her communication needs (like those of all children) are likely to change.

Good relationships with parents and carers

Most play settings have a relationship of one kind or another with the parents and carers of the children who attend. As the main carers of their children, parents and carers have a right to full information about the setting and events within it. Parents have an interest in ensuring that the play setting meets the needs of their children and will usually have the final say in whether their child attends or stays. The parents give permission and often pay the fees where fees are payable. They can also provide your strongest support. While you, as playworker, have much to contribute to the well-being of the children in your care, you need to communicate with parents, respect their rights and work in partnership with them.

Some games use gestures to communicate

What do we mean by parent?

Throughout this section, where the word 'parent/s' is used, it is taken to mean the adult or adults who has or have the main responsibility for the child at home. In some cases, we have used 'parent or carer' to emphasise this point, but in other cases, this became impossibly clumsy. The person or persons who take the parenting role will not necessarily be the biological parents. Children may live with a lone parent, a grandparent or other relative, gay or lesbian parents, adoptive parents, stepparents, a foster parent or social workers in a children's home.

Communicating with parents and carers

Communicate with parents right from the start and let them know how and when they can communicate with you at work. When a new child visits the play setting for the first time, a friendly welcome to the parents as well as the child makes a good start. It is also important that you provide a welcoming atmosphere at the start of each session.

ACTIVITY   Welcoming parents

1 Each play setting is different. Make sure you know who has responsibility in your play setting for welcoming visitors and showing people around, and when and how this takes place.

2 Make a list of the questions you think a parent might ask when visiting a play setting with a view to enrolling their child. What answers would you give?

Parents have known their children a lot longer than you have. Parents know their child's cultural, medical and social history, her likes and dislikes and past experiences, good and bad. If they are able to share some of this knowledge with you, it can help you to get to know the child more quickly, smooth the settling in time and avoid the pitfalls that can come from making incorrect assumptions.

Parents may drop in unexpectedly to get information or view the play setting when you do not have the time to show them around. In this situation, you could invite them to look around by themselves and ask questions later, refer them to someone who can show them around or arrange an alternative time for them to visit. Be polite and have some written information for them to take away.

ACTIVITY   Working with parents and carers

Find out in your play setting:

- how parents get information about the setting
- how they can express their views on what goes on there
- ways in which the parents can alter what goes on in the play setting
- what opportunities there are for a parent to discuss a child's progress in the play setting and be involved in planning future play opportunities.

Make time for communication with parents

Communication with parents is equally important after the child has settled and throughout the time he remains in the play setting. Parents need to know when you can discuss any issues or concerns with them that require more than a minute or two. Communication is important both ways. Only you and your colleagues know how the child is getting on within the play setting as seen from an adult point of view and you may spend more time with him during his waking hours than the parent does. Not all parents will ask about how their child is getting on, even if they do have questions, because they recognise that you are busy and have many children in your care. They may see you as a professional (however friendly) and believe they do not have the right to take up your time. Make it clear in your communication with parents that you welcome discussions with them. You might want to suggest the best time to talk to you, when you are least likely to be busy.

Good communication can help you to plan better for individual needs and circumstances and to share any achievements or concerns. If you keep records of the children's development or activities, make time to share your observations with the parents of the child concerned. Draw the parents' attention to particular achievements – 'Have you seen Sunita's puppet? It took her three days to make it. The children want to use it in a puppet show next week'; or 'Sam braved the aerial swing today – it took a lot of courage'; or 'Ashley has been particularly helpful in looking after the two new children this week – showing them where things are and involving them in the games.'

The ways in which you involve parents can be very simple, like having a suggestions box in the entrance to your play setting (and acting on the suggestions – which can be less straightforward). You might have an open diary or logbook. Make sure it is in a place that is accessible for parents to look at regularly and perhaps add their own comments.

 ACTIVITY   Tell the parents?

Consider the following situations.

1 Liam is 6 and unhappy. When asked what is wrong he says that his cat got run over.

2 Imran and Rashida are 10 and 11. They have taken a great interest in preparing snacks and cooking in the play setting. Over several weeks, they have also involved the younger children in setting up 'cafés' in which to serve their food.

3 In your play setting, you overhear three or four children aged 13 and 14 talking about joyriding and how their mates want them to join in driving stolen cars.

4 Rosa and Paul are 15. They will soon be too old to come to the play setting. Recently they have inspired numerous artistic projects within your setting, including airbrushing T-shirts and elaborate face painting with younger children. They are looking for a work experience placement from school.

Now ask yourself:

● As the playworker in each of the situations, what, if anything, would you say to the children's parents? Ask a colleague to take the part of the parent, and practise what you might say.

● What activities would you plan or what action would you take within the play setting to meet these children's needs?

Equal opportunities

Children live in different types of family. It is important for the children that their own and other families' values are respected within the play setting. As far as possible, all parents should have the same opportunities for communicating with you and becoming involved. This may mean that you need to get written information translated into another language, arrange for an interpreter for a consultation meeting or, in the case of a housebound parent, do a home visit or send a child home with a diary to share – a notebook or scrapbook which the child takes between home and play setting in which she can record (draw, stick, write) things which she wants to remember to tell or discuss with her parent or her playworkers.

Open access and older children

If your play setting is an open-access or drop-in facility, or caters only for older children, it may be that you rarely, if ever, see the parents of the children. Communication with the parents will then be indirect through the children, but consent forms for trips and so on will still need the signature of a parent. Information about the setting, its policies and practice should be made available whenever and however possible – on noticeboards (within the play setting and in the wider community), in leaflets for children to take home and through good publicity (more on this in Chapter 14).

Providing information

Information can be passed from you to parents in many forms:

- verbally through the children
- through notes, letters or newsletters
- in a prospectus or information sheet
- by notices on a noticeboard

Give parents and children clearly presented information to take away with them

- more formally during meetings and consultations
- informally if and when the parent brings or collects the child.

All these are useful opportunities for sharing different kinds of information. Choose the method of communication that seems most suitable for the information you wish to share, the age of the children and your type of play setting (see activity 'Sharing information with parents'). You might, for example, decide you could redesign the noticeboard with photographs of staff, programme of activities, important notices and displays of children's work. Alternatively, you could involve your colleagues in changing the organisation of the start and end of the session to allow you more time for informal chat with parents. Remember to consider the needs of parents who do not speak fluent English. You might be able to enlist the help of a bilingual member of the family to interpret, translate some of your written material for wider circulation or learn key words yourself.

Written information

Sometimes it is important that information is written down. This is the case for all policies and procedures and for information that might need to be regularly referred to by staff, management and parents. Written information enables parents or carers to:

- have accurate information about the group
- understand the reasons why the setting operates in the way it does
- decide whether your setting is likely to be suitable for their child
- become more involved and share responsibility for the care and the quality of play experience for their child.

Written information for parents helps ensure that management and staff:

- give the same information to all parents
- have decided what policies are needed for the group and the kind of service they wish to provide
- know the policies of the group and give accurate information to others
- take the same line in a given situation.

ACTIVITY · Information sheet for parents

Draft an initial information sheet or booklet for new parents, to include:

- aims of group – who it serves, what is on offer – activities, care, age of children, where it runs
- opening hours
- fees or cost, if any
- admissions – how to book a place or get on the waiting-list if there is one
- staffing and management: who runs the group, staff–child ratios
- policies and procedures – how can parents find out what approach the group has on equal opportunities, children with special needs, health and safety, behaviour limits set and methods of discipline, child protection issues.

Provide a brief statement on each of these and information about where the fuller policies are held:

- What other information do you wish to include?
- If you already have an information sheet or booklet, think of improvements that could be made – perhaps including some of the suggestions made here.

CASE STUDY What is the play setting's admissions policy?

Two mothers come to the play setting, each wanting to put her child's name on the waiting list. There is only one place likely to become available during the following six months. The first mother says that her child should have the place because he is older than the other child. Also, they have no garden at home. The second mother says her child should have priority because she is working and needs the childcare.

In the case study 'What is the play setting's admissions policy?', a worker from a play setting that has a clear policy about admissions will know on what basis places are awarded and how needs are prioritised. She will know what answer to give. If her play setting has no admissions policy, the worker responsible for the waiting list will carry sole responsibility for such decisions. She will be open to accusations of favouritism, bias and discrimination, whatever decision she takes.

SPOTLIGHT ON Sample admissions policy

The aim of our play setting is to provide play opportunities for local children and childcare for working parents:

- Our play setting takes children between the ages of 5 and 12 in the geographical area of (state catchment area if there is one).
- Places are awarded to children on the waiting list in order of date of birth.
- To book a place, please contact the waiting list organiser.
- The waiting list organiser is: [name of person responsible who may also be a playworker, a management committee member, secretary]. She can be contacted at: [telephone number, email address or when available in play setting].
- Priority will be given to siblings of children who attend or have already attended the scheme and children or families with other circumstances that give rise to a referral from another agency (health, education, social services or voluntary support group). (Such referrals must be consistent with the aims of the setting.)
- A number of places are reserved for children in these categories (for example: five for children of parents working for a local employer who has purchased places; three for emergency referrals).
- If your child is disabled, but you do not have contact with a referring agency, please contact the waiting list organiser who will be able to advise you. (If a child may be entitled to a priority subsidised place, the waiting list organiser should know the procedure and who to contact in social services if a referral is needed.)

- All questions relating to booking places or the waiting list should be addressed to the waiting list organiser, or in writing to: [name and contact address of the chairperson or manager].

This example will not be appropriate for all play settings. Open-access facilities, for example, have particular requirements for their policies and procedures. They do not have waiting lists. If you work in such a play setting, you are likely to have less contact with the parents of the children who attend. Regular children may arrive with a group of new friends one day. You will need to know what to do when more children attend than has been expected: how will you ensure safe and adequate supervision, space, materials and equipment?

Conditions of attendance

Conditions of attendance may form part of an admissions policy. They will include information about any circumstances in which a child could lose his or her place. If fees are payable, information should be given on any assisted, supported or sponsored places available, concessions or discounts for siblings. Conditions of attendance may include payment in advance, period of notice required on leaving and arrangements for holidays and sickness. If you work in an open-access play setting, you will need to inform children and their parents as appropriate (in information leaflets, on consent forms or on noticeboards) that it is not a childcare facility and that children are free to leave when they wish. If the play setting becomes dangerously full, it may be necessary to refuse admission to more children on a particular day.

All parents and carers should know about the policies of your play setting

Initial information given to parents about the play setting should contain statements that summarise the policies. Parents should know how they can obtain copies.

Involving parents in the play setting

The Children Act 1989 and the Care Standards Act 2000 stress the importance of involving parents. Providers should make sure that there are sufficient opportunities for parents and

Children's play opportunities can be enriched by sensitive adult involvement

the people who work with the child to discuss his progress and plan for future activities. Information must be shared. Certain parental rights enable parents to influence the nature of their children's play environments. To this end, the following opportunities for parents should be considered:

- to acquire information about the play setting
- to express their view on the play setting
- to alter the play environment of their child
- to choose between alternative childcare environments (Children Act 1989).

Through their involvement, parents can also become more informed about the value of play – both for their own children and for children and society in general.

Parents as volunteers and management committee

If you work in a voluntary or community group, it is more likely that parents of the children make up most of the management committee and have a major influence on how it is run. Some parents will need help and encouragement to feel confident about taking on management tasks. If a parent is unwilling or unable to sit on the management committee, she or he may be happy to be part of a small working group to look at a particular aspect of the play setting that needs development, such as fundraising or building new play structures. Playworkers can help to ensure that any parental involvement is consistent with the aims and principles of playwork.

Parents publicising play

Parents who see the benefits to their own children of the play opportunities provided in your setting can give the best word-of-mouth publicity. Such parents may also become involved in campaigning for and supporting play facilities and the rights of children within the local community.

Sharing practical skills

Many parents will have particular skills that they may be willing to share. They may work in healthcare and be able to give a talk or share information with the children on a health-related issue. Perhaps they have practical skills to offer – carpentry, sewing dressing-up clothes, art, craft, sport or cookery – or they may have time to help out. Ask for contributions for a newsletter (written, artistic or simply informative). Parents with computers or access to photocopying or printing facilities may help you to produce it. Think about skills that may be useful to the play setting – and let parents know of your needs.

Social events

Social events can be a good way to enable parents to get to know you, other staff, other children and their parents. Many play settings invite parents to barbeques, festival celebrations or social evenings or to accompany them on trips or camps.

Encouraging parents' feedback

Feedback from parents, children, staff and visitors is an invaluable means of helping you evaluate the service you are providing. You can encourage feedback by providing a prominently placed book or box, stating that your play setting welcomes any comments. Once you receive feedback, you can then decide if any changes need to be made. For example, a parent may suggest that the play setting needs some music. The next step will be to talk to the children to see if it is a popular idea, talk to the staff to get their ideas and you may need to talk to the person who has overall control of the budget. If you follow up on the suggestion, you will have made changes to the physical resources. Other changes might affect:

- specifications, such as opening hours
- working methods, such as adopting a key worker system
- human resources, such as having volunteers at the play setting
- communications, such as letting parents know when the next meeting will be held.

Some suggested changes may not be possible due to factors such as space, money or safety, but often someone with energy and initiative can make the changes happen. You will need to assess the advantages and disadvantages of any proposed changes. Let the person who provided the feedback know in what way you are responding to their suggestions. If changes have been made, keep an eye on how well they are working.

Dealing with complaints

Parents should have a written complaints procedure for the setting, which includes the contact details of the person who deals with complaints. A clear complaints procedure helps define responsibilities and prevents you being drawn into discussions about matters you are not in a position to deal with. Be clear about what kinds of complaints you can deal with yourself and when to pass complaints or concerns on to a senior colleague.

 ACTIVITY Dealing with complaints

Consider the following situations:

- Mr Price is upset that his daughter ripped her coat while playing outside yesterday. He thinks the play setting should pay for a new one.
- Mrs Ho says her son has been bullied by an older boy. She says if you don't sort it out she will.
- Miss Bellini wants to know why she has to pay for her daughter to attend the play setting when the Greens get free places. She knows they have loads of money. 'Have you seen the car they bought last week?' she says.
- Mr Douglas has heard that one of your colleagues is gay. He doesn't think 'such people' should be allowed to work with children.

1 How would you deal with each situation immediately? How would the complaint be followed up?

2 Discuss with a colleague to check that you are in agreement about appropriate action and who has the responsibility for following the complaint through.

3 Role play the situation with a colleague to develop your confidence in dealing with situations such as these.

A parent making a complaint needs to know that he or she will be listened to, but should be politely referred to the person who is responsible for dealing with it. An upset parent may need the space and time to calm down and be reassured that their complaint will be taken seriously. This does not mean that the playworker should make false promises or agree to any action beyond the procedures of the setting. The points about communication made in Chapter 10 about listening, expressing yourself clearly and paying attention to body language and tone of voice apply here too.

It is important for staff, management and children that parents are given accurate and consistent information at all times. Parents and playworkers are partners in the care of the children and both have the welfare and well-being of the children as their common starting point.

Summary

The relationships we create with children affect how comfortable they feel within the play setting. Providing a warm welcome, developing trust and communicating positively can all help to develop positive relationships. Mutual respect is created when playworkers make efforts to listen to, understand and involve the children. Parents and carers are key partners in children's lives and therefore in the play setting. This chapter also sets out a variety of ways in which playworkers might communicate with and involve parents. Positive relationships with parents have wide-ranging benefits for families, children, parents and playworkers – and for the setting as a whole.

Reference

Saint-Exupéry, A. de (1991) *Le Petit Prince (The Little Prince)*. Mammoth.

Further reading

CAN DO series of activity books, published by Thomson Learning: many of these books are particularly written for playwork settings.
Dynamix and Save the Children (2002) *Participation – Spice it up!* Save the Children.
Logue, J. and Jones, S. (2004) *Play Talks: Fun Ideas to Promote Communication through Play*. SCOPE. (SCOPE also produces a free 'Communication Passport Template', a simple, practical guide to help people communicate with a non-verbal child available at http://www.scope.org.uk/earlyyears/assets/comm_passa5.pdf.)
Petrie, P. (1994) *Play and Care: Out of School*. HMSO.
Wade, H. and Badham, B. (2003) *Hear by Right – Standards for the Active Involvement of Children and Young People*. NYA/LGA. Also available to download on the National Youth Agency website: www.nya.org.uk.
www.surestart.gov.uk/_doc/0-2D1402.pdf – information on children and body language.

CHAPTER 7
Behaviour in the play setting

Children are not the people of tomorrow but people today. They are entitled to be taken seriously and treated with tenderness and respect as equals. They should be allowed to grow into whoever they were meant to be. The UNKNOWN person inside of each of them is the hope for the future.

(Janus Korczak, Polish author and philanthropist, 1878–1942)

In order to play and develop within the play setting, children need to feel safe. This chapter looks at children's behaviour in the light of the key principles of playwork (see Chapter 2). In this chapter, we will consider:

- Behaviour and development
- Encouraging children to behave positively
- Behaviour and safety
- Helping children to resolve conflict
- Dealing with unacceptable behaviour
- Looking at adults' behaviour

Behaviour and development

Behaviour is closely linked with development and is largely determined by a child's experiences and role models. It can be affected by other factors such as inherited or acquired physical and mental abilities and impairments, illness, trauma, cultural background and family circumstances. You can expect different behaviour from children at different ages and stages of development. Some we consider acceptable, desirable even, others we may not approve of. For example:

- A 5 year old in an after school club may well be getting used to starting a long day at school. He may be physically exhausted and less able or willing to join in some of the more active play opportunities. Another 5 year old may use offensive language without any understanding of its meaning (and therefore the offence it causes).

- A 9 year old may consider the approval of her friends more important than the approval of the playworker. This may lead to increased cooperative behaviour and understanding of the rules of a game, but it may also lead to playing 'chicken' or getting involved in other physically dangerous dares.

- A 14 year old may have developed a greater sense of responsibility. He may be able and willing to care for younger ones or lead a cooking activity. He may also see smoking or experimenting with drugs as part of the transition from childhood to adulthood.

By the age of 5, most children will understand that different kinds of behaviour are acceptable and expected in different settings. What may be accepted at home is not necessarily tolerated at school. The behaviour expected in the supermarket is different from that allowed in the park. Young children will have varying levels of experience of different settings. They may well not understand the reasons why they are encouraged to run around in the park but are told off (or receive greater punishment) for doing so in the supermarket or why they can draw whenever and whatever they like at home but are expected to sit still and finish colouring in a pre-designed sheet at school.

It takes time for children to learn the codes of behaviour that many older children and adults take for granted. They may need to have the rules explained to them many times and to be frequently reminded about what is acceptable and unacceptable behaviour in a particular setting.

Playing together

ACTIVITY | Adults' views on behaviour

Try this activity first on your own, then with colleagues (perhaps at a team meeting):

1 What do you see as positive behaviour? Write a list of the kinds of behaviour that you would encourage within the play setting. Are these types of behaviour consistent with:
   - the values and principles of playwork?
   - the aims and objectives of your setting?
   - the age and stage of development of the children?

2 What is unacceptable behaviour? Write down as many examples of unacceptable behaviour within the play setting as you can think of within three minutes. Take each example in turn and ask why it is unacceptable. Try to distinguish between rules that relate to health and safety (e.g. no smoking, no unsupervised access to the kitchen, not more than two at a time on the aerial swing) and types of behaviour that are unacceptable because they violate another person (physically, socially or emotionally) or limit the shared use and enjoyment of the play environment.

3 Look at your first list. Do you approve of the same positive behaviour in adults? Look at your second list. Is the behaviour you find unacceptable in children the same as the behaviour you find unacceptable in adults? What are the reasons for your answers?

This activity is often undertaken with children in play settings as part of laying down the 'ground rules' – see the next activity, 'Children's views on behaviour'.

ACTIVITY | Children's views on behaviour

Go back to the activity 'Adults' views on behaviour':

1 Try it with the children in your play setting (perhaps in groups of different age bands). Make sure you have planned this in advance with the rest of the staff. Encourage in-depth discussion about why particular kinds of behaviour are unacceptable. You could follow up these discussions with relevant stories, drama or artwork (for example, about a child who has to deal with discrimination or bullying).

2 Compare what you hear from the children with your own attitudes and those expressed by your colleagues. Do you need to revise your behaviour policy?

Factors that can affect behaviour

Children can sometimes be inconsistent in their behaviour. It is useful for playworkers to try to find the underlying reason for any unusual negative behaviour (or particularly 'clingy' behaviour). Depending on the age or stage of development of the child, it could be a result of one or more of the following:

- changes, problems or upheavals at home
- peer group pressure
- the child testing and challenging as part of his natural development
- type of food eaten (or hunger)
- new, reduced or changed medicine
- copying a character from computer games or from television
- the child may wish to discuss an issue but has not found the right words or way to raise it with you
- abuse from parents, other adults (including another staff member) or other children.

Observation (see Chapter 2) is a good first step in ascertaining the factors that might be underlying unusual behaviour. Gentle, sensitive questioning can help you find out more, and can provide a chance for the child to discuss any issue (if there is an issue). If unexplained changes in behaviour continue, you could also ask other staff in the setting for their views – or the child's parent or carer if appropriate.

Encouraging children to behave positively

The kinds of behaviour you want to encourage in your play setting will be those that encourage the maximum opportunities for children to determine their own play, and might include cooperating with each other, looking out for others, being creative and adventurous, attempting new activities, challenging their own 'best score'. Examples of unacceptable behaviour will be those that inhibit the opportunities for play in others through intimidation or lowering their self-esteem and include violence, stealing, racism, sexism, destroying equipment and name calling or other verbal abuse. Make sure all the staff agree on what is positive and what is unacceptable behaviour – this will form the basis of the setting's ground rules for behaviour. Also agree on the approach the staff should take towards behaviour – this will form the basis of the setting's behaviour policy.

Ground rules and behaviour policy

Some children, and indeed some adults, will bring unacceptable behaviour into the play setting. It is therefore necessary to establish a framework for acceptable and unacceptable behaviour and for how staff are expected to respond to unacceptable behaviour. What is considered acceptable and unacceptable behaviour in your play setting may be influenced by:

- the views, beliefs, experience and backgrounds of management and staff – including your own

What types of behaviour do you want to encourage?

- the views, beliefs, experience and backgrounds of children and families who use the setting
- the nature of the setting and its aims
- other people with an interest in the premises, service or community (Ofsted or other regulating authority, local authority, landlord etc.)
- the law.

Everyone involved in the play setting needs to be able to understand and follow the behaviour policy. The policy should be drawn up in consultation with management and staff, children and parents. The more the children are able to participate in this process, the better understanding they will have, although the way in which you involve them will depend on their age and understanding. It is useful to provide information about the behaviour policy in written information for parents, carers and older children. This can take the form of a written statement about general principles – see the following example.

SPOTLIGHT ON | **Example statement of behaviour policy**

Welcome to Fun, Etc. After School Club! All children coming to the play setting have a right to play and enjoy what is on offer without fear. This is a safe and caring place for play and adventure. Everybody is respected and bullying, intimidation or lack of respect for others is not allowed. For further information, please ask for a copy of our full behaviour policy.

Your full behaviour policy should be available for all children, staff and parents to see and refer to. This will include information about what action will be taken if a child breaks the ground rules. Different actions will work for different age groups. (See more about this further on in this chapter under 'Dealing with unacceptable behaviour'.)

Involve the children in creating the ground rules about acceptable and unacceptable behaviour. If you do, the children will be more likely to remember them and take responsibility for keeping them. They will also remind each other about them. The agreed list of ground rules can be drawn or painted by the children and put up as a reminder on the wall.

Children can help each other to remember the ground rules

Some rules about rules

- Try to word most of the rules positively, such as, 'Please walk when you are indoors' instead of 'No running.' 'Please keep the toilets clean' instead of 'No messing about in the toilets.' The positive rules give the children an 'image' of how to behave. Negative rules about messing about in toilets give children an altogether different 'image' in their heads.

- Make them with the children's full participation and agreement. Let the children give their own suggestions. If you need to prompt them about a particular issue, say something like, 'What about swearing, what shall we say about that?' The children will probably say, 'No swearing!' You could suggest that you word it positively, such as, 'Please speak politely and respectfully to each other.'

- Limit the number. Children will remember very few of the rules if there are too many. Try a maximum of 10.

- Display them prominently, ensuring that all the children, including those who use wheelchairs, can read them.

- Refer to the rules frequently. This helps everyone to remember what they agreed, and, as a result, they are more likely to be applied.

- Review them together regularly, adding and removing rules as appropriate.

Behaviour policy in shared premises

The premises and nature of your play setting will have a bearing on your behaviour policy. Some out-of-school clubs and playschemes are set in schools or community centres. This can cause problems if codes of conduct are imposed on the play setting by other groups. The play setting needs to be able to develop its own identity. Children in the play setting will choose their activities, have access to resources and relate to adults in a different way from how they would in a school, place of worship or other setting.

Playworkers will need to be clear about the objectives of their setting that are the reasons for adopting a particular behaviour policy. There needs to be continuous communication with other users of the building, so that these objectives can be explained. Negotiation and some compromise will often be required.

Praising the positive

Make a conscious effort to spot and comment on children behaving positively. This helps children to know what behaviour is valued at the play setting:

- 'Thank you, Katie, for holding the door open.'
- 'You two look like you are having fun!'
- 'Well done everyone, you did a great tidying up job.'
- 'Joseph, thank you for helping Jay to tie his shoe laces.'

Most children like adult attention from time to time. Alongside praising children, another effective idea is to ignore some of the minor negative behaviour. If you ignore some of the trivial negative things, children will come to realise that if they want your attention, they are more likely to get it if they behave positively.

A word about praise

It is natural for adults to use praise to encourage children to do things in a certain way. However, it is worth noting that too much praise may teach a child to always look for an adult's response in order to prove their actions 'worthy'. Self-esteem comes from feeling pleased with *yourself* – needing to please others can have the opposite affect. Also, try to be aware of which aspect of behaviour you praise. For example, if you say, 'Well done – you jumped really high!', the child may then think that it is important, when jumping, to jump high. This takes the focus away from listening to or observing what the child thinks is important or fun. In other words, changing it from a *play* activity to one that puts a focus on *outcomes* and *achievement*. Used properly, though, praise can be an extremely powerful tool in helping children to feel good about themselves and others – which is likely to result in more positive behaviour.

SPOTLIGHT ON **Spotting positive behaviour**

A child who has attempted a piece of artwork or modelling for the first time or with particular effort can feel rewarded by having the finished product displayed. You may like to comment about it not only to the child, but also to other staff, children or parents.

A child who has joined in a cooperative game for the first time without attempting to mess it up can be asked if she would like to choose or lead the next game. You can acknowledge and reward a child who has shown particularly responsible behaviour in one area (looking after the woodwork tools, for example) by giving more responsibility in other areas (tending an open fire, running a library area or tuck shop, lighting the cooker), albeit still with appropriate adult supervision.

Rewards

Rewards should build up the self-esteem of the child displaying positive behaviour and give an incentive for that child to continue. Rewards for positive behaviour can include giving praise, thanks or encouragement and should offer opportunities for the child to build on the positive actions he or she has taken.

The rewards you offer need not encourage competition. They should be based on the individual needs and merits of each child. Learning to catch a ball is a great achievement for one child; for another it is easy. It takes some children more time to learn to cooperate in their play. Your rewards should be consistent with the aims of your setting and the principles of playwork.

Praise can be a very powerful tool

and fellow citizens. The children in play settings with this approach were actively involved in discussions and negotiations about what is fair and unfair and in finding just solutions to problems. They were encouraged to take responsibility for their own behaviour and its consequences. The second approach appeared to be a broadly democratic approach in that the playworkers also appealed to the children's sense of fairness about keeping other people waiting or spoiling other people's fun. The difference here was that the emphasis was on group control and keeping children amused:

> *Children were seen to some extent as passive, as customers or perhaps more accurately as the children of customers.*
>
> (Petrie 1994)

The third approach was a more punitive one, where the emphasis was on work rather than choice. Children were seen in a different light:

> *These children were not citizens with rights, nor customers to be wooed, they were subordinates, rather who were to be obedient to the staff; they had no autonomy and no right to adult respect for their point of view.*
>
> (Petrie 1994)

The underlying principles of playwork (as outlined in Chapter 2) suggest that behaviour management in playwork should hold the rights of the individual children and their opportunities to play as central and should support enabling children to find their own solutions to problems arising within the play setting.

A chat can help to sort out conflict

ACTIVITY   Different approaches to behaviour management

There are different approaches to behaviour management in play settings and these are influenced by the aims of the play setting (what it sets out to achieve and for whom) and the approach of the staff (how they view children and the meaning they attach to what it is to be a child and the importance they attach to facilitating the play process):

1 Look at your setting's behaviour policy and ground rules. Look also at how staff at your setting approach behaviour 'management'.

2 Which of the three of Pat Petrie's observed approaches (outlined in the text) comes closest to the policy and practice of your play setting?

Dealing with unacceptable behaviour

Dealing with unacceptable behaviour and 'discipline' are frequently seen by playworkers as major concerns. The role models you provide and the rewards you offer can encourage positive behaviour within the play setting and can reinforce the values of respect and providing for individual choices and needs. This approach can only succeed with the cooperation of all involved.

Every play setting will have its share of negative or unacceptable behaviour. Playworkers in the setting need to agree what action is appropriate for particular kinds of behaviour. Children, parents and workers need to know what action will be taken and in what circumstances it will be applied. Actions can include:

1 *Ignoring.* Some kinds of non cooperative or disruptive behaviour (a 5 year old making insistent rude noises, for example) are best ignored, at least in the short term. The behaviour may be a bid to get extra attention. Extra attention is usually best directed at positive behaviour. Be aware that the child still wants attention, however, and be sensitive to 'cues' to involve you in play. Working as a team helps: another playworker could distract a disruptive child into a different activity. A longer term strategy would be to help the child to develop more positive ways to gain the attention he needs.

2 *Challenging.* Bullying, intimidation, racism, sexism or other discriminatory or abusive behaviour need to be challenged *at the time*. Explain why the behaviour is unacceptable and, if necessary, what will happen if it is repeated (as laid out in the agreed framework for behaviour of your setting). Be sensitive. Don't judge or interpret too quickly what you have seen or been told. Give priority to supporting the recipient of the abusive behaviour, who can all too easily be forgotten while the perpetrator gets all the attention (even if it is in the form of a challenge about why his remarks or behaviour are not acceptable).

3 *Exclusions.* Exclusions from activities, trips or the play setting are more extreme measures and should only be applied in consultation with the senior member of staff. Parents will also usually need to be informed, particularly in a childcare setting. A child may need to be excluded if she consistently presents a danger to herself or others or prevents others from benefiting from what is on offer.

The approach used in your play setting and the way in which they are applied will depend on the nature of the setting and the age of the children. The following example is used at an after school club for children aged 5–12 years.

CASE STUDY   **Three warnings system**

Westfield After School Club have tried out different approached to negative behaviour over the years. The one they have found works best is a simple system of 'three warnings'. It is easy for the children to understand, easy to apply and the children can see the consequences of their actions. Children are given a chance to change their own behaviour before a warning is issued (for example, 'Justin, if you do that again, I will have to give you a warning.').

First warning: The child is given a verbal warning that her behaviour breaks the rules of the setting. It is explained why that behaviour is unacceptable and that if she breaks the rules again, she will be given a second warning. (The playworkers try to end the conversation on a positive, encouraging note about the child's behaviour. This helps both to draw a line under the episode, shows the child that they trust her to behave positively and ultimately is more likely to result in positive behaviour than ending on an angry or frustrated note.)

Second warning: A second warning results in the child's name being written in a book. The child is reminded of the consequences of a third warning. (Again, the playworkers try to end the conversation on an encouraging note about the child's behaviour.)

Third warning: A third warning results in the child's parent or carer being told about the behaviour. How to proceed is discussed with the parent and the child. An effort is made to agree with the child how she will behave in future. The playworkers end with a focus on a positive aspect of the child's behaviour or character, such as their helpfulness or that they are great fun to have at the setting. This helps the child go away with a positive glow and makes her more likely to make an effort to get more positive comments in future.

As a result of this system being used (in a setting with respect for the children, exciting play opportunities and activities and a focus on positive behaviour), no child has ever had to be excluded from Westfield After School Club.

Violent or physical punishments or those that involve shaming or humiliating the child are not acceptable in the play setting or in keeping with the values of playwork. There may be occasions where physical force is required to restrain a child from causing harm to himself or others. Stay calm and always use the minimum amount of force to hold the child until the danger has passed or help and support arrive. Remember, your aim is to safeguard the child and anyone else present. Safe techniques for holding children whose behaviour may cause them to endanger themselves or others are best learned through training and practice through role play. Similar issues need to be considered in the event of unwelcome intruders from outside the play setting.

ACTIVITY   Dealing with difficult situations

1   Ask one colleague to take the part of the child and another colleague to act as observer.

2   Think of a situation you have found difficult in the past in which you have had to challenge a child's unacceptable behaviour. Explain the situation to the person taking the part of the child – how he or she behaved and a little background to the incident.

3 Role play the situation for a few minutes. The observer should keep time and tell you when to stop. The observer tells you:

- three things you are doing well (e.g. keeping calm, making eye contact, listening, explaining)
- three things you could improve (e.g. speak louder or more quietly, make eye contact, adopt a different body position, say more or less).

4 Continue the role play for a further few minutes or until the situation is resolved to your satisfaction. The observer announces the end of the role play. Make sure you detach yourselves from the roles you have been playing. Then discuss the role play, asking:

- how each player felt during the role play
- whether the observer has any new comments to add.

5 Agree on three things you can do to help you to deal more confidently with a similar situation in the future. Write them down.

This activity may work best if each person has an opportunity to take the part of the observer, playworker and child, with a new situation being role played each time.

Good communication is important

Good communication is essential in establishing and maintaining a framework for behaviour: it allows you to negotiate and explain rules and codes of behaviour. When dealing with unacceptable behaviour you will need to:

- gain the attention of the child(ren) concerned
- listen to what the child is saying about what happened, what led up to the incident and the reasons behind the actions
- explain what the child has done wrong and why
- criticise the behaviour not the person, for example 'That is a racist thing to say' not 'You are a racist'; 'That was an unfair thing to do' not 'You inconsiderate child!'
- explain what will happen as a consequence of the action
- have good communication, consistency and support from other team members
- ensure that the child has the opportunity to make amends and continue to be part of the group once the incident has been dealt with.

There should be no further recrimination from staff or other children. Body language is also important. Try to make sure you are on the same eye level as the child when discussing important issues such as behaviour. Threatening body language such as towering over a child or pointing or shaking your finger at him may make him feel unsafe and unable to contribute. After dealing with a situation involving unacceptable behaviour, your friendly pat on the shoulder or hug can help reaffirm that you still like the child, even though you did not approve of his behaviour.

Developing your skills in dealing with difficult situations

Dealing with unacceptable behaviour is never easy. You may find it difficult to challenge racist or sexist remarks or intervene in a potentially violent situation. It is useful to practise ways of dealing with such situations before they actually occur. When you are dealing with a conflict situation, it is easy to let anger, fear or embarrassment interfere with your ability to deal with it effectively. Practising your strategies for dealing with difficult situations can build your confidence and ability to deal with the real thing. If you can practise with colleagues, it can also increase your understanding of each other and the ways in which you each react in conflict. This will enable you to be more supportive and consistent with each other in your work in the play setting.

ACTIVITY   Dealing with unacceptable behaviour

Look at the following examples of unacceptable behaviour. Discuss different strategies for dealing with each situation with another playworker. What (if any) immediate action would you take in the following situations:

1 You find two children aged 11 and 12 sniffing glue behind the shed.

2 You overhear a 7 year old say to another child, 'Go away, I don't like brown people. You can't play.'

3 You ask a 9 year old to help to clear away an activity he has been involved in. He tells you to 'get lost'.

4 You come outside to find two children locked in a fight, rolling on the floor. A group of other children has surrounded them and is cheering them on.

What follow-up action would you take in each situation?

Consider the scenarios described in the activity 'Dealing with unacceptable behaviour'. There are no right answers in deciding how you would deal with such incidents. Each situation will be different in practice and you will need to judge and assess the situation on the spot, drawing on your knowledge of the children and the environment, the support available and your past experience. You can however consider your approach and practise what you would say and do in a similar situation. Ask yourself what might cause particular types of behaviour. Can you do anything to increase the child's understanding of why the behaviour is unacceptable and therefore perhaps prevents it happening again?

In some cases, you will need to attend to safety considerations. In the first situation in the activity 'Dealing with unacceptable behaviour', it is important that you assess the physical and mental state of the children sniffing glue before dealing with the behaviour issue itself. You might need to call for medical assistance.

In the second situation, you will need to challenge what has been said immediately. You might say, 'That is a very unpleasant thing to say,' then explain why it is unpleasant. You will also need to show support to the child who has been rejected, perhaps by putting an arm around him or her. Over the following days, look for opportunities to build up this child's self-esteem by praising his or her positive skills and attributes. Follow up the reasons behind why the incident occurred. Look at your resources, think about the activities you offer. Encourage discussion and develop those activities that give positive value to differences in children and the world as a whole.

In the third situation, you may not be able to insist the 9 year old clears away the activity. You will need to consider the reasons behind why he or she was rude to you and also be clear about whether you consider it the children's responsibility to clear up or the playworkers'. Remember the playworker's first responsibility is to be at the service of children's play and that sometimes, by insisting on tidying away while the child is still immersed in their play, you might not be fulfilling this role. However, there is also the need to be practical within time constraints and requirements of the premises. And learning to tidy up your own mess is a useful life skill!

In the fourth situation, you will need to diffuse the situation by distracting the supporting crowd of onlookers before separating and dealing with the children who are fighting. Again, you might need to seek the support of a colleague.

In all cases, remember also that the children may have learned the behaviour from other adults or older siblings who are important to them. Be sensitive in how you challenge behaviour. Your aim should be to increase the child's understanding of other views, not to censure the child or his family.

Dealing with persistent unacceptable behaviour

Negative behaviour can be a symptom of underlying problems for the child (see also 'Factors that can affect behaviour' earlier in this chapter). It can be caused by the child's lack of self-esteem, developmental difficulties or anger or confusion about being unable to live up to expectations made of him. Alternatively, perhaps other people or events have not lived up to his expectations of them. Try to identify the causes for persistent negative behaviour:

- *Listen to the child.* Listen to the parents. Listen to other members of staff.
- *Is the child unhappy?* What reasons might there be? Do they stem from home, school, play setting or other environment? Does the child choose to come to the play setting?
- *Are the play opportunities varied and stimulating?* Are they relevant to the child's age and stage of development? Could new play opportunities be developed based on the child's particular interests?

ACTIVITY **Observing extreme behaviour**

Choose a child within your play setting whose behaviour gives you cause for concern. If this child's behaviour is extreme, or frequently unacceptable, you may like to go straight to section B. If it is less extreme but gives you ongoing concern, complete section A first, and then try section B.

Section A
Observe this child every 20 minutes for a period of five minutes. Record what he is doing with whom. Write up your notes. Ask yourself:

- What were the main activities he engaged in?
- Who are the people (children and adults) he relates to most?
- Is the child unhappy?

Repeat this on several days over a period of two or three weeks to build up a fuller picture. Share your observations with a colleague or senior member of staff.

Section B
Observe the child only at times when he is behaving unacceptably. Get colleagues to deal with the child when you are observing. After several observations, consider:

- What events led up to the incidents?
- Is there a pattern to them?

- Are there any warning signals, e.g. the child becomes withdrawn or particularly noisy. (One child we know gets bright red ear tips shortly before he 'blows'.)
- Do the incidents occur at a particular time of day (e.g. before or after food, before going home, on arrival, during large group activities)?
- Do they involve other people? Are they the same people (children, member of staff) every time?

If you identify a pattern, discuss with colleagues the reasons for it. Can the pattern be predicted and therefore prevented? What strategies can you think of to help this child deal with his or her own behaviour?

Sometimes a child will show deeply disturbing or consistently unacceptable behaviour within the play setting and you may need specialist advice. Such a child may require psychodynamic or therapeutic support to enable her to find the causes of her problems and to develop manageable behaviour patterns. In extreme circumstances, you may need to exclude the child from the play setting for a time. The reasons for this must be clearly explained to the child and parents. If it is a first exclusion, keep it short, such as one day – you want the child to return so that she can benefit from the play setting. Give the child clear, simple, positive expectations of behaviour for when she returns. If possible, end on a positive note, perhaps about something she can look forward to when she returns to the play setting.

CASE STUDY   Playing with guns

Westfield Play Club has changed its 'zero tolerance' approach to children playing with guns. In the past, no toy guns, weapons or weapon-like objects were allowed to be brought in or made within the setting. The playworkers had believed very firmly that allowing the children to play with guns would increase the amount of violent, negative play and that, by banning weapon play, the children's play would be 'channelled' into more positive activities. Playworker Gary explains:

Before we banned guns, some of the children (mainly boys but some girls as well) would spend the whole time shooting, killing, dying, and so on. We tried to tempt them to try other play activities, but they weren't interested. Then one day one of the smaller children got hurt in the boisterous play, and we decided to ban all play with guns or other weapons.

Things worked out well for most of the children. They just played with other equipment, did some craft activities, and were not really bothered that they were not able to play with guns. But there were a few children who found it very difficult to adapt. Even after four months, you could tell that they still wanted to play fight. Their behaviour, if anything, had actually worsened since the gun ban. They were constantly getting into trouble with the other children, or else wandered around aimlessly. The playworkers agreed to do some observations, to see why their behaviour was so negative.

The main observation was that the children were unhappy, and that their natural play direction was being distorted by our weapon rules. Talking to them unveiled the fact that they had a strong 'drive' to play with weapons. We discussed and discussed the matter at our team meetings, and with the parents and carers. We read the book *We Don't Play with Guns Here* by Penny Holland. This in particular gave us the confidence to make the decision to lift our outright ban on guns.

The first few weeks were pretty chaotic, to be honest. Everyone wanted to play with guns and swords! More than once, we thought we had done the wrong thing. But then a change happened. Most of the children lost interest after the initial excitement and went back to doing other things. The original group of children who had shown such interest in playing with weapons were like different children. Their eyes shone with delight, and they interacted very playfully.

Initially we applied a few rules to the weapon play. These included not shooting at people (only at objects) and no frightening children who were not playing your game. These rules became more relaxed as we all saw that children were able to contextualise the play – they knew it was play and not real. We make sure that we discuss issues such as 'hurting others' and 'death' with the children, and often the children come to us for a chat and some 'time out' from the onslaught.

I would say it is worth thinking about relaxing attitudes to gun play. We did it because we trust children to decide on the direction they take their own play.

Looking at adults' behaviour

We try to ensure that children do not bully, shout, leave people out or call names. We also ask them to avoid selfish, rude and sarcastic behaviour. Of course, we must also endeavour to follow these rules – if we shout, belittle or call names (even 'in jest'), children will assume that it is acceptable.

The underlying core of your judgements, values and motives is based on everything you have experienced in life so far. Aspects such as your upbringing, your relationships with your parents and other external factors have influenced the person you are now. If your parents were extremely calm and fun-loving people, that is likely to have had an influence on your character. If one or both parents were aggressive, that is equally likely to have had an influence on the person you have become.

The 'jigsaw pieces' of your experiences affect the thoughts you have and the way you behave. They also give you a very personal view of the world – which can sometimes give a partial or distorted view of reality. A reflective playworker looks back at events in the play setting in order to see if they have acted in the most positive way for everyone, and if they could have done things differently. An environment that promotes positive behaviour from children *and* adults is altogether calmer and happier – leaving more time for the serious business of play.

Summary

Chapter 7 focuses on behaviour within play settings. Playworkers can increase positive behaviour within the setting by being a good role model, spotting and praising positive behaviour, ignoring minor negative behaviour and applying agreed ground rules. These actions are also likely to decrease incidences of unacceptable behaviour. A behaviour policy sets out the approach the staff should take and also the actions that will be taken in the event of persistent unacceptable behaviour. A playful, respectful, consistent approach is in keeping with the principles of playwork and will lead to increased positive behaviour within the play setting.

References

Korczak, J. (1999) *A Voice for the Child: The Inspirational Words of Janusz Korczak.* HarperCollins.
Petrie, P. (1994) *Play and Care out of School.* HMSO.

Further reading

Finch, S. (2003) *An Eye for an Eye Leaves Everyone Blind: Teaching Young Children to Settle Conflict without Violence*. Save the Children.
Fine, N. and Macbeth, F. (2000) *Playing with Fire – Creative Conflict Resolution for Young Adults*. New Society Publishers.
Holland, P. (2003) *We Don't Play with Guns Here.* Open University Press.

CHAPTER 8
Including everyone

Whether you think you can or think you can't, you're right.

(Henry Ford, 1863–1947)

This chapter looks at how your play setting can welcome children from a variety of backgrounds and who have a wide range of abilities and needs. There is discussion about why we need to include all children, both from a play point of view, and from a wider perspective. Our own attitudes towards prejudice are put under the microscope and we look at developing anti-discriminatory practice in play settings. In this chapter, we will consider:

- Play for all
- Celebrating differences
- Looking at your own beliefs and values
- Prejudice and discrimination
- Legislation affecting playwork and discrimination
- Developing anti-discriminatory practice
- Including disabled children in the play setting
- An equal opportunities policy for your setting

Play for all

Play is for all children. Playwork has always embraced ideas of equal opportunities. That is because the concept of equal opportunities is about fairness and fairness is very important to so much of children's play. That does not mean that playworkers know it all or can afford to be complacent. There are many examples of good and bad practice in respect of equal opportunities within play settings. We still hear playworkers saying: 'We believe in equal opportunities, we treat all the children the same.' 'Equal opportunities' is not about treating all children the same. It is about recognising that we are all different and have different things to offer and different needs to be met. It is about recognising and respecting each child as an individual with his or her own life story, needs and expectations. If this is the approach you take to your work, you have an understanding of at least part of what it means to practise equal opportunities in a play setting. But working towards achieving equal opportunities in a play setting requires more than a child-centred approach alone. 'Equal opportunities' is about recognising that there are many groups of people who face discrimination in our society and the world over – on the grounds of gender, skin colour, nationality, race, disability, age, sexual orientation, religious persuasion or other factors. Playwork is concerned with meeting the needs of individual children and helping them to meet their full potential through play.

CASE STUDY | 'It doesn't apply to us'

Mrs Green runs an after school club in a church hall in a suburban town south of Manchester. She says: 'All the children in the club come from the same kind of family. They are all white. So are the children in the school. Equal opportunities aren't important in our case.' What do you think?

Play settings enable children to try out different ways of being

Celebrating differences

People are discriminated against because they are different from the majority or those who hold the power. We are all sometimes afraid of the unfamiliar and the unknown. We can jump to conclusions about why people look, dress, behave as they do. The world would be a boring place if we were all the same. It is the differences between us that create the interest, the challenge and that enable us to change and develop ourselves.

Differences can be cause for exploration, discovery and celebration. Many play opportunities can encourage children to accept and value differences in each other. A child who can speak another language or use sign language has a valuable skill to share. Dressing up allows children to try out different roles and images. Talent shows can be opportunities for some children to display their 'hidden talents' but need to be sensitively handled so that they do not become a platform for only the children who are already bursting with confidence. The best kind of talent shows we have seen have been organised on the spur of the moment. A playworker discovers with delight that the usually quiet and withdrawn 13 year old Nada with mobility difficulties can juggle with five balls or that 8 year old Andrew, who has tried to learn to whistle since he was 5, has finally cracked it. With the agreement of the new 'star', a small audience is hastily drawn together to watch and show appreciation and applause.

Your play setting will be a richer, more exciting place for all the cultural materials from all over the world that you bring into it. If you have children from families of different cultural backgrounds you are fortunate to have a firsthand resource. Encourage the children to talk about and, if they are willing, bring examples of different customs, festivals, languages, food, music and clothes. Whatever is topical and currently popular in your play setting, you can encourage the children to expand and enliven it by introducing ideas and materials from different cultures.

ACTIVITY **Play and identity**

1 Plan two ways in which you can introduce ideas and materials from different cultures into an activity that is currently popular in your play setting. For example, if building houses and dens is currently popular, you could begin by discussing with the children the different kinds of building people live in: flats, bungalows, terraced and so on. Ask if any children have lived in any other kinds of accommodation? (In a play setting we visited recently, one child lived on a canal boat, another in a caravan and one had lived in a house on stilts in Indonesia.) Use books to research other kinds of dwellings – a North American tipi or a Mongolian yurt. Some children might be interested in trying to build a copy of one of these dwellings in the play setting, which may well lead to other kinds of imaginative play, stories and research into appropriate dressing-up clothes, cooking utensils or musical instruments.

2 Choose a festival that is coming up soon – the Chinese New Year, the birth of Haile Selassie, Chanuka or Diwali, for example. Plan how to introduce this festival to the children of your play setting – with music, craft, food, props, stories, costumes? Can you enlist the help of some of the children, parents, your colleagues or members of the local community? Beware of making the play setting into a classroom. Concentrate on play opportunities and involving children in activities that interest them. Learning new information will be a valuable bonus.

Everyday events and times, which can be great starting points for play that includes multicultural resources, are:

- *food* – mealtimes, snacktimes
- *carnivals* – dressing up and fashion shows
- *festivals* – children's birthdays, Easter, Eid
- *families* – the ones in your setting, but also TV programmes and stories about others
- *clothes* – the ones we wear and dressing up in others
- *music* – on the CD player, being a disc jockey or MC, using instruments.

You will be able to think of many more. The point is that any theme will be experienced differently by different cultures and each will be able to contribute another outlook and a variety of ways in which to express it. Even if you do not have children from a variety of cultural backgrounds in your play setting, you will still be able to research and introduce play materials from other cultures. It is perhaps even more important for these children, with no direct daily experience of other cultures, that they have opportunities to develop understanding of the multicultural world in which they live. These days, children may well not stay in the area they are brought up in – familiarity with other cultures and acceptance of difference equips them to deal with future life experiences.

SPOTLIGHT ON   Festivals calendar

A festivals calendar is a poster that shows the special days of many of the world's religions. It may be useful in a number of ways. You will know if any of the children at your play setting has a special or festival day and can share it with them. For example, you will know the reason why some or all the Muslim children do not come to the setting on a particular day (Eid, for example) or why they are wearing special new clothes. If you do not have children from a variety of cultures in your play setting, you will be able to take the opportunity to introduce a taste of the wider world into their lives. (The SHAP Working Party on World Religions in Education produces a calendar of religious festivals – see appendix.)

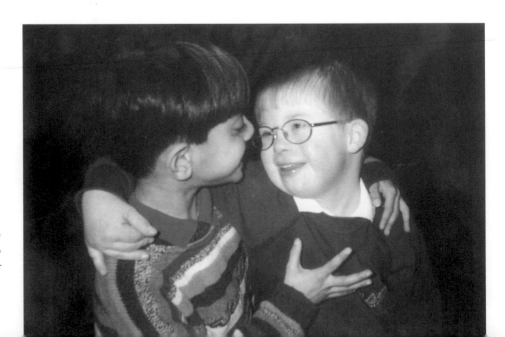

Children can encourage and inspire each other

Educational and play materials supply catalogues now offer a range of multicultural materials from dressing-up clothes to musical instruments, dolls, songbooks and cooking equipment. Make contact with specialist 'multicultural resource centres' (your local authority might be able to help you). Make or develop personal contacts with people from different cultures. Ask them if they are willing and able to share with you their skills, knowledge and understanding. Perhaps you know someone who is prepared to come into the play setting to tell stories, cook with the children or help you celebrate a festival. However, do not assume they know everything about their own culture.

ACTIVITY   Observation of gender

1 Observe a boy and a girl between the ages of 5 and 8 involved in 'free' play (that is when they are engaged in a freely chosen activity not organised by an adult).

2 Observe each child on three separate occasions for a period of several minutes.

3 Write up your notes on your observations.

Think about:

- Were there any differences in the nature of play and the play types that the boy and the girl engaged in?
- Did either or both tend to play more with children of their own sex?
- Do you think there was a difference in opportunities for play open to them?

If there were differences, what might be the reasons for this and is there anything you could do as a playworker to extend the opportunities open to each?

Read *Gender Matters* by Sandra Melville (see Further Reading) for ideas on countering gender stereotypes in the play setting.

Looking at your own beliefs and values

Each of us develops values and assumptions about the world we live in and our own possibilities or limitations within it. Using our own experiences and sharing experiences

Masks

with others, we develop and enrich our understanding of the world and of what it means to be a human being. For each of us the meaning of 'childhood' and 'play' will be different. Values change over time and are closely connected to culture. The Channel 4 series 'Childhood' explored in depth the differences in the values attached to childhood by cultures in different parts of the world. In the Baka tribe, the children played and learned the skills of survival in the rainforest alongside older siblings and adults. The homeless street children in a city in Mexico created their own 'family' and support network between peers as a means of survival. The family in the USA had children who attended daycare from babyhood.

SPOTLIGHT ON   Children's life stories

Children have individual and different life stories and expectations. As a playworker, you will need to consider how the opportunities you provide will meet the needs of the different children who come to your setting. How can you meet the individual needs of many different children?

There are often many different cultures represented in one smaller community – a city, a town, a village or your play setting. Each child and family has their own story. Do not assume that everyone shares your values. For example, you may think it is important for all children to sit down and eat their packed lunches together, sharing conversation and the company of others. Your colleague may not agree – preferring to encourage the children to choose where to sit and when to eat.

It is important to look at the underlying values of your work to understand and be able to explain why you think certain things are important. It is equally necessary to be open to change as new experience, new understanding and new children come your way. By sharing experiences and ideas with other professionals, with friends and with children you can show others what playwork means to you and gain understanding of what it means to others. And by being aware of your own values and beliefs, you can make attempts to eradicate any discriminatory behaviour you may have learned yourself.

Prejudice and discrimination

You have probably experienced some from of discrimination in your own life, perhaps due to your age, gender, skin colour, background, ability or impairment. Maybe other children in the school playground would not play with you because of your background or maybe you could not get into your bank because there was no access for wheelchair users. Any discrimination can make you feel upset, angry, frustrated, isolated and powerless. Persistent discrimination is likely to reduce your feelings of self-worth and make you feel like an outsider in society.

Prejudice usually stems from a lack of understanding about a person or people or a lack of knowledge about their lives and beliefs. Discrimination occurs when people act on this prejudice. A child who grows up in a family or society that is prejudiced against others is likely to believe that that is the right thing to do and may hold the same prejudices himself. Contrawise, if the child grows up in a family and a society that respects every individual, the child is likely to understand and value other people's differences.

Look at your own play setting.

- Are all children able to play equally?
- Are all play resources available to all children?
- Do the staff make an effort to ensure that all children are able to join in (if they want to) to the best of their ability?
- Does the environment prevent any child from playing in any way?

You may find when you look closely at your play setting that some children are discriminated against, even though you had not realised it before. You can then take steps to change the situation. You could invite others to keep their eyes open, too – routinely ask the children for ideas; enable the staff to speak out informally or at meetings; provide a 'suggestion and comments' box for children, parents, carers and staff to use. People feel valued when they are listened to – and people *are* valued when their ideas are acted on and changes are made.

ACTIVITY Local resources

Find out what sources of information and advice are available in your local area and on a national level. Use your local authority, telephone directory and the useful contacts in the appendix at the end of this book. Look to your community workers, schools, community leaders, the local mosque, church, temple or synagogue. Start your own directory of helpful organisations and contacts and how each might be helpful in the work of your play setting.

Legislation affecting playwork and discrimination

The Children Act 1989 was the first legislation regarding childcare that specifically refers to a child's religious persuasion, racial origin and cultural and linguistic background and actively encourages good anti-racist and anti-discriminatory practice. It promotes the idea that good childcare includes meeting the needs of individual children, providing resources that are of value to them and promoting positive images of children from different family types and backgrounds. Other relevant legislation that affects people's rights and makes discrimination illegal includes:

- The Disability Discrimination Act 1995 (Amendment) Regulations 2003 makes it illegal for employers to discriminate against disabled people applying for jobs or against existing disabled staff. In general, it is also illegal for anyone providing goods, facilities or services to discriminate unjustifiably against a disabled person.

Dressing up. Some activities encourage children to try out other ways of being

All companies and organisations that provide services to the public are required by the Disability Discrimination Act to ensure that those services are reasonably accessible to disabled people.

- The Special Educational Needs and Disability Act 2001 (SENDA) requires all schools to ensure that they do not discriminate against disabled people in any of the services they provide. They must also ensure that they do not discriminate against prospective disabled users who may wish to use the services. This highlights the fact that disabled children have a right to play together with their non-disabled peers and is good practice for all play settings, whether or not they are using school premises.

- The Sex Discrimination Act 1975 (Amendment) Regulations 2003 makes it unlawful to discriminate on the grounds of sex or marital status.

- The Race Relations Act 1976 (Amendment) Regulations 2003 makes it unlawful to discriminate on the grounds of colour, race, nationality, ethnic or national origins. You are also required to have a race equality policy that is linked to an action plan. It is unlawful to discriminate directly or indirectly. An example of direct discrimination would be to refuse to admit a child to the play setting simply because he is black or white. An example of indirect discrimination could be conditions that might be seen on the surface as being fair, but that put certain groups at a disadvantage – for example, if places are allocated to children whose parents are part of a circle of friends who have spread the word among themselves. This would be unlawful if it excluded a particular racial group and could not be justified.

- The Human Rights Act 1998 incorporates provisions from the European Convention on Human Rights into UK law.

SPOTLIGHT ON   **Play against discrimination**

In Chapter 2 we looked at how some children may be at greater risk from play deprivation than others. Play settings may compensate for children's lack of free play opportunities in the wider world. We also know that play has therapeutic value. Can play opportunities also counterbalance some of the effects of discrimination in the wider world?

No two children will have the same skills, understanding and experience

Developing anti-discriminatory practice

Anti-discriminatory practice is not just about avoiding discriminatory behaviour within the play setting. It requires active thinking, planning and evaluation by you, the other staff members and your managers. A commitment to equal opportunities is essential. But how do you put this into practice? There are suggestions throughout this book and more information and in-depth consideration will be found in the books listed in the further reading at the end of this chapter. Some of the areas you will need to consider include the following.

Choosing resources and avoiding stereotypes

As well as using play materials from different cultures, you will need to look at how people are portrayed within the books, posters or other images in your play setting. From an early age, children become aware of the 'boxes' that different people are put into by society and the labels that are attached to them. Unless these stereotypes are challenged, children will grow up believing them to be true. Common stereotypes include:

- 'Girls can't play football.'
- 'Disabled people are helpless.'
- 'Asian women are docile.'
- 'Homosexual people get AIDS.'

These are common and very simple stereotypes. The point about all stereotypes is that they are generalisations – often based on ignorance and prejudice. In the play setting, you can counteract some of these common stereotypes by choosing resources and stories that show disabled people, women, girls, black people and people from different cultural backgrounds in a variety of roles with positive value attached. Your own attitude and example is important too. You will need to be aware of the language you use and the role models you and your co-workers provide. As a male worker, are you always expected to take more responsibility than the female workers for repairs and construction, organising team games or sports and maintaining discipline? Or do you also care for injured or upset children, prepare and serve refreshments or wipe the floor? As a female worker, have you developed skills in woodwork, construction or team sports? In this way, our behaviour can help to counteract stereotypical beliefs.

Challenging discrimination

By the time the children are old enough to come to your play setting, many of them will have learned what it is like to be a victim of prejudice and will have had their self-esteem damaged by such experiences. As a playworker, you have a responsibility to challenge racist, sexist and other forms of discriminatory language or behaviour within the play setting. If it is left unchallenged, the perpetrator and victim of such behaviour, as well as any children standing by, will assume that you find the behaviour acceptable. The

The trust and quest for adventure that makes playing (and living) exciting and meaningful

way in which you challenge will depend on the circumstances of the incident, your knowledge of those involved and the age and development of those involved. Discriminatory language and behaviour may be unintentional and unconscious and learned through imitating adults who are important in the life of the child.

ACTIVITY   The language we use

Consider the following situation:

1 Ronnie, Ahmed and Julia are on the same team. They are friends and have invented their own relay race game. It is Ahmed's turn to run. Ronnie starts shouting, 'Run. Hurry you stupid Paki. Get a move on!' Ronnie and Ahmed have been friends for a long time. They are both aged 6. You have never heard Ronnie use the term 'Paki' before. How would you react? What would you say to both boys?

2 Get two colleagues to play the part of the two boys and practise what you would say to them as a playworker. If possible, get a fourth person to observe and comment, with positive suggestions for other possible ways of responding.

In the situation described in the activity 'The language we use', Ronnie may well have been unaware that his language was racist. He may have learned it from people who are very important to him. You will need to be sensitive in the way you challenge and in the way you support. When you are challenging discriminatory behaviour, your body language and tone of voice are important. Aim to be relaxed, informative and unthreatening and to achieve the following three goals:

1 To raise the awareness of the person responsible for the incident – say clearly what you find unacceptable and why.

2 To change the behaviour of the person responsible to ensure that it does not happen again.

3 To be supportive of the person who is on the receiving end of the discriminatory behaviour by showing clearly that you find it unacceptable and to help rebuild self-esteem.

You can provide a good role model if you are open to challenge of your own behaviour and language. We all have our own prejudices and areas of ignorance and people can be very defensive about this. They are worried that they will say the wrong thing. Others can be dismissive by saying, 'I don't believe in all this politically correct language nonsense.'

Language, including social labels, popular jargon and what are considered to be acceptable terms, changes over time and as our thinking and awareness changes. We need to be sensitive in the language we use. Language carries meaning – and often the meaning it has for the listener is different from and more damaging than the meaning that was intended by the speaker. In the activity 'The language we use', do you think Ahmed understood the term 'Paki' in the way it was meant or intended by Ronnie? If you are unsure about whether a word you use might cause offence, ask the person to whom or about whom you are speaking.

SPOTLIGHT ON | Disabled people's list of acceptable terms

The following is a list of some of the terms used by disabled people. Although many disabled people prefer these terms, some disabled people may prefer to use different terms – take your cue from them about what language they find acceptable.

Acceptable term: disabled person (conveys that society disables the person)

Unacceptable term: handicapped, crippled (conveys neediness or deformity)

Acceptable term: wheelchair user

Unacceptable term: wheelchair bound; confined to a wheelchair (this conveys restriction, whereas a wheelchair often provides freedom and liberation)

Acceptable term: a person who has, for example, cerebral palsy

Unacceptable term: suffers from, for example, cerebral palsy (most disabled people do not regard themselves as 'suffering')

Acceptable term: non-disabled person

Unacceptable term: normal (this would convey that disabled people are 'abnormal')

ACTIVITY | Positive or negative words?

Look at the following words. Do you consider them positive or negative words? What images do they conjure up?

> special   disabled people   brave   cripple   the disabled
> deaf   wheelchair bound   sufferer   inclusion   wheelchair user
> disabled toilet   accessible toilet

Discuss with a friend or colleague which terms you are comfortable using and why.
Remember language changes over time and terms that were acceptable in one society at one time can become insulting in another society or time and visa versa.

We can help each child to discover his or her own possibilities

Raise the subject of language at a staff meeting, preferably before an incident arises. Try to create an atmosphere within the play setting where it is acceptable for staff and children to question and challenge language that they think might be offensive to others and where they can explain why they think it is offensive.

Including disabled children in the play setting

Disabled people are only 'disabled' because society obstructs them in some way. If we lived in a society that ensured that disabled people had full access to all services and could move around freely, they would not be 'disabled' at all. The view that it is 'society' that disables people, not their impairment, is often called the *social model of disability*. This approach assumes that it is the responsibility of society to change to include everyone. This is in contrast to the *medical model* approach that tries to 'fix' the impairment with medical procedures, therefore suggesting that the disabled person has to change in order to fit into a society designed for non-disabled people. The medical model approach is often accompanied by the idea that some disabled people should be segregated, kept apart from non-disabled people, because mainstream services are not suitable for them. In reality, mainstream services can often be designed to include everyone. For example, some adventure playgrounds have led the way in developing a fully inclusive attitude. Their design, construction, equipment, staff, training and attitude give all disabled and non-disabled children the chance to play equally.

Including disabled children in your play setting can give each child an opportunity to experience play in whatever way is open to them. You can help each child to discover his own possibilities. All children benefit from having children with different needs and abilities around them and being part of their play. They have the opportunity to become more sensitive to the needs of others and to overcome ignorance and prejudice.

Despite this, there are often barriers to disabled children participating, or participating fully, in play settings. These barriers fall into three categories:

- *physical* – unsuitable access and toilet arrangements, transport, insufficient resources or inappropriate equipment
- *attitudinal* – anxiety, prejudice, laziness, lack of interest, understanding, concern or training of key members of the play setting
- *organisational* – the routines, rules, supervision, aims and activities of the play setting.

If you do not have any disabled children, what are the reasons for this? You may need to raise the issues with your supervisor or manager – for example, the need to make adaptations to premises, materials, equipment and activities in order for some children to be able to participate fully in play with their peers. Some children may need extra adult support, medical care or supervision to ensure their safety and give them equal opportunities within the play setting. You may need to consider whether your play setting is accessible – wide doors, ramps, transport and so on. Remember that the Disability Discrimination Act makes it the duty of anyone providing a service to the public to make reasonable adjustments to ensure accessibility for disabled people.

Look for positive ways to meet children's communication needs

Including everyone

Is your play setting available to all children? List the things that might help or hinder inclusion of children with impairments within your play setting. Divide your list under the following three headings:

- physical
- attitude
- organisational.

An equal opportunities policy for your setting

Does your play setting have an equal opportunities policy? If so, do you review the policy at regular intervals to make sure it is still relevant, up to date and useful? Or perhaps it was written in 1975 and you know it's around somewhere, you just haven't had time to look at it recently? Whether you are writing or reviewing your equal opportunities policy, it is important that you and the rest of the staff understand the need for such a policy. You can do this by discussing it at staff meetings or by attending equal opportunities training. Or you could ask for advice from your local play association, or from one of the national play organisations, such as 4children (see the appendix). Only by understanding the policy will you be able to put it into practice.

Once you have written the policy and put it into action, it is important that you monitor the policy and your practice to make sure you are including everyone. It is also good practice to prepare your setting for any future children who may come along. For example, if a child who is blind came along to your setting for the first time, how would he feel? Would he feel welcomed and relaxed because the staff are confident and supportive about his impairment and some of the equipment is specifically designed for children who are blind or partially sighted? Or would he feel disoriented and unwelcome while the staff run around trying to decide how to include him? Would he have to stay in a 'safe' area of the play setting while the other children are free to come and go as they please? Or would there

Playworkers need time to consider their own values and attitudes

be opportunities for him to explore, play freely and encounter exciting challenges with the rest of the children? By monitoring and evaluating your policy with the staff and with the children – and making the necessary changes at your play setting – you will have a policy that is really useful – and really worth the paper it is written on.

ACTIVITY 'Of course, I had to say no'

Consider this situation:

Your manager comes to a team meeting. She says, 'I was asked if we could take an 11 year old girl with epilepsy. She is also profoundly deaf. Of course, I had to say no. We simply don't have the expertise or staff to cope with a child like that.'

- How could you challenge the phrase 'a child like that'? Did your manager meet the child? Did she find out exactly what the needs of this particular child were?

- What arguments could you use to convince your manager that it is important to find a way to offer this child a place and the potential benefits this would have to the play setting and everyone within it?

- How can the Disability Discrimination Act help playworkers to include everyone?

Training and evaluation

Playworkers need time to consider their own values and attitudes. You will need time to share concerns, ideas and understanding and to learn about new ways of working. It is important that the values of your play setting are clearly stated in the form of policies that are understood by all. It is equally important to find ways of monitoring to ensure that the policies are put into practice. You need time to reflect on your playwork practice and refresh your ideas. You can do this by choosing a particular topic or policy to discuss during a staff development meeting. One or two workers may attend external training in a particular area and bring new ideas back to the rest of the team and the play setting as a whole.

Summary

Play is a great leveller. When children play, the realities of everyday life often do not apply. Although this is a very healthy and positive starting point for anti-discriminatory practice, playworkers must do everything possible to make sure that discrimination and prejudice do not interfere with each individual child's right to enjoy and feel accepted in their play. You can do this by:

- being aware of the issues surrounding equal opportunities and discrimination
- looking at your own attitudes and prejudices
- talking about anti-discrimination with all the children, staff and parents
- creating a policy for equal play
- putting this policy into action.

Further reading

Melville, S. (1994) *Gender Matters*. Playboard. Available from www.playboard.org.

Oliver, M. (1995) *Understanding Disability: From Theory to Practice*. Palgrave Macmillan.

Scott, R. (2000) *Side by Side: Guidelines for Inclusive Play*. Kidsactive. (Kidsactive now called Kids, also have some very useful fact sheets about accessible play – Tel: 020 7359 3073 or email: pip@kidsactive.org.uk.)

Children's rights

www.therightssite.org.uk UNICEF UK's youth website, which includes a summary of the UN Convention on the Rights of the Child.

Legislation

Much of the legislation mentioned in this chapter, such as the Disability Discrimination Act and the Race Relations Act, is available in full at www.hmso.gov.uk.

CHAPTER 9
Developing reflective practice

Compared with what we ought to be, we are only half awake. Our fires are dampened, our drafts are checked, we are making use of only a small part of our mental and physical resources.

(William James, in Siegel 1991)

This chapter suggests ways in which you can reflect on:

- What you do in the play setting.
- How you do things and who else is involved.
- Why you do things the way you do and how others see what you do.
- What you learn along the way and when and whether to change things.

The way in which you work is affected by your personal history and experience. Thinking back to past experiences, including from your own childhood will help you to become more aware of your own responses to situations that arise in the play setting. It can also help you identify where you have learned things and how you learn best. You will also become aware of things that have maybe blocked your learning. In this chapter, we will consider:

- Starting with yourself
- Reflecting on your own work
- Developing resourcefulness and broadening your experience
- Working with colleagues – getting feedback from others
- Management support and review

- A personal development plan
- Work–life balance

This chapter also encourages you to look at developing your own resourcefulness as a playworker and to gain a deeper understanding of how your actions impact on the play setting and the children and adults using it. You can do this by using your observations of children when they are playing, your own experiences of playing and by testing out your thinking through learning with others (staff development and training) and using theoretical perspectives to extend and analyse the way you think about your work. Reflective practice begins however with self-awareness.

Starting with yourself

As a playworker, you need, among other things, enthusiasm, flexibility, imagination, stamina, patience, sensitivity and a sense of humour. These qualities will help you to plan, provide and engage in play that is life enhancing for the children and young people with whom you work. There will be times when you get tired or when situations present themselves in the play setting that you do not fully understand or when you are not sure of the right way to act or proceed. You need to know what resources are available to you to support you and to help you reflect on the work you do and to develop personally and professionally within your role. A good way to begin this self-reflection is by drawing a lifeline.

Being and working with children can be a privilege, a joy or a chore. If you observe babies and very young children, you cannot fail to notice their qualities of openness, wonder, receptivity, interest and enthusiasm for life. In some children, these qualities are buried from a very early age behind a wall of defences build up from experiences of criticism, fear and perceived failure. As a playworker you are also a 'role model' for the children you work with. How do you as playworker maintain and develop your own desire to dream, discover and explore through play? A play setting can be a place that enables children of all ages to rediscover and maintain the spontaneity, the trust, the self-esteem and the adventurousness that make playing (and living) exciting and meaningful. Your job in the play setting is to be of service to the children in their play. In order to do this successfully you need to think where and how you get the nourishment to keep you 'awake' to playfulness and fit for the job.

ACTIVITY   Lifeline

1 Think again about what and who helped you in your childhood to develop the knowledge, skills and understanding you have now. When and how did you develop the skills you now use as a playworker?

2 Write or draw a picture or chart of this information. This is sometimes called a lifeline, and can be done in any way you wish. One group of playwork students chose to depict their lifelines in many different ways: a flower, a river, a key, a spider's web (page 150).

3 Write down three of your major strengths or skills as a playworker. Think about what helped you develop them.

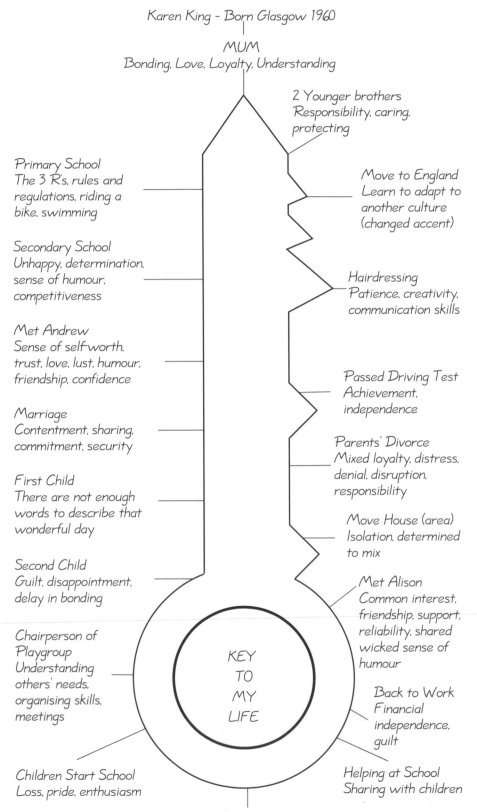

PLAYWORKER'S LIFELINE

Karen King – Born Glasgow 1960

MUM
Bonding, Love, Loyalty, Understanding

2 Younger brothers
Responsibility, caring, protecting

Primary School
The 3 R's, rules and regulations, riding a bike, swimming

Move to England
Learn to adapt to another culture (changed accent)

Secondary School
Unhappy, determination, sense of humour, competitiveness

Hairdressing
Patience, creativity, communication skills

Met Andrew
Sense of self-worth, trust, love, lust, humour, friendship, confidence

Passed Driving Test
Achievement, independence

Marriage
Contentment, sharing, commitment, security

Parents' Divorce
Mixed loyalty, distress, denial, disruption, responsibility

First Child
There are not enough words to describe that wonderful day

Move House (area)
Isolation, determined to mix

Second Child
Guilt, disappointment, delay in bonding

Met Alison
Common interest, friendship, support, reliability, shared wicked sense of humour

Chairperson of Playgroup
Understanding others' needs, organising skills, meetings

KEY
TO
MY
LIFE

Back to Work
Financial independence, guilt

Children Start School
Loss, pride, enthusiasm

Helping at School
Sharing with children

Start work as playworker in After School Club

It is vital for you as a playworker to make time to develop your own resourcefulness. As well as being 'a job' your work within the play setting is a personal and professional journey and you need to think about the support you will need to make you fit for the journey and to sustain you on your travels. The children who come to your play setting are your travelling companions and you need to look after yourself if you are going to be able to look out for them.

ACTIVITY   What makes good play?

Individual children will have different ideas about what makes 'good play'. Think about when you were child and what you considered your 'best play' experiences then.

How old were you? What were the key ingredients? Was it outside or inside? Were you with other children or were you alone? Were there any adults around – what were they doing? Interview a couple of friends or colleagues about the same questions and make comparisons.

SPOTLIGHT ON   Self-awareness and motivation

Why did you choose to become a playworker?

What needs in you are fulfilled by your work?

What motivates you to continue being a playworker?

These are important questions for you to think about if you are to develop reflective practice. The answers are likely to change as you develop as a playworker. Children will be quick to pick up on your motivation and on whether you are there to support and facilitate their play space and their play. If you are there more for your own needs – because you like to play yourself, for example, or if you don't really want to be there at all – will it affect how you do the job?

Reflecting on your own work

Not everyone enjoys change, but as a playworker you will need to adapt to fulfil the diverse needs of the children. So, where do you start? A good place is by evaluating your own work – trying to be as objective and honest as you can. Think about the times when you feel you do a very good job and the work seems to 'flow'. What is happening during those times? What are the key factors of success? Now think about the occasions when you feel you lack the skills or knowledge to give the job your best.

There are many models of reflective practice but most are based on a version of Kolb's learning cycle: Plan–Do–Review.

The learning cycle

Whichever model you use you will be asking yourself questions such as:

- What did I expect or plan to happen in this play session?
- What actually happened – what might others have seen happening?
- What else was going on – what was I thinking and feeling – what might others have been thinking and feeling?
- What can I learn from this experience and how it will affect the way I plan to work in the future?

Of course, as play is largely spontaneous, your planning will be very open ended. The important thing therefore is to think about what happened and how this might affect your actions and behaviour in the future. You might like to focus on particular aspects of your work, for example:

- How you engage with the children in developing the play environment and organisation of resources.
- Your relationship with particular children or your work with your team of colleagues.
- How you have responded to a child with a particular impairment starting at your setting.
- Critical incidents: your responses to particular play cues or a difficult situation that has occurred at work

---

ACTIVITY   **Keeping a journal**

Try keeping a journal – writing down your experiences and thoughts about your work on a regular basis.

You could include drawings and photos. It can be a very simple account, diagram or map of the things that happened during the day: the tasks and activities that you undertook. Alternatively, you might want to note the feelings and interactions that went on during the day – between you and the children, between the children and the children and between you and your colleagues.

CASE STUDY   **Different styles of working**

During the course of his work on the playscheme, Robin was aware that he didn't like the days when he worked with Anna because there always seemed to be a lot of tidying up to do. Anna was always suggesting that the children use new or different resources and then not encouraging them to put things away. As a result, the playworkers were left to do it at the end of the session (the hall was used by others in the evening), making Robin late home. Finally, he plucked up courage to speak to Anna, 'Anna I find it difficult when we have so much clearing up to do at the end of the session that it makes us late. Could we get the children to help clear up a little earlier?' An interesting discussion followed where Anna expressed the view that playworkers should not disrupt the flow of play and should be prepared to stay afterwards to clear up. Robin explained his need to get home on time due to family commitments. They reviewed the way they worked together and also with the children so that more play material could be left out from one day to the next, but also winding down the play session earlier so that they could get home on time.

Learning to appraise yourself is the first step to reflective practice.

Developing resourcefulness and broadening your experience

Learning from others is important for all kinds of work – and especially work with children. It is useful to test out your evaluation of your own work and the thoughts and observations of your colleagues against a broader reference – through reading books and journals for published ideas on 'best practice' or by using one of the many accredited quality assurance schemes (see Chapter 3).

Most playworkers these days will have been on some kind of training and will see continuous professional development as an important part of the job.

You will probably know how you learn best – through watching other people and working alongside more experienced playworkers (shadowing or visits to other play settings), through informal discussions with colleagues or more formal training courses or through reading books, journals or researching on the internet.

Playworkers can use a range of these techniques for keeping up to date and getting new ideas on the way they work. Theoretical perspectives on your work can sometimes seem too dry or abstract to digest on your own. Perhaps you could have a regular slot at a team meeting where one of the playworkers prepares a short activity or presentation about something he or she has read and found useful in thinking about work. If you have a small

A playwork resource library

team it may be that you can link up with other playworkers in your area. Do you have a local play association or playwork network? You can encourage them to set up seminars and invite visiting speakers or to organise trips and visits to other play settings (more on this in Chapters 4 and 14).

You can also broaden your experience by meeting and training with people who work with children in other settings – schools, health centres, youth service, social work, psychology who will have specialist expertise to offer to help you broaden your understanding of the children you work with and the wider context of their lives. You will also have expertise on facilitating play and creating play environments for example, that will be interesting to others – such as those developing children's centres or extended schools or community and leisure centres.

ACTIVITY   **Resources**

Develop a resource file for yourself with lists of useful web pages, interesting quotes or articles that make you think about your work.

Alternatively, you could develop a resource library for the setting as a whole. You could use the appendix at the end of this book, as well as the ideas for further reading at the end of each chapter as your starting point.

Ask colleagues what they find most useful. Do they have a favourite book of games or have they read any particularly interesting articles lately?

Working with colleagues – getting feedback from others

There are many ways of getting feedback from others. It is important that your play setting enables you and your colleagues to work together in an open and non-judgemental fashion where it is OK to make mistakes and to learn from them together. This kind of approach is consistent with playwork principles (see Chapter 2) and enables you to give and receive feedback without feeling criticised or defensive. There are many ways this can happen, for example:

- formal and informal observations from colleagues
- keeping a logbook or shared diary for colleagues to write things as they occur during the session
- keeping a suggestions/comments book for children and/or parents to write in
- team meetings and development days
- management support and review.

Observations

Tutors and supervisors will often observe playwork students during the working day as part of a training course or during assessment for NVQ. They will then give feedback to the students on what they have observed. Although it can be uncomfortable at first to have someone watching you, it is a very useful way to get feedback on how others view your work. Try to welcome it as a useful tool for you own development and continue to use it on a regular basis. (It may be necessary to arrange for staff cover during such an exercise.)

Before you are observed, make sure you agree with the person who is observing you how long the observation will go on for and what kind of feedback will be given. Are there particular things the observations should focus on? The observer might, for example, be looking at how you interact with children or colleagues, how effectively you communicate and how you offer praise or manage difficult behaviour. Alternatively, you might be focusing on the quality of the play environment and your role in facilitating this through organisation of resources, pace and timing and response to play cues from the children.

When you get feedback, be sure to listen, asking for clarification or specific examples if you do not understand. Be prepared to accept any valid criticism, focusing on the need for development rather than the criticism itself.

Start making notes about areas for your development. Some may be simply organisational, such as 'make sure there are enough glue tubs for future craft activities'. Others may be more complex or take a bit longer to put into action, such as 'develop more assertive communication with parents'.

You can use a table, similar to the sample table for making observations of your own (or a fellow playworker's) work.

Date: _____

Purpose of observation: Feedback to MG on engagement with children and organisation of resources

Key incidents	Points to consider	Notes in response
Three girls playing with paints on tabletop — start doing handprints — paper covered — start on newpaper and table top (looking at playworkers on other side of the room and giggling)	Took good 3 or 4 minutes before children's giggles were loud enough to attract attention by which time several others had joined in attracted by growing energy and laughter Missed cue? Distracted by parent?	The session observed lasted well over an hour. The children were engaged in play with paint for extended period and my interventions were intended to enable the 'flow' of play to continue with minimum disruption. I missed the first cue re hand painting and need to extend as I was distracted by a parent. Need to be more assertive with parents wanting to chat during session times
MG intervenes with suggestion of using newsprint roll	Imaginative engagement by MG extending opportunity — asked for table to be wiped before laying out newsprint	The resources could be better organised in the craft area to enable children to access them themselves more easily
Two girls ask for glue to make collage	MG responds to request. Girls help get glue	
Glue spilled as too many try to use the same pot At MG's request the boys go off to get glue from stock cupboard but they do not return	MG intervenes (uninvited) and asks two boys to get more glue Flow interrupted? Boys do not return with glue — they have started another game outside	Needed to intervene as developing into potential health and safety issue. Boys seem more reluctant to ask for resources and did not know where glue is stored. Consider engaging boys in ordering new craft resources

You can then use these notes to develop your personal development plan, but also to raise issues with colleagues that may mean changing existing practice as a whole.

Team meetings and whole team development activities are also important ways of getting feedback and planning for the future. There are more ideas on this in Chapter 10.

Management support and review

Many play settings will have a system of regular meetings between playworkers and their line managers and for reviewing their practice. This is sometimes called supervision and appraisal, or 'one-to-one' meetings and annual review. Whatever the system used at your work, there should be planned times and opportunities for you to meet with your supervisor or manager on a one-to-one basis to review our work and plan what development activities you need. Although this should be formal in terms of being planned in advance and having some structure to it, these kinds of meetings should be relaxed occasions – a positive time for you to focus on your own role and needs.

You might for example look at your overall practice and how you feel about how it's going:

- What are the things that have gone particularly well at work?
- Have there been any particular highlights and achievements?
- What things have gone less well?
- Have there been any particular difficulties or complaints? How are they being addressed?

 CASE STUDY | Annual review

The following example is the documentation used by playworker Morgan Green (MG) and her supervisor for her annual review.

Part 1 Review of current work

Overall highlights of the last year:

MG particularly pleased with the way that the wild area has developed over the last 3 months. The children have developed several new temporary shelters within the shrubs, using plastic tarps and other scrap building material which became available during the course of sorting out the stock cupboard. Another highlight is developing relationship with SD who used to be very withdrawn and passive within the play setting but now often 'cues' MG in her play and engages in conversation.

The play environment

MG has been particularly successful in developing this aspect of the work. MG thinks that there is insufficient time allowed to bring play to an end and clear away resources at the end of the session. MG has found her reading on 'play types' to be particularly helpful and would like the opportunity to share some of her ideas on this with other staff.

Action/goal: two items for future team meeting agendas:

- play types
- pace and timing in relation to end of session and organisation of resources at team meeting.

Working with colleagues

MG joins in well in planning meetings, providing lots of ideas. Sometimes arrives late for sessions and meetings

Action/goal: improve time keeping.

Organisation of resources

Morgan has led the reorganisation of the stock cupboards so that resources are much more accessible. Several of the children were involved in this and now take more responsibility for getting things out and putting them away. MG also suggested the use of the scrap materials for developing shelters in the 'wild area'.

Action/goal: in discussion with children plan to expand range of craft materials and the system for maintaining an inventory of resources.

Relationships

MG has good relationship with children, staff and parents. Some difficulty in dealing with unwanted behaviour – particularly from older boys.

Action/goal: consider best support to develop more confidence in dealing with unwanted behaviour in a play setting, and developing relationships with D and S.

Health and safety

Very thorough in making safety checks and identifying hazards. Uses positive methods for promoting children's health – e.g. planning healthy eating.

Part 2 Review of job description

Job description satisfactory.

MG agreed no changes needed (note – see Chapter 10 for more on job descriptions).

Part 3 Feedback from MG

Level of support received

MG feels that levels of support are adequate in most areas, but would like further support in dealing with unwanted behaviour.

Level of responsibility

MG feels that her current responsibilities are satisfactory and that she is fully stretched.

Job satisfaction and work–life balance

MG is generally content in all areas of work. Would like to consider a later start some days as MG has additional care responsibilities at home at the moment. Would like time to visit other play settings for fresh ideas, and suggested a work exchange with another club.

As a result of reviewing your practice you might identify things that you need to work on or find out more about. It may be that the way you work in the play setting has changed over time. This might be prompted by asking yourself questions such as:

- Are you up to date with any new legislation or regulations that affect the work in the play setting?
- Does your job description accurately reflect the work you do? Are there any changes that need to be made?

These meetings should also be a time for you to think about your personal interests and to plan further development or training.

- What are the main professional development goals for you personally or for the development of the play setting for the next period?
- What training or other support would help you to develop in your role and to achieve your goals?

A personal development plan

Your reflection on your own practice and feedback from others will help you to plan the sorts of development activities you need. Even if your setting does not have a formal supervision and appraisal scheme, it is useful for you to have a regularly reviewed personal development plan. This is where you record your agreed actions arising from your review. Once you have agreed your actions and priorities they need to be set out in a SMART format. That is, they should be:

- **S**pecific (clearly understood actions and not too broad or general).
- **M**easurable (how will you know when you have completed your action?).
- **A**chievable (you need to be confident that it is within your power to undertake this action – even if it will need support);
- **R**ealistic (not so ambitious that it makes you feel overstretched or stressed).
- **T**ime bound (sets out specific times by which you expect to have completed the action).

The following case study is just one example. There are many other formats for recording appraisals and also for personal development plans. Whichever format you use, the focus should be on your ability to do your work as effectively as possible and should identify any support you need for this.

CASE STUDY Personal development plan

Development plan with actions arising from MG's annual review

Area identified	Who/what	By when
Increase confidence in behaviour management of older boys	Shadow PD in work with older boys MG to attend training course	May March
Expand range of craft materials and the system for maintaining an inventory of resources	MG to work with children to develop inventory and order resources	June
Time keeping to be improved	Agreed late starts on Mondays and Wednesdays (3.30)	Immediate effect
MG to share understanding of play types and pacing of the end of the play session	Following items for team agenda: • play types • pace and timing in relation to ending play MG to introduce topics and lead discussion and PD to support	July September
Visits to other play settings	PD to arrange worker exchange for 1 week with adventure playground	August

Work–life balance

It is important to remember, however, that your professional and personal life are interlinked. Stress in one area will affect the other. If things are difficult at work it is important to find ways to relax and 'switch off' when you get home. Equally, if things are difficult at home due to a health problem, childcare, money or relationship difficulties for example, it may be important for you to make your manager or supervisor or a trusted colleague aware of this. They may be able to support you as appropriate by making allowances if you need time off for appointments or need to come a little late for a while. They may also know agencies or sources of advice that can help you solve your difficulty yourself. Ultimately, however, you are responsible for looking after your own physical and mental health and well-being. If you do not do this, it will have a negative effect on your work and on the children with whom you work. Playwork is an active job that requires good physical health and emotional maturity and stability.

ACTIVITY   Work–life balance

What kind of New Year's resolutions do you make? How good are you at implementing them?
Make a list of:

- things you do to relax and wind down after work
- things you do to keep healthy.

Discuss these with a colleague and make sure your personal development plan pays attention to your own needs as well as the demands of work. If you are healthy and happy outside of work, it will affect your ability to do the job fully and to the best of your potential.

Summary

This chapter includes a range of ways to ensure that you continuously reflect on your work and develop as a playworker. Make sure that you have access to good information about the range of training and professional development opportunities in your area as well as

Sharing a laugh

articles and books that can stimulate discussion and thinking about best practice in playwork. It is also important that the setting you work in takes this aspect of the work seriously and builds in time for you to share and talk about and reflect on your practice and to use this experience to build on for the future.

Reference

Siegel, B. (1991) *Peace, Love and Healing*. Arrow Books.

Further reading

Hughes, B. (2001) *Evolutionary Playwork and Reflective Analytic Practice*. Routledge (especially a very useful Annex 3 with case studies, which can be used for collective problem solving and discussion).
Hughes, B. (2001) *The First Claim – A Framework for Playwork Quality Assessment*. PlayWales.
Isles-Buck, E. and Newstead, S. (2003) *Essential Skills for Managers of Child-Centred Settings*. David Fulton.
Palmer, S. (2003) *Playwork as Reflective Practice* (Chapter 12 in Brown, F. *Playwork: Theory and Practice*) Open University Press.
Stobart, T. (2002) *Take 10 More for Play*. National Centre for Playwork Education.

CHAPTER 10
Teamwork

Conflict is part of life and growth. Without conflict there would be no change and no challenge.

(Fine and Macbeth 1992)

When a group of people get together to work towards specific aims and objectives they are a team. Playworkers usually work as part of a team. Teams can be effective or not effective in achieving their aims, depending on how well they work together.

This chapter will help you look at how your team works and at your own contribution to the team and ways of responding to difficulties and conflict. In this chapter, we will consider:

- Identifying your team – hearing the music
- Developing shared aims and values
- Defining roles and responsibilities
- Recruiting playwork staff
- Working together – team dynamics and relationships
- Communication within the team
- Giving and receiving feedback
- Effective team meetings
- Dealing with conflict
- Your rights and continuous professional development

Identifying your team – hearing the music

A manager's job has been compared to that of a conductor of an orchestra. A playwork team could be compared to a group of musicians making music. The 'music' is what happens in the play setting. The musicians (or playworkers and the children of the play setting) need to agree on what tune they are playing. Each musician needs to know his or her part, although sometimes they produce excellent music by improvisation. If one member plays too loud, the music is distorted. If one member plays out of tune or out of rhythm with the others, the music is spoilt. You must listen to one another. Each musician has particular skills and knows his or her instrument. Some instruments emphasise the rhythm, others the melody. In a larger team such as an orchestra, the conductor helps the

Brushbury Park Leisure Centre

Centre manager   *Permanent staff members*   *Casual workers*

Kridlington Kids' Club

The committee   *Paul* *Violet,*   *Sasha*   *Mary,*
                             the coordinator   *17 year old*
                                                                volunteer

Two team structures

musicians work together. The conductor knows the music well, understands what each musician can contribute and what can be achieved out of each instrument even when she or he can't play it. It takes practice to play together well, but the music that can be created by playing together is far greater than the sum of its individual parts.

Whatever your role you need to know how the team works so that you can carry out your job as an effective part of it.

CASE STUDY | What kind of playworker are they looking for?

It takes a lot to be a playworker. Each play setting will have its own approach to roles and responsibilities of its playworkers. Looking at differences in adverts and job descriptions for playworkers is interesting in order to gain a greater understanding of the different approaches across the field of playwork as a whole. Adverts and job descriptions will vary depending on the nature and ethos of the play setting.

Example 1: *Playworker – Kridlington After School Club*

At different times our playworkers find the need to fulfil the following roles at our friendly, thriving after school club: manager, cook, counsellor, sports and games player, artist, referee, first aider, craftsperson, singer, actor and peacekeeper. Our playworkers enjoy the diversity and challenge of working with children; they are enthusiastic and have bags of energy. If you like working with children and want to know more, please contact xxxxx.

Example 2: *Playworker – Cranmore Play Centre*

Do you have imagination, a sense of humour and enjoy being with children? Are you passionate about play and have an understanding of child development? Are you able to facilitate and support a range of varied and adventurous play opportunities to meet the needs of a diverse group of children with different backgrounds and abilities? If you can answer yes to these questions and have some experience of working with children, please contact xxxxx.

Although you may see the children you work with as a vital part of the play setting 'team', it is also important to focus on how you and the other playworkers and staff (secretary, caretaker, management committee, etc.) work together.

Developing shared aims and values

The main purpose of your team will be to ensure that you work together in the service of children at play. Exactly how you aim to do this and how you judge what is 'the best possible practice' will depend on the type of play setting you work in. Although team members are individuals who come with their own set of beliefs and experiences, each member of your team should be clear about what your setting aims to provide and about the principles that underpin the work. This is covered more fully in Chapter 2. The overall purpose and aims of the project are often set out in a governing document, brochure or policy document. However, the principles and values of a setting are more often 'felt' than explicitly stated. The things that affect the 'feel' or the 'ethos' of a play setting are to do with the overall environment and the way in which people relate to each other and care for the setting. Developing a positive 'ethos' is the responsibility of all the people who work there – the team.

Defining roles and responsibilities

Once the managers have agreed the aims and objectives, they need to know how to make them happen in reality. What skills are needed within the workforce and how are responsibilities divided?

You need clear guidelines about how you are expected to carry out your work and what the priorities are. You may need to know specific procedures for the action needed in particular situations, such as if there is an accident or complaint. You need to know who is responsible for taking the appropriate action and, if it is not you, how you refer information to the person who needs to know.

The policies and procedures of your setting are signposts and guidance for how your team needs to work together. If you are going to work together effectively, you need to know who is expected to do what and how best you can support each other to do the jobs required. Have you got a job description?

The range of duties in your job description will depend on your type of play setting, and the aims and objectives of your setting. See Chapter 2 for more on this.

ACTIVITY   Roles and responsibilities

How clear are you about who should do what in your play setting? Write the name of the person or people within your play setting responsible for carrying out the following tasks, which are the kind of tasks playworkers often need carry out over and above their main responsibilities of facilitating and responding to children's play:

- collecting fees (if fees are payable)
- preparing the play environment, including setting up particular activities every day
- showing visitors or new children around
- dealing with accidents
- carrying out safety checks on equipment
- dealing with complaints from parents
- ensuring all equipment is safely stored at the end of the session
- overseeing the safety of the setting during the session
- dealing with a child's unacceptable behaviour
- banking money
- planning changes to the play environment or obtaining new resources
- dealing with wages
- attending planning meetings
- dealing with disclosed, reported or suspected child abuse
- ensuring children's records are complete and up to date.

If you are unsure about who is responsible for any of these tasks, find out from the rest of the team. You might wish to refer to other sections of this book.

Recruiting playwork staff

Preparation and selection process

You may be asked to be a member of the selection panel who will interview for new staff members. When a staff vacancy occurs, it is important to employ the best possible person to fill it and that this is done in a fair and efficient way. The selection panel should consist of at least two people, who will put together an information pack, consisting of:

- A job description – get examples from other play settings or read 'What is a playworker?' in Chapter 2, page 24.

- A person specification or selection criteria, which set out the skills, knowledge and experience needed to do the job – the kind of person you are looking for.

- An application form and/or details of what is required from applicants – cover letter, curriculum vitae, referees etc.

It is important that you do not discriminate in your selection criteria by making reference to age, gender, religion, marital status etc. It is also important that you think about how you will check whether the person meets the criteria:

- 'A good understanding of playwork principles' is easily tested at interview.

- 'At least 3 years playwork experience' or 'a level 3 playwork qualification' can be tested by application form, copies of certificates and references.

- 'Reliable' can be tested by references.

- But 'a good sense of humour' or 'practical' are less easy to check fairly in a selection process.

ACTIVITY   **What is your job?**

Consider each task within your job description in turn. Ask yourself:

- Do I have the skills required to successfully undertake these tasks?

- Are all the tasks reasonable and in line with the overall aims and objectives of this play setting?

- How closely do the tasks relate to the playwork principles outlined in Chapter 2? How many tasks are 'play' focused and how many tasks are administrative or management focused?

- Do I frequently have to undertake tasks that are not in my job description?

If you lack confidence or are unclear about any of the tasks, discuss this with your supervisor or manager. Should your job description be amended? Do you need training to enable you to fulfil any of the requirements of your job description?

If by any chance you have never been given a job description – try writing your own:

- List all the tasks you undertake in the course of your work and any others that you might be required to undertake in particular circumstances.

- Make time to discuss it with your supervisor or manager.

You need to decide on the selection process to be used. Will you ask candidates to take part in a play session so you can observe their interaction with the children? Will you ask them to give a presentation or be part of a team discussion? Whatever you decide you need to be clear what you will be looking for and how you will assess the candidates fairly.

The information pack may also include general information about the play setting, your equal opportunities policy and dates of interviews and whether the playworker will be expected to undertake any other activities as part of the selection process.

Make a list of places to advertise the vacancy. Do you want to advertise locally, regionally or nationally? There are some places, like the job centre and some shops, where you can place your advert free of charge. Newspapers and most internet sites charge for placing an advert, but this widens the field for potential applicants. Your advertisement should include the name and address of your organisation, job title, details of the job vacancy, hours per week, salary, closing date for applications, date of interviews and a contact telephone number for an information pack.

Shortlisting

Once the closing date for applications has passed, the selection panel should draw up a shortlist of suitable candidates, making sure they meet the selection criteria in the person specification. Information in the applications should be treated as confidential. Candidates who have not been shortlisted should be informed straightaway and thanked for their interest.

Interviews

Nearly all selection processes include an interview. You may need to organise the use of a suitable room for interviewing, making sure it has access for disabled candidates. The next step is to plan a timetable for the interviews, allowing sufficient time for each candidate. Candidates should be given at least a week's notice for interviews. A letter inviting each shortlisted candidate should include the date, time and approximate length of the interview, details of the selection panel, a map and advice about travel and a telephone number with a request that candidates confirm that they will attend. Obtain references on shortlisted candidates before the interview. Prepare a list of suitable interview questions and decide which of the selection panel will ask which questions.

The day of the interviews

Arrange for someone to meet the candidates as they arrive, and to show them to the waiting area. Place a 'Do not disturb – Interviews in progress' sign on the door of the interview room and, if possible, divert any telephone calls. Each member of the selection panel should have:

- a list of candidates
- copies of application forms
- copies of references
- a copy of the job description
- a copy of the person specification or selection criteria
- a copy of the information pack
- a sheet for making notes about each candidate.

Try to keep to schedule but if a slight delay is unavoidable, explain and apologise. During the interview, try to make the candidate feel at ease. Introduce the selection panel and explain the structure of the interview. Avoid asking 'closed' questions, that is, those that require a 'yes' or 'no' or a one-word answer. Instead, use 'open' questions, which encourage and enable the candidate to talk freely. 'Open' questions may begin with What…?, How…? or Why…? Aim for the candidate speaking for 80 per cent of the time. Listen to what the candidate has to say, asking for clarification where necessary and try not to make assumptions. Make only brief notes, allowing you to concentrate on listening to what the candidate has to say. End the interview by asking the candidate if he has any questions. Tell him what will happen next and how you will inform him of the outcome. After the interview, write up your notes more fully, referring to the person specification.

Final selection and wrapping up

The best candidate is the one who most closely matches the person specification. At the end of the day and after discussion and comparing notes, the selection panel may be ready to choose one candidate for the job. You might choose a second choice in case the chosen candidate declines the job offer. If there are no suitable candidates, it may be necessary to re-advertise the post. A nominated member of the selection panel should contact the successful candidate and offer them the job. If the candidate does not have satisfactory criminal records bureau checks, then make it clear that the job is offered subject to clearance. Once the chosen candidate has accepted the job, you can then contact the unsuccessful candidates. If you make the job offer by telephone, follow it up straightaway with a letter of appointment. Keep all forms related to the interviews in a safe and confidential place. Make up a contract of employment for the new employee (if you do not have a standard one, get examples from other settings or take advice on this from an organisation such as 4Children – see the appendix).

Arrange for a suitable period of induction, so that the new employee can get to know the ropes.

Working together – team dynamics and relationships

A team is one particular type of group. Groups function in different ways in terms of how individual members interact and communicate, how they assume power or influence the group and how they form relationships and create change. This is called 'group dynamics'. Groups function as entities in their own right and an individual's behaviour and ability to perform their tasks well or less well will be affected by the group. A group's efforts will be more than the sum of its parts – a group that works well together will be more effective than if its members work individually.

How well do you think your team works together? What do others think? The following suggests some of the things that will contribute to good team working.

Specification of a good playwork team

- There is good communication between its members.
- Team members share and understand common aims and co-operate to achieve them.
- Team members share a commitment to playwork principles and regularly review and share views on their work together.
- Team members feel able to make mistakes sometimes and learn from them without blame.
- Interactions between colleagues can be playful.
- There are clearly defined tasks and responsibilities within the team.

- Work planned can be achieved within the limitations of time and money.
- Work is fairly distributed according to skills and abilities of team members.
- Work is shared within the limits of individual roles and responsibilities.
- Individual team members' strengths and weaknesses are acknowledged and team members support each other in times of stress.
- Team members trust each other personally and professionally.
- Team members respect each other's views, beliefs, family backgrounds, individual circumstances and needs.
- All members are encouraged to contribute to planning, evaluation and making suggestions for new working methods.

ACTIVITY   Evaluating your team

You can do this activity on your own, but it is better if you do it with the other members of your team, in order to share your views and possible solutions for working better together:

1 Give at least five answers to each of these questions:

- What does your team do well? For example, 'We all attend meetings'; 'We share workloads in times of stress; 'We are clear about what we each have to do.'
- What does your team do less well? For example, 'Some members turn up late' or 'We sometimes complain about colleagues behind their backs.' You could also give your team marks out of 10 for each point on the 'specification for a good playwork team' list.

2 Think about:

- how you can build on the positive aspects
- what the causes are of the negative aspects
- what you can do to improve team working.

If a team does not work well together, it is unlikely to achieve its aims. Unresolved conflict or breakdown in communication can lead to sniping about or between team members, the formation of opposing cliques and subgroups. It can also lead to stress, dissatisfaction, absenteeism and unreliability by individual team members. It is only by working together effectively that you can provide the best opportunities for good play experiences for children. It takes self-awareness and hard work to ensure that a team works together well and because a team is made up of individuals with a diverse range of ideas and experiences, things will not always go smoothly. The way in which you communicate and resolve conflicts is important and relationships need to be based on mutual respect and trust. A conflict of ideas can be healthy if it leads to constructive critical evaluation and change in practice. A conflict in personalities is often much more difficult to resolve.

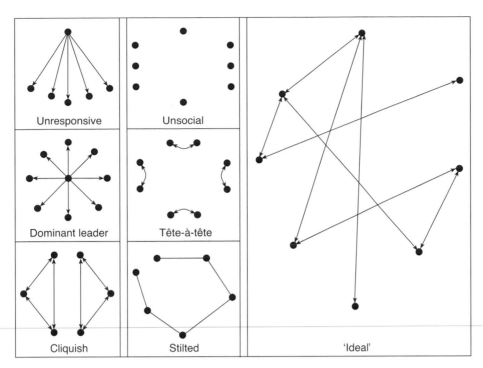

Different patterns of group communication

Communication within the team

Communication takes many forms: verbal or non-verbal (body language, sign language, written), formal or informal. Different patterns of communication can emerge within a group, which affect the way people work together. Many of the principles of good communication raised in Chapter 6 on forming relationships with children and parents also applies to working with colleagues.

Ideally, all team members should have plenty of opportunities for face-to-face communication so that ideas can be shared, concerns aired, and a cross-fertilisation of new ideas can take place. This may mean allowing time at the beginning and end of work to talk informally, as well as regular meetings with a set agenda.

So what is meant by 'good' communication'? Think about the following points:

- listening
- body language
- expressing yourself clearly
- giving and receiving feedback and criticism
- written communication.

Listening

At work, try to listen to what is *actually said* rather than what you *think* is said. Check that you have understood what is being said by summarising what you have heard in your own words and asking if you have got it right. Don't be too quick to agree or disagree. Good listening is a skill that can be developed. It forms a large part of many counselling courses.

> ### ACTIVITY   Listening
>
> Try this exercise with a friend or team member.
>
> **1** Your colleague spends three minutes (timed) talking about something that is important to him or her. You are the listener and should not interrupt. Listen only to what you are told without interpreting, judging or putting yourself into the speaker's shoes. If the speaker comes to a stop, you can show that you are paying attention by keeping eye contact, nodding or smiling. Interjecting words such as 'Yes', 'Mm', 'Right', 'I see' or 'I know' in pauses can also show that you are listening. If necessary, ask questions relating to what you have just heard.
>
> **2** Once the three minutes is up, summarise what you have heard, without adding any of your own thoughts or interpretations. Ask the speaker how close the summary is to what he or she actually said.
>
> **3** Listener and speaker then swap roles and repeat the exercise.
>
> *Note*: Many people do not find it easy to listen to someone even for three minutes without wanting to add their own thoughts or give examples of agreement from their own experience. If this is the case in your role play, discuss possible reasons.

Body language

Take note of body language. If you are fidgeting, looking at your watch or slumped in a chair with your eyes half-closed you will not appear to be listening, even if you are, and this will not encourage communication. Is the speaker's body language consistent with what they are saying? Inconsistent body language could be saying, 'Yes that's great news' while having a downcast facial expression and posture; or, 'I don't mind staying on to help' while looking at your watch or edging towards the door. Take account of the fact that different cultures give different meaning to body language. Maintaining eye contact can be a sign of insolence rather than attentiveness in some cultures, for example, and nodding does not always signify agreement.

Expressing yourself clearly

Even very good listeners are not mind readers. If you do not say what you think or feel, you cannot blame others for not understanding you. For example, if you have health problems or a domestic crisis that affects your work, you should explain this, without necessarily going into any details. Otherwise your sudden need to leave punctually or to take time off could be interpreted as loss of interest, unreliability or taken as a personal slight. If you frequently find that you are doing things you don't really want to or don't have time to do, think twice before agreeing quite so readily next time. If you are constantly pressured into doing things out of your own feelings of guilt, fear or the need to be popular, you will not do them as well as something you chose to do. It is better to say 'no' or even 'maybe' to a request for help, than 'yes' now and then have to find an excuse as to why you are unable to see it through. Give honest responses to requests. Try using phrases such as 'I choose to' rather than 'I have to'. Say 'I don't want to' rather than 'I ought to'.

For example, try saying: 'I choose to work late because I can support better play opportunities within the play setting if I put in more preparation,' not 'I have to work late because otherwise the work doesn't get done.'

The second sentence may be true but no one can make you work above your contracted hours. If you find that you are expected to stay longer than your contracted hours on a regular basis or that there is too much work to do in the time allotted, you need to raise this issue with your manager. There may be a need for greater shared responsibility for the workload between the team or in employing another member of staff. Alternatively, the solution might lie in setting more achievable goals within the time and resources available. If you feel you are constantly misunderstood or exploited, or that you cannot express yourself clearly, it may help to attend an assertiveness course.

Written communication

A daily logbook or diary can also be useful in keeping team members, particularly part-time workers, informed and in touch. There are other types of written communication that can be particularly helpful:

- A brochure or leaflet explaining what your play setting does, who it's for, when it opens and what children, staff and parents can expect.
- Written policies and procedures.
- Notes of meetings.
- Records of compliments and complaints.

(See Chapter 13 on playwork paperwork for more on this.)

Giving and receiving feedback

Being positive

If there is an open and honest ethos within your setting and a level of trust and good communication between the team, it will be easier for you to give and receive feedback from each other about practice within the setting and how you feel about it. Critical feedback is always easier to receive from someone who knows your strengths and who values you as a colleague. Just as children need praise to develop independence and self-esteem, adults need to feel valued if they are to be confident and content in their work. Therefore, make sure you take time to let your team members know the things you appreciate about them. For example: 'I really like the way you work with Paul – he was so hesitant when he started at the play setting, and now he comes in and is straight away telling you his latest joke.' Or, 'thanks for helping me out with clearing up the paints yesterday – I would have been really late home otherwise.'

Giving criticism

There will be times when you feel critical about the words or actions of another team member within the work setting. This may be:

- A minor irritation (you don't like the way C always opens all the windows without asking whether anyone else finds it too warm – in fact you often get cold).
- Something more serious relating to a colleague's work practice (you think B is discriminating against an individual child or that she shouts too often and inappropriately).

In either case, it is important that you raise the issue with the person concerned, either informally between yourselves or at a team meeting if extra support or arbitration is needed. Try not to be condemning. Criticise the action or incident, not the person. Be specific. Say, 'I feel cold with the windows open. Would you check with the other staff members before opening them next time?' instead of 'You're so insensitive, just opening the windows whenever it suits you.' Try to use a moderate tone of voice and stand in a relaxed way. Give the person to whom you are making the criticism the opportunity to respond. Behaviour which involves discrimination or inappropriate childcare practices should always be challenged. It may also need to be referred to the person responsible for dealing with grievances according to the policies and procedures of your play setting.

Receiving criticism

If someone criticises you, listen to what they have to say. Ask for clarification or specific examples – 'What exactly did I say or do to a parent that you felt was rude?' Decide whether the criticism is wholly or partially valid. Accept any facts, but not personal judgements or interpretations – 'Yes, I did ask Mrs B to come and see me another time, but I do not agree that my manner was rude. Her question was not urgent and I explained that I was very busy and would see her at the end of the session.' Be prepared to accept valid criticism and admit mistakes. If relationships are open and honest and there is a 'no blame' culture, team members will feel more confident about admitting to and learning from mistakes and also raising difficult issues before they start affecting the overall atmosphere of the workplace (see also Chapter 9 on developing reflective practice for more about giving and receiving feedback).

Effective team meetings

A meeting is an opportunity for you to spend time with other team members away from the day-to-day work situation, to share ideas and make decisions about your play setting. Meetings can have different purposes and be formal or informal.

An agenda and a chairperson or facilitator

All meetings should have a purpose and an agenda – a list of things that need to be discussed. All team members should be able to put items on to the agenda before the meeting. The meeting will need a chairperson or facilitator – someone who:

- ensures the meeting starts and ends on time
- introduces the meeting

Planning together

- makes sure all items on the agenda are discussed
- gives everyone the chance to talk and ensures that no one dominates the discussion.

If you work in a voluntary sector setting you are likely to have a management committee which is legally responsible for the management (employment, health and safety, finance) of the group. It will have a formally appointed chairperson; in other situations it may be the manager or the supervisor who 'chairs' or facilitates the meetings. In some cases, team members take turns at facilitating meetings. This enables all team members to develop facilitation skills and prevents fixed patterns of communication developing, such as one or two people doing all the talking or always having the final say. However, meetings led by an unskilled or inexperienced facilitator or chairperson can be very frustrating, particularly if there is a lot of business to get through or if major decisions must be made when there is no agreement.

CASE STUDY | **Meetings at Kridlington Kids' Club**

Weekly staff and children planning meetings

The coordinator (who is also a playworker) and the three other playworkers of Kridlinton Kids' Club meet every Friday. All the workers make notes of things they want to bring up at the next meeting during the week and write them down in the team diary. Issues discussed every week include:

- overview of the week – what went well, what did not?
- planning for the following week.

Other issues that are discussed as they arise may include:

- individual children's development and play experiences or needs
- gripes or grievances between colleagues
- sharing information about local community events or training relevant to playwork or the play setting.

The first part of the meeting about reviewing and planning involves the children. They participate either personally or by writing down, or asking someone else to write down, suggestions/ideas to go in the box for discussion. The second part of the meeting, involving discussions about individual children, concerns or grievances, happens after club hours when the children have left.

Bi-monthly team meeting with managers

Once every other month the playworkers meet with the management committee to discuss issues of finance or policy. The coordinator meets informally with the chairperson of the committee at other times.

Keep it playful

Remember that your work is about being of service to children at play. Your own ability to be playful and respond to children's play cues is an essential part of what needs to be considered in your work with the team. Make time to talk about your own experiences of play with your colleagues and about how the play within the play setting affects you. Some playwork teams use games to 'warm up' at the beginning of a meeting to open up communication or enable people to relax before they start or to wind down at the end. Team development days can also be a good opportunity for deeper conversations about the main focus of playwork: being in the service of children at play. One way of doing this can be to engage in some creative activity together such as painting, making music or clowning or through cooperative games at the start or end of the session.

Notes and minutes

All meetings should be recorded in the form of notes or minutes and one person will do this. Records of the meetings should include the main points discussed, any decisions taken, action that needs to be taken as a result of these decisions, whose responsibility for taking such action and when it should be completed by. Enough detail should be recorded to enable the person responsible to be clear about what needs to be done. All team members should receive a copy of the minutes in time to carry out any actions specified.

Small working groups

If the team is small – a dozen people or fewer – meetings can be a useful forum for sharing ideas, planning and evaluating the work. In a larger team, it may be better for these activities to be undertaken in smaller groups, with full meetings being used only to make final decisions, fulfil legal and business requirements and take votes.

Too often, every meeting is taken up with business or day-to-day planning or organisational issues. Meeting and working groups can enable playworkers to focus on particular aspects of practice such as:

- How are *resources and materials* selected to ensure that they promote play and support the play needs of the children? How do you judge whether they are interesting, enjoyable and reflect the multicultural world in which we live?
- How can *stereotyping* be avoided?

A regular staff development meeting or training session, with a prepared programme for looking at a particular area of policy and how it relates to practice – health and safety, equal opportunities, child protection – will ensure that staff continue to look at how the policies of the setting relate to their practice within it (see also Chapter 9 on developing reflective practice). You can also use this as a chance to network or bring in someone from outside of the team (e.g. a psychologist, health worker or community police officer) to give you the benefit of their experience or perspective and for you to share what you do with them.

 Staff development and training and Kridlington Kids' Club

Four times a year the playworkers have a staff development day. Half of this day is used for forward planning of play opportunities within the setting. The playworkers share ideas for themes to be explored, aspects of the play environment they would like to develop, training they wish to attend, equipment needed and so on. They sometimes invite other people to join them – for example, a musician who is going to help run some music sessions in the play setting at the request of a group of children who want to form a band. The second half of the day is spent either looking at how they work as a team – practising their group work and communication skills or looking at a particular aspect of playwork they want to develop. Topics for these sessions have included equal opportunities (gender, race, disability) within the play setting, observing children and understanding and supporting different types of play (cooperative, solitary, exploratory) and so on. Again, they sometimes invite someone from outside the team with special skills, knowledge or understanding to lead the session.

The coordinator also meets individually with the playworkers for regular one-to-one meetings and picks up ideas on team development from them.

Dealing with conflict

All teams have their share of disagreements and conflict. It is healthy for a team to contain different and sometimes opposing views if it leads to a new and better understanding or improved ways of working. This requires good communication between team members and a need allow time for discussions to take place. Disagreements between colleagues that arise during a working session should be dealt with after the session and/or during the next team meeting. Resolving conflict often calls for negotiation – a willingness to compromise or meet halfway, so that both sides feel that their views have been taken into account. There may be need for someone to take the role of facilitating this discussion or 'mediating' to encourage each party to listen and communicate effectively.

A conflict of ideas can be easier to resolve professionally if it does not develop into a conflict of personalities. Diversity in a team is a good thing. It means that the children will have role models and access to playworkers who between them have a fuller range of understanding and experience, attitudes and abilities. By working together a diverse team can contribute more to the play setting than if all the playworkers come from similar backgrounds or have similar beliefs. However, tensions can arise through lack of understanding or respect.

The causes of conflict can vary. Conflict may be caused by poor communication, lack of clarity about roles and responsibilities, policies and procedures, lack of shared aims and values about how the play setting is managed or about the approach to working with children, behaviour management, etc., or it can be caused by personal reasons, such as likes, dislikes, differences in values, social circumstances or beliefs.

 SPOTLIGHT ON   Approaches to conflict

Everyone responds to conflict differently, and different approaches may be suitable depending on the situation. For example, Nelson (1995) suggests five different responses:

- *Direct approach*: This approach challenges the conflict head on, and brings issues out in the open straight away. Issues are faced as objectively as possible and a positive solution to the problem is sought.

- *Bargaining*: This is useful when both parties have ideas on a solution yet cannot find common ground. Often a third party, such as a team leader, is needed to help find the compromise. Compromises involve give and take on both sides, however, and can end up with everyone feeling equally dissatisfied.

- *Team rules or disciplinary procedures*: This response is best only used as a last resort to avoid conflict spilling over into the play setting and affecting children's opportunities to play. It is usually only needed when there is a major breakdown in the way the team functions or when one or more individuals are not team players and have values and principles at odds with the play setting.

- *Retreat*: Some people would always prefer to use this approach than face conflict directly through one of the other approaches. Simply avoiding the conflict or working around it can often delay things long enough for the individuals to cool off and the problem to disperse. However, in most cases, if conflict is not dealt with directly and openly it will fester and cause bigger problems in the long run.

- *De-emphasis*: This is similar to the bargaining or negotiation approach. It seeks to establish areas of agreement rather than focusing on the disagreement, so that a new direction can be found which is acceptable to all – sometimes called a win/win solution.

Even with the best of intentions and with good support and facilitation, some conflicts cannot be resolved easily. If this impacts negatively on the work of the play setting, the managers may have to take formal action, such as bringing in outside arbitration or disciplinary proceedings.

Conflicts should not be allowed to drag on, but need to be dealt with promptly to avoid individuals becoming unduly stressed or worn down and de-motivated or angry. It is particularly important that conflicts between team members are not allowed to disrupt the work of the play setting.

Your rights and continuous professional development

Terms of employment

Your conditions of service should be clearly laid down in your contract of employment. You should know about the hours you will be expected to work, your pay and any notice required if you wish to leave or notice due to you if you are asked to leave. If you think you are being unfairly treated, your play setting should have a management member responsible for personnel issues and possibly a formal grievance procedure. Any decisions taken should be in line with legislation and the overall policies of the organisation. All play facilities that employ staff must comply with employment law in terms of recruitment and selection, conditions of service and employees' payment and rights. You can get more information about how these laws relate to you and your rights as an employee from your local Department of Employment office, citizens' advice bureau or neighbourhood advice centre if you have one (see also further reading at the end of this chapter).

Continuous professional development and team building

Every member of the team has the right to respect from their colleagues and to support for his or her professional development. It helps if there is a formal way of doing this – such as one-to-one meetings (sometime called supervision) between a manager or supervisor and less senior members of staff – as well as informal praise being given when it is deserved (see Chapter 9 for lots more on this).

It is important to recognise the skills, cultural and religious practices and contributions of others and to have your own contributions and needs recognised and understood. As team members, you can help each other reach your full potential within the work setting. Make opportunities to increase your self-confidence and find any other sources of help or support required. Challenge any evidence of discrimination against another team member and give support to the person discriminated against to help them to assert their rights and sustain their confidence and self-esteem.

 **SPOTLIGHT ON** **Six thinking hats – looking at a problem from many points of view**

'Six thinking hats' is a tool invented by Edward De Bono (2004) to help people recognise and value the strength of different points of view. It enables you to move outside your normal way of thinking. The following is adapted from De Bono's original scheme.

Each 'thinking hat' is a different style of thinking. These are explained below:

Blue hat

The blue hat thinkers are able to take control of an issue. Blue hats might be good at chairing meetings – they can bring in the other hats and ensure that everyone gets a chance to be heard.

Green hat

The green hat stands for creativity. Green hats will be good at problem solving and thinking 'outside the box'. Many playworkers find this comes quite easily because play is particularly good at encouraging this kind of thinking.

Grey hat

Grey hat thinkers are cautious. They will see the potential negative impact of any new proposals. This is useful for risk assessment and business planning and to make sure you have thought through any pitfalls before implementing changes.

Red hat

With this thinking hat, you use intuition and respond more emotionally. Red hat thinkers might be particularly sensitive to the 'feel' of the setting and able to predict individuals' responses to changes you might be planning to the play environment.

White hat

If you are a white hat thinker, you like to look at the information and knowledge available to you – you like to make decisions only after you have all the facts or data. White hat thinkers can help the play setting analyse admissions and whether the children coming to your setting are representative of the local community.

Yellow hat

Yellow hats think positively. Their optimism will always put the bright side and see the silver lining to a dark cloud. This can help energise the team when the going gets rough.

Which hat do you normally wear in the team? You could introduce this tool to your team at a team meeting and try taking turns to wear different hats and bring in a different perspective when tackling a difficult issue. If you are lucky, your team will have members who are particularly good at thinking from different perspectives.

Summary

For a team to be effective, you need to communicate and cooperate with a positive attitude, valuing each other's contributions. Individual team members need to support each other within their roles and responsibilities. All team members should have the opportunity to make suggestions for change in working practice and to be part of the process of evaluating and reviewing the work of the team (see also Chapter 9 on reflective practice).

References

De Bono, E. (2004) *Six Thinking Hats*. Penguin.

Fine, N. and Macbeth, F. (1992) *Playing with Fire: Training for the Creative Use of Conflict.* Youth Work Press.

Nelson, M. (1995) 'Interpersonal team leadership skills', *Hospital Material Management Quarterly* 16(4), 53–63.

Further reading

Adirondack, S. M. (1998) *Just About Managing*. London Voluntary Service Council. www.actionlink.org.uk. A practical booklet aimed at voluntary organisations, including sections on teamwork, stress and conflict.

Gawlinski, G. and Graessle, L. (1999) *Planning Together – The Art of Effective Teamwork*. Planning Together Press.

Isles-Buck, E. and Newstead, S. (2003) *Essential Skills for Managers of Child-Centred Settings*. David Fulton.

Legislation and the law

Books on employment and the law can be complex and expensive. The following websites may be useful to you for finding sources of support or reference material:

www.actionlink.org.uk
www.citizensadvice.org.uk
www.croner.co.uk
www.nacvs.org.uk

Keeping it playful

Burton, P. (2002) *Serious Fun: Games for 10–14s*. Thomson Learning. (You can use these games with adults too – they are great for 'breaking the ice' at team meetings.)

CHAPTER 11
Child protection

There is danger in this world we live in, and we only increase our jeopardy by dealing in illusions – by pretending that only strangers are dangerous, that the danger is 'out there' somewhere, not here close to home where we live, love work and play.

(Peg Flandreau West 1989)

The approach taken throughout this book has been that children should not be viewed as objects of concern. They are individuals with rights and expectations and a developing understanding of themselves and the world around them. But children can be in a vulnerable position within their families and society at large. Child abuse is relatively rare, but playworkers should be aware that it does happen and that you have a duty to be observant and to take appropriate action if you have concerns about a child's welfare. In this chapter, we will consider:

- The changing face of child protection
- What is child abuse?
- The role of the playworker in child protection
- Child protection procedures in the play setting
- Anxieties about making a referral and dealing with parents
- The role of the play setting in preventing abuse

The changing face of child protection

In the last few years, there have been several high-profile cases of abuse leading to the death of a child. Most notable is the death of Victoria Climbié in 2000 and the subsequent inquiry led by Lord Laming, which showed that the systems in place failed to offer her protection due in part to ill-trained and unsupported staff with insufficient support from managers. A series of changes to the way services are organised and the way different agencies share information have been set out through a range of government policy documents and new legislation. It is vital that playworkers are aware of their responsibilities with regard to child protection and that they keep up to date with training and current guidance. The websites listed at the end of the chapter will have regularly updated guidance documents. It is also essential for all playwork settings to have a child protection policy in place and to be familiar with local arrangements, including the main contacts within the local authority for training and for reporting concerns.

What is child abuse?

Child abuse is difficult to define. Any definition will be subject to change as thinking and practice develops. Abuse has been categorised into different types: physical, sexual, emotional, neglect and bullying, but these are not mutually exclusive – an abused child may well be suffering more than one type. The categories are useful in coming to a working definition and identifying particular features – physical or behavioural – which may be associated with abuse. But be aware that many of the symptoms described in the following, in particular the behaviours, can be caused by a variety of other factors that are not related to child abuse.

Physical abuse

This is any form of actual injury inflicted (or knowingly not prevented) by a person having custody or care of the child. Sometimes called non-accidental injury, it includes bruises, cuts, fractures, burns, scalds, scratches, bites or administration of poisonous substances. The symptoms of physical abuse are often the most easily recognisable – although you should remember that children frequently bruise and injure themselves accidentally.

Injuries which may signify abuse are:

- bruises in places unlikely to be caused by falls – inside thighs, behind ears, groin area
- bruises with an unusual shape – fingermarks caused by violent gripping or slapping
- weals caused by straps or other implements
- cigarette burns.

You should also be concerned if the explanation of how the injury occurred given by a child or adult is inconsistent or unlikely given the appearance of the injury or if there has been a delay in seeking medical treatment. A child who is suffering physical abuse may appear fearful of adult reactions, have poor concentration or be unwilling to undress (for swimming, for example) and expose marks hidden beneath clothing.

Sexual abuse

Sexual abuse is the exploitation of children to meet the sexual demands of adults. Exploitation is the key word here, as sexual abuse is also about power and control.

Direct sexual abuse can involve genital contact, oral, anal or vaginal penetration, masturbation or ejaculation onto the child's skin. Indirect sexual abuse includes genital exposure ('flashing'), using children in, or exposing children to, pornographic material or encouraging two children to have sex. While sex between adolescents under 16 years of age or between an older person and a child under 16 is unlawful, it is not considered to be abuse if exploitation is not an issue, that is, if both parties were consenting, force was not used and there has been no misuse of power based on age difference (five years or more) or other form of authority.

Signs of sexual abuse can include:

- bruising on breasts, inner thighs or buttocks
- stained underclothes
- genital injuries, soreness or rashes
- urinary tract infections
- frequent headaches and stomach pains.

The playworker should be concerned if a child has difficulty walking or sitting, shows sexually explicit behaviour (including compulsive masturbation) or if they have inappropriate sexual knowledge for their age. Other behaviour that may indicate sexual abuse includes terror of particular people or one person, anxiety, feelings of worthlessness or over-compliant behaviour.

Emotional abuse

Children need love, attention and stimulation as well as physical care if they are to develop into healthy adolescents and adults. They gain their cues on how to behave from adult role models around them. Verbal attacks, isolation, humiliation, extremes of inconsistent care or over-protectiveness lead to loss of self-confidence and the ability to form relationships with others. Such psychological damage can be as harmful to children as some physical abuse in that it can permanently damage the child's ability to form relationships and take part in social activities.

Symptoms of emotional abuse can include:

- communication difficulties
- lethargy
- stunted growth
- constant wetting or soiling
- poor self-esteem
- rocking back and forth
- aggression
- unresponsiveness
- complete withdrawal from activities in the play setting.

Neglect

Neglect is the denial of a child's right to food, warmth, medical care or other aspects of care including supervision to ensure that they are not exposed to dangers such as heaters or traffic before they are old enough to cope with them. Neglect can result in the child suffering preventable injuries or being unable to thrive due to poor nutrition, lack of essential medical care and lack of adult attention, stimulation and support.

Symptoms of neglect may include:

- low weight
- voracious appetite

- unclean appearance or smells
- inappropriate clothing, such as sandals in winter.

The child may show a lack of interest in what is going on in the play setting or the carer may show a lack of interest in the child.

Bullying

Bullying can take many forms, including verbal, physical, emotional, sexual, racist or any form of discrimination. Adults as well as children can be described as bullies if they use their power to frighten, threaten or hurt. Bullying makes many children's lives miserable, but you can help to prevent it at your play setting by implementing anti-bullying strategies, such as:

- creating an anti-bullying policy (perhaps part of your behaviour policy)
- having clear procedures for what to do if bullying happens
- providing good-quality training for staff
- talking the issues over with the children and making it clear to them that bullying will be taken seriously
- sending information home to parents
- providing positive images such as posters
- being good role models.

Bullying, like all the other forms of abuse, is unacceptable and good training will help you to spot the possible signs. A child who is being bullied by adults or children may show signs of nervousness, insecurity and withdrawal. Further information and practical ideas on the prevention of bullying, the reasons for bullying, possible signs of bullying, victim support and self-assertiveness can be obtained from Kidscape (see appendix).

Notice that the same symptoms may appear in different categories of abuse. Be aware, too, that abuse may be occurring when there are no outward signs to observe. If you notice any of these symptoms in a child, remember that there may be a reasonable explanation that is not related to abuse. But never ignore any observation that suggests there may be something wrong, particularly if a number of symptoms are noticed or there is a marked change in behaviour. It is your responsibility as an adult and as a playworker to share your concerns with the appropriate person, following the procedures of your setting.

Playworkers can be a source of trusted support

ACTIVITY   Local training

If you have not been on any child protection training, find out where such training is available in your area (ask your local children's services department in the local authority). They can also let you know about the procedures of your LSCB (local safeguarding children board), including guidelines outlining the procedures for child abuse referral and investigation in your area. Ask to discuss child protection training at your next team meeting if you or any of the other staff members need to update your knowledge.

The role of the playworker in child protection

Your play setting has a particular place within the life of each child who attends. As the playworker, you are one of the adults who provide a role model for each child and you are a potential source of trusted support. You may observe symptoms such as unexplained injuries or changes in behaviour that give cause for concern (suspected abuse); someone may tell you that a child is being abused or that they are abusing a child themselves (reported abuse); a child might confide in you that she or he is or has been suffering abuse (disclosed abuse). You have a duty to discuss your concerns if you have reason to believe that a child has been or is being abused. Attending good quality, up-to-date training about child protection will help you to carry out this duty. Playworkers need to know about:

- The possible signs and symptoms of different types of abuse (outlined earlier).
- Who to contact if you have concerns about a child's welfare (both within your organisation *and* in your local authority children's services, social services or police).
- Your play setting's procedures for dealing with suspected, reported or disclosed child abuse – your own responsibilities; the responsibilities of others and the action to be taken.
- The procedures of your local authority area (children's services, social services, health and police) for investigating possible abuse – what action they will take when you or another member of staff contact them with concerns about a child's welfare (this is called making a 'referral'). In some areas your local NSPCC team can also take referrals. Both the local authority children's services department and the NSPCC will work with the police if a criminal offence is suspected.
- Sources of help, advice and support.

Dealing with personal feelings about abuse

Attitudes to different kinds of abuse vary and are affected by individuals' own experiences (including perhaps firsthand experience of abuse as a child) and cultural and family values. One person may see public humiliation or shaming as more abusive than a private beating. Another may see sexual abuse as far worse than neglect. What disgusts one may seem tolerable to another.

It is not the role of the playworker to judge, assess or investigate suspected abuse. However, if you have to respond to an incident or suspected incident within your work setting, you may need personal support to help you deal with the feelings it brings out in you.

Identifying and getting support

Create your own support network by:

1 Choosing three people you can trust and talk to about the issues raised in this section (these could be a friend, a member of your family, a colleague at work, a contact in social services or the NSPCC).

2 Discussing with them what their role is in relation to child protection within your work setting. A friend or family member could give personal support in relation to your own feelings. A senior worker would be the first person to go to if you have any immediate concerns about an individual child. If you are the senior worker, a contact in the children's services department of the local authority is essential for reporting suspected or actual abuse. How important is confidentiality? What does confidentiality mean in this context?

3 Keeping the contact names and numbers of your support network where you can get access to them quickly.

4 Attending training in child protection.

Child protection procedures in the play setting

Since the inquiry into the death of Victoria Climbié, procedures for dealing with cases of potential child abuse have changed. Local Safeguarding Children Boards (LSCBs) have been set up in each area, with an emphasis on the many different agencies involved with children working in partnership. The child protection policy and procedures for your play setting must link with the procedures of your LSCB.

If you suspect a child is being abused

Within your play setting, the most senior worker should have the responsibility for making referrals – that is, contacting the local authority with concerns about the safety of a child. If the senior worker is not present, and the situation is potentially life-threatening or the child is severely injured, another worker will need to know how to contact the hospital or duty social worker, preferably in consultation with a member of the management of your play setting. If the situation is not life threatening and you or your senior worker think that the symptoms giving cause for concern may be caused by abuse, it may be appropriate to take one or all of the following courses of action:

- If appropriate, discuss your concerns with the child, using suitable language for their age and level of understanding. Avoid asking 'leading' questions such as, 'Did you fall?' or 'Did someone hurt you?' Ask open, neutral questions such as, 'That bruise looks sore – how did you get it?'

- Share concerns with other members of staff. Have they any observations or insights?

- Make notes of observations that have given rise to concern, including dates, times and sign them. Distinguish between what you have directly observed and what was reported by someone else. Make notes of discussions with your colleagues, decisions taken and reasons for the decisions. Do not record personal judgements or opinions. All such records are strictly confidential and must be kept in a safe, secure place that cannot be accessed by anyone other than yourself or a senior colleague. You may need to share records with the appropriate authorities if there is an investigation.

- Ask for an informal discussion with your contact in the local authority children's services department or NSPCC to help decide whether you need to make an immediate referral.
- Share your concerns with the parents or carers of the child concerned (but see next section).

Sharing your concerns with parents

A senior worker may decide to share concerns with the parents of the child. This will require a great deal of sensitivity. If you notice bruises or injuries, it would be useful to ask the child and parent how the injury happened. There is likely to be a reasonable explanation. If a child is displaying aggressive, withdrawn or over-compliant behaviour, again the parent or child may be able to suggest reasons – conflict at home or a bereavement, for example. However, it is important not to take on the role of an investigator. Do not question the replies you receive, or attempt to probe or cross-examine. It may be that the parent is the abuser or a close relative or partner of the abuser. There may be a risk that the child will be blamed for your concerns, or that additional pressure will be placed on the child 'not to tell'. The abuser may make efforts to hide any further abuse. In extreme cases, it could put the child in further danger. If in any doubt, make the referral immediately, but stay calm and do not panic.

Responding to a child's disclosure of abuse

If a child tells you that he or she is being abused, stay calm. Your reaction to such disclosure is very important. It is important to contain any feelings such as shock or distaste. If you find you are unable to deal with the disclosure yourself, ask someone else to take over, staying sensitive to the child's needs.

Listen to the child, without probing or rushing, trying to understand their perspective and without jumping to conclusions. Support and reassure the child, and respond to any signs of distress. Reassure the child that he or she was right to talk to you. You may say, 'It's OK to tell me' and 'I am glad you have told me.' Use language appropriate to the age of the child and talk at the child's pace. Allow the child to talk and don't pressure the child into revealing more than he or she wishes to; you only need to know enough information to make a decision about referral. You should not physically examine the child or ask leading questions. A leading question is one that suggests to the child that you suspect or expect a particular answer. Examples of such questions are: 'Did someone do this to you?' or 'Has so-and-so been hurting you?' This could intimidate or confuse the child and complicate and undermine the role of the local authority or the NSPCC team if a referral is made.

Avoid making promises that you may not be able to keep. Do not promise confidentiality; reassure the child and explain that you will need to share the information with others who can help. Refer the information to the senior colleague responsible or to the local authority (children's services department) or the NSPCC as soon as you can.

Record everything that was said and done as soon as possible after the disclosure, with the date and time and keeping the report as factual as you can. Be clear about the evidence you have personally observed and any information you have received from other sources, such as background information. Keep all the information confidential, preferably in a locked cupboard. Remember that it is *not* the playworker's responsibility to investigate.

Some preparation will enable you to deal better with disclosure. You can prepare by getting to know the child protection procedures at your play setting, getting support for yourself, being mentally prepared for what a child may disclose to you and by attending good child protection training.

Making a referral

Initial contact

The senior playworker should know the contact number of the local child protection agency (usually the local authority children's services department or social services, but

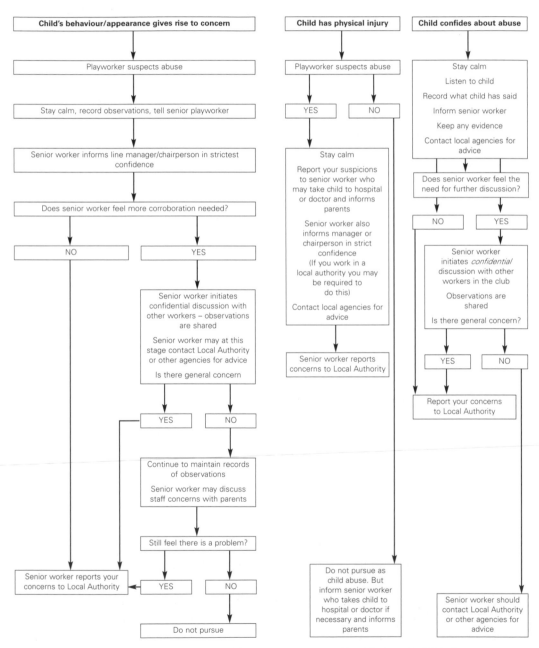

Flow chart of actions following an incident, or suspected incident, of child abuse

could be NSPCC or the police), and will usually be the person who makes the referral. Out of hours, or if the child protection workers are not available, the duty social worker will be able to take the referral. If you cannot speak to the person you want, ask to speak to his or her senior. Keep trying until you speak to an appropriate person. If the child is already known to the local authority, try to speak with the allocated social worker.

Make sure you have the details (name, address, date of birth) of the child to hand and that you can give a clear description of the incidents or observations that have led you to make the referral. Ask for the name and the job title of the person to whom you speak and ask what will happen next. Keep a record of your conversation and the name of your contact. Agree what the child and parent will be told, when and by whom. You should follow up your telephone referral in writing within 48 hours. The children's services department will then acknowledge your referral within one working day of receiving it. If you have not heard from them within three working days, contact them again.

What action will the local authority take?

After acknowledging your referral in writing, the local authority will make an 'initial assessment' – this helps them to decide if the child is in need and if a more detailed 'core assessment' is required. If the incident is very serious or potentially life threatening, the social worker may come to your setting immediately and talk to you and the child. You will need to organise the time and space for this. It is more likely that the investigation team will make other enquiries to help them build up a fuller picture. This may take some time, as they may want to speak to the child's school, health visitor or doctor before approaching the parents or carers and child. The local authority should contact you in writing about their decision. If you are anxious and have heard nothing, you can telephone your contact to find out what is happening.

If anyone telephones you asking for information in connection with a child protection investigation, ask for their name and telephone number and tell them you will call them back. This way you can check that they are who they say they are – and not give out information inappropriately. If you need time to think about what you want to say, take the telephone number and arrange to ring back later. If you are in any doubt, give no information and refer the matter immediately to your supervisor or your contact in the local authority.

What happens after the initial assessment?

When the local authority have made their assessment, they will decide what further action is necessary. If a decision is made that the child is suffering or likely to suffer significant harm, they will arrange a 'strategy discussion' – a forum for exchange of information and discussion about the alleged or suspected abuse with all the relevant agencies (which may include a representative from your play setting). The strategy discussion will provide an opportunity to:

- work cooperatively and share information
- agree what immediate action is needed to safeguard the child
- decide what information to share with the family and when
- decide whether or not to undertake s47 enquiries (Section 47 of the Children Act 1989 places a duty on the local authority to investigate the circumstances of a child at risk). This may include a 'core assessment' and a 'child protection conference'
- agree tasks for those involved
- agree what further help or support may be needed.

ACTIVITY   Making a referral

Find out:

- how you make a referral in your local area
- what happens after a referral has been made
- (if you are the senior worker) who you can talk to informally within children's services department of the local authority to get informal advice and support if you are concerned.

CASE STUDY   Anxieties about making a referral

Hazel, a senior playworker, has had to make her first referral to the local authority. Here she discusses how she felt:

Having run our after school club and playscheme for 11 years, I recently made my first ever referral to the child protection team at our social services department. It is one of the hardest things I have ever had to do. I nearly didn't do it, I was scared about what might happen – I didn't know the process and I was worried about what the parents and other family would say. And I was really scared of being wrong. But now I know I did the right thing, judging from what the child protection team have said. The rest of the playworkers have been great – very supportive and caring, which is helping a lot.

I still feel upset about it. Sometimes I even feel that maybe I shouldn't have said anything – but I just have to think about what that child went through, and what I have stopped, and it reminds me I did the right thing. Deciding to make a referral wasn't an easy thing to do by any means, but I talked it over with my manager and social services before I made the referral – and they helped me to know if things needed to be taken further. They have been very professional and supportive.

Anxieties about making a referral and dealing with parents

You may be aware of stories in the national press about children being taken away from their homes in the middle of the night, or about over-zealous social workers taking children into care only for it to emerge that allegations of abuse were unfounded. You may have a good relationship with the parents of the child and be reluctant to discuss your concerns behind their back. You might worry about the consequences of a parent finding out that you have made the referral and even fear for your own safety.

In such situations, remember these points:

- your first responsibility is for the welfare of the child
- many parents will recognise this and appreciate that you made the referral out of concern
- it is not your responsibility to make judgements – only to share your concerns

- if someone else has already expressed concerns about the child to the child protection team, your views might be essential additional information in building up a complete picture.

Don't rely on someone else making the referral. Remember: 'The consequences of reporting suspected abuse and being wrong can be difficult. The consequences of not reporting suspected child abuse could be fatal' (*Protecting Children*, NSPCC).

It may be helpful if you ensure that parents are aware of your legal responsibilities from the beginning. Include a statement about your child protection procedures in the written information you give to parents when the child first comes to your play setting, alongside statements on equal opportunities and health and safety. This could read:

- 'Like all childcare workers, we have a responsibility to protect the children in our care, and will share our concerns with the local authority if we fear a child may be suffering abuse or neglect.'

or:

- 'The staff are always ready to discuss with you any concerns you have about your child. Our first responsibility is to the children in our care. If we have any concerns about the welfare or safety of a child, we have a duty to share these concerns with the appropriate authority.'

The role of the play setting in preventing abuse

Support for families

Play settings can provide a vital role as part of the support that can be offered to families or children under stress. Parents know that within the play setting their children are well cared for and receive stimulation and support from peers and adults that may not always be possible at home. Parents whose children are cared for within a play setting may be gaining time to pursue other work, training, rest or support. This may be essential for their own personal development and self-esteem and necessary for them to be able to continue their parenting role in a way that encourages the healthy development of their children.

Support for children

You may have children in your play setting who have been abused or who are on the child protection register. The role of the playworker as an important and caring professional in the lives of such children is increasingly recognised.

Play itself can be very therapeutic in enabling a child to come to terms with all kinds of traumatic or distressing experience, but play therapy is a specialist area and you should not attempt to become an amateur psychologist in setting up or interpreting a child's play for therapeutic purposes without training, help and support.

Protective behaviour for children and playworkers

Relationships based on openness and trust

All children need to learn about human relationships, trust, affection and love. What is appropriate physical touching depends on the nature of the relationship – mother and baby, father and daughter, brother and sister, teacher and pupil, doctor and patient, two toddler friends or adolescent lovers. Children who are abused are made part of relationships that are distorted from those considered acceptable by the rest of society.

This damages the trust built up within the relationship of the child and someone more powerful than themselves and they may find it difficult to establish the ground rules for future relationships.

In your play setting you can encourage relationships based on openness, honesty and trust, where keeping secrets is *not* positively valued and telling tales is not penalised. You can discuss the difference between happy secrets or surprises and secrets that make children uncomfortable or unhappy. You cannot agree to keep what a child says confidential until you know what it is about. Explain that you may need to talk to someone else in order to help.

Personal safety

Help children to recognise situations that make them feel uncomfortable and to learn that it is alright to say, 'no'. This applies to any activity within the play setting that makes them feel uncomfortable or unhappy but should not prevent you from finding ways to gently encourage the child to participate in activities which are challenging. Peg Flandreau West of Protective Behaviours Inc. links concepts of personal safety with adventurousness:

> *We cannot promise ourselves, or make a promise to others, that we can be safe all the time. We can promise that we can act to feel safe all the time. The extension of this attitude is that we can feel safe and empowered even while dealing with physically dangerous situations.*
>
> (West 1989)

You can encourage the children to feel good about themselves and their bodies. Play opportunities such as drama, role play and activities related to a topic, for example 'myself', can promote self-awareness and respect. Discuss what language and behaviour are abusive and what to do if you encounter it, such as being assertive or reporting it to an adult. Go over the ground rules of the play setting at regular intervals, and discuss what behaviour is unacceptable.

Through play, children can test and challenge their fears and anxieties. They can develop strategies and get support to overcome their anxieties and know when to say, 'yes' as well as when to say, 'no'. Play opportunities that give children choices and empower them to make decisions and take the lead can enable them to recognise and express their feelings. With support, they can develop strategies to face challenges, overcome fears and develop confidence and adventurousness.

Play helps children feel confident to express themselves

> ### ACTIVITY — Recruitment procedures
>
> Find out what recruitment procedures are used in your play setting. Are they the same for paid staff and volunteers? Examples:
>
> - take-up of references, examining past experience to check the reasons for any unexplained gaps in work records
> - interviewing for appropriate skills, understanding of and interest in playwork
> - criminal record bureau checks
> - a probationary period where a new worker or volunteer works under the close supervision of another member of staff.
>
> Discuss with a senior staff member or manager whether and how the procedures safeguard against appointing abusers.

Looking at your own behaviour

Male playworkers in particular are often anxious about how their behaviour might be perceived. Physical contact when playing with and caring for children is important. Good recruitment procedures of staff *and volunteers* can include some safeguards against appointing abusers.

Children may demand physical affection beyond what you feel is appropriate. An older child or adolescent may develop a 'crush' on you, want to hold your hand all the time or to sit on your lap or be kissed. A younger child may want to sit on your lap for a story or on a swing or constantly involve you in rough and tumble play. It is your responsibility to set clear boundaries in your relationships with the children and to deal with any inappropriate advances assertively, without rejecting the child. Explain to the child clearly what is or is not appropriate and why. For example, you might say: 'I don't want you to sit on my lap, it is not comfortable for me and stops me from talking to the others. Would you like to sit next to me here?'; or 'I'm glad that you like my company and I've enjoyed our game. I am going to work with some other children now but I think Terry might like a game.' You may need support from other team members in this, to back you up or to ensure that children who need physical contact are not rejected.

Matters of personal hygiene – taking a child with special needs to the toilet, for example, or changing for swimming – may also be an issue. Some childcare and play facilities have a policy that there should always be two workers present in these situations or that the door should always be left open. However, the child's right to privacy must also be considered. You could have a policy of always letting another member of staff know when you need to accompany a child to the toilet and of making sure that this is not always left to the same member of staff. When taking children on trips it is important to have both male and female playworkers so that the children can be escorted to public toilets or helped with changing for swimming.

Discuss any concerns you might have about the expectations of others and your own role. The procedures of your play setting should protect against the possibility of child abuse within the play setting and protect you from being open to false accusations.

Summary

Abuse of children is relatively rare, but anyone who works with children should be aware that it does occur – and should attend good-quality training to help spot the signs of abuse and the appropriate actions to take. Your play setting's child protection policy must link in with the policy of your local safeguarding children board (LSCB), and every member of staff should know the appropriate procedures to take in the event of suspected, reported and disclosed abuse.

Your play setting can help support staff, parents and children by displaying a statement stating your duties with regards to child protection. Through play, children can learn 'protective behaviours' – such as recognising uncomfortable situations, trusting their instinctive feelings and saying, 'no' to something when they feel uncomfortable. Play and playwork can also help children develop confidence, security and self-reliance.

Reference

West, P. Flandreau (1989) *The Basic Essentials: Anti-victimization and Empowerment Process*. Protective Behaviours, Inc. (US), Essence Training and Publication Pty Ltd.

Further reading

Fair Play for Children (2002) *Child Protection in a Playwork Setting*. Fair Play for Children. Available from www.arunet.co.uk. Includes a model child protection policy.
Hobart, C. and Frankel, J. (2005) *Good Practice in Child Protection*. Nelson Thornes.

Websites

www.doh.gov.uk – the following key documents are available to download: 'What to do if you're worried a child is being abused' and 'Framework for the assessment of children in need and their families'.
www.kidscape.org.uk – very useful website with resources (many downloadable) about preventing bullying and child abuse.
www.protectivebehaviours.co.uk – information about helping children to feel safe.
www.there4me.com – interactive website from the NSPCC for 12–16 year olds, including confidential online advice.
www.worriedneed2talk.org.uk – another NSPCC website for young people, includes support notes for professionals.

CHAPTER 12
Health, safety and well-being

The fishermen know that the sea is dangerous and the storm terrible, but they never found these dangers sufficient reason for remaining ashore.

(From *Dear Theo*, autobiography of Vincent Van Gogh)

There are potential dangers all around us. Fishermen learn how to assess how hazardous the sea is in different conditions and take precautionary measures – a sound boat, skilled crew and lifesaving equipment – to minimise the risks to their safety. Children must also learn how to become responsible for their own safety and need opportunities to develop their skills and judgement to do this. Through play, children try out their skills and gain understanding of their own abilities, achievements and limitations. An awareness of health and safety issues belongs to all aspects of playwork. This chapter looks more closely at how playworkers can ensure the health and safety of children in the day-to-day activities and use of the play setting and how they can help children to develop their own awareness of health and safety matters. In this chapter, we will consider:

- A healthy, safe and secure environment for play
- Playwork and children's health
- Food preparation
- General hygiene matters
- Promoting healthy living
- Emergency procedures

A healthy, safe and secure environment for play

Children need to feel secure about their play setting. They have the right to expect that playworkers will make sure that the premises, activities and play materials do not expose them to unacceptable risks to their health and safety. However, it may not always be clear what are acceptable and unacceptable risks in play. Some play settings feel compelled by fear of accidents and possible litigation to reduce and control the play opportunities they provide. As a playworker, you can find yourself in an uncomfortable position. On the one hand, the principles of playwork and your role put the case for children to be able to play in their own way and for their own reasons. This may well involve getting dirty, making a mess and undertaking some activities that challenge boundaries – their own and others' – as their right and as part of their essential learning and development. On the other hand, you know that the buck stops with you in terms of responsibility and the blame you might get from a child, parent, employer or solicitor if something goes wrong and you are perceived to have acted negligently or without due care and attention for the children.

Every year an estimated 1.2 million children under 15 visit a hospital accident and emergency (A&E) department in the UK following an accident away from home (the figure for home-based accidents is also over a million). Children aged 5–14 have 86 per cent of non-home child accidents. Only around 8 per cent of these happen in sports areas and approximately 10 per cent in recreational areas, far lower than educational areas (34 per cent) and transport areas (14 per cent). Streets and car parks are particular danger areas for young children away from home. Every year, over 200 children are killed in road accidents and thousands are injured. They are at greatest risk as pedestrians.

So, while playgrounds are statistically relatively safe places for children to be, playworkers need to be aware of safety issues and understand their responsibilities under the law. They need to have a commonsense approach to accident prevention. A definition of an accident in a play setting is 'an unplanned and uncontrolled event which has led to or could have caused injury to persons, damage to premises, equipment or other loss'. Much of what happens in play is by definition 'unplanned and uncontrolled' and it is therefore particularly important that injury or other negative consequences are avoided through skilled risk assessment and supervision.

Play may well involve some activities that challenge boundaries and enable children to take risks

Identifying hazards and assessing risks

To prevent accidents, you must identify what is likely to cause them. Safety issues need to be discussed within your team so that you can reach agreement on what are acceptable and unacceptable risks and the roles and responsibilities of individuals for health and safety matters. When looking at the safety of your own play setting you will need to decide what might be a danger to the safety of the children and what to do about it. Initially you should identify the hazards and assess the risks.

A *hazard* is something that could cause harm to someone. A *risk* is how likely it is that a hazard will cause actual harm. Your play setting will probably contain lots of hazards and what you and your colleagues should decide is whether the risk involved is acceptable or not.

You can involve the children in identifying hazards by playing 'dangerous places' where children are asked to look around the space either indoor or out and are asked to go and stand in a space or next to something they think could be dangerous. The group then discuss the potential dangers and how they could reduce the risk. This is a good game for encouraging children to assess risks themselves. Factors that might affect the level of risk include:

- age and stage of development of the children (for example in using tools)
- experience of children (for example in building and tending open fires)
- weather conditions (for example in using some outdoor equipment)
- level of supervision and staff/child ratios (for example in trips to open water)
- experience of supervisors (for example training in first aid/life guarding).

Playwork can take place in a variety of situations and you need to be able to undertake risk assessments wherever you are working with children – including open-access parks, woodland or by open water such as rivers or the beach.

ACTIVITY   Identifying hazards and assessing risks

1 Walk around your play facility. Look at the buildings, from floor to ceiling. What things in the building might cause harm to children? How might this occur? Make a list.

2 Discuss with your colleagues and managers which things on your list present an acceptable risk and which need to be removed or replaced. (See preceding examples.)

3 Do the same in your outside play area and with your play equipment.

4 Now imagine the following situations. What immediate action would you take in the following situations?

- You are in the outside area of your play setting before the children arrive and you find broken glass bottles near the perimeter fence.

- You are chatting to some children playing on a tyre swing and you notice the rope is frayed and thin.

- As you are looking around the play setting before leaving, you find that two sharp woodwork tools have been left on the floor.

- A child brings in a glass-painting kit that used to belong to his sister, but which he has said can be donated to your play setting. The instructions are lost, but the child knows what to do and asks, 'Can we do some today?'

- What follow-up action would you take in each situation to try to ensure it was not repeated?

SPOTLIGHT ON   The role of risk taking in children's play

Risk taking is a part of everyday life. Without taking risks, we are not challenged and do not have the opportunities to develop new skills, explore what is possible or discover our potential. Almost every decision we take involves some level of risk.
   Questions a playworker might ask are:

1 How can you provide opportunities within your play setting that enable children to take risks and make choices about these risks that develop their skills of judgement and give them personal responsibility?

2 How do such opportunities differ from unacceptable risks in the play setting?

Identified hazard	Risk assessment
Climbing frame	While there is always the possibility that a child could fall from the climbing frame, everything has been done to minimise the risk. The structure complies with health safety standards, it is checked regularly for signs of wear and tear or vandalism, it is mounted on an approved surface, children are supervised appropriately and know and understand what is acceptable and unacceptable (dangerous) behaviour. If the climbing frame were removed it would limit the opportunity for children's play. In these conditions the climbing frame is an acceptable hazard and should stay
Broken glass in outside play area	Obvious hazard with unacceptable risk. It limits children's play opportunities and is a danger to them. Outside area should be checked before every session, and broken glass and other rubbish removed
Frayed rope on tyre swing	Danger to children. Unacceptable risk – needs to be replaced immediately
Matches	Potential danger to children. Necessary in play setting for cooking and maybe candles or bonfires? Need to consider when can children use matches themselves and what supervision is required. Secure storage so that children cannot get hold of and use matches inappropriately. Acceptable risk given these points
Cleaning materials	Cleaning materials will be necessary, but need to consider safe storage and who will have access to them (see COSHH Regulations, page 209)
Woodwork tools	Can cause injury but can also encourage and extend children's play opportunities. Need to consider age and ability of children using the tools, supervision, safe behaviour, appropriate use and storage and maintenance of tools

The BSI Kitemark means that the product has been tested by the British Standards Institution and will be regularly checked by qualified inspectors to ensure it reaches the agreed standards for safety

The CE mark means that the manufacturer claims that the products meet the standards of the relevant European Union directives

SPOTLIGHT ON The BSI Kitemark and CE marks

The BSI Kitemark means that the product has been tested by the British Standards Institution and will be regularly checked by qualified inspectors to ensure it reaches the agreed standards for safety. The CE mark means that the manufacturer claims that the products meet the standards of the relevant European Union directives. As a playworker using the product you must still follow instructions and ensure it is properly used, stored and maintained.

Who is responsible?

Children have the right to expect that the playworkers have taken steps to prevent them from coming to any harm in the play setting. Playworkers' views on what these steps are will vary from one worker to another. You will have your own views on what is an 'acceptable risk'. By law, all employers are responsible for making the workplace a healthy and safe place to work. Employees have the duty to take reasonable care of themselves and others affected by their work, and to cooperate with their employers on all matters relating to health and safety. If you share the premises and occupy a building owned by another group, you are also legally bound to have regard for the safety of yourselves and others using the premises. If your play setting is run or managed by a large organisation such as a local authority, you will have your own health and safety representative who can be called on for advice. A large organisation will also have health and safety policies and procedures that you must follow. In a smaller organisation, such as a voluntary community playscheme, it is important that clear health and safety guidelines and procedures are drawn up by management and staff and given to all those who are affected. Such guidelines and procedures should make clear who is responsible for doing what.

The following activity will help you identify clearly who is responsible and what your own responsibilities are. You can use a grid or checksheet as illustrated on page 199. If you do not know the answers to the questions in this activity, discuss them with your senior colleague or manager. While you yourself may not be responsible for most of these activities, you need to know who is so that you can report any problems, breakages, hazards or concerns promptly to the right person.

ACTIVITY Who is responsible?

1 Write down who is responsible in your play setting for:
- carrying out checks of premises and play materials

- ensuring buildings and materials are properly maintained and in a good state of repair
- reporting breakages or replacing worn items
- monitoring that health and safety policies are being followed by all concerned
- reviewing health and safety policies if they are not working.

2 Make a checklist of all aspects of your premises and equipment that need checking for reasons of safety – daily, weekly, once a term or once a year.

3 Write on the list who should check each item and what you should do if you find a problem with any of the items on the list.

4 Where it is your responsibility to check a particular item, write down how often you should check and how you will check each time (see example on page 199).

Arrivals and departures

The times when children arrive at and leave the play setting are often those during which accidents are most likely to occur. This is because there are frequently many other people on the premises, such as parents and carers collecting or delivering children. You and your colleagues are busy with setting out or tidying up play materials or giving or receiving information about children. Points of access and departure can in themselves be hazardous if, for example, people are able to leave prams or buggies in narrow entrance halls or if the play setting is close to a busy road or car park. If you work in a playcare setting, you need to know who has permission to collect each child at the end of the session. You must not let the child go with any other person unless you have authorisation in advance from the child's usual carer. You also need to know who to contact if a child does not arrive when expected or is not collected. Do not take the child to your home. As a final resort, if no contact can be made with the carer, call the duty social worker at your local authority children's services department.

 ACTIVITY Observing arrivals and departures

1 Spend 20 minutes at the beginning and at the end of a session observing the arrivals at and departures from your place of work.

2 Ask yourself:

- Is the supervision of children adequate at all times?
- Do children know where to collect their coats?
- Are there opportunities for playworkers to communicate with parents or carers on urgent matters?
- Do children know what they can do if they have to wait for their parents or carers to collect them or to talk to the playworkers?
- Are there any problems with traffic congestion or road safety outside the setting?

3 Discuss your observations with colleagues. Is there any way in which arrival and departure times should be changed to improve safety?

EXAMPLE

NAME OF GROUP:

DATE:

Safety checklist

What needs checking	Who will check	How to check	How often to check	Action if faulty/who to report to
Building				
Floors (trip hazards etc.)	Supervisor	Visual check	Daily	Remove hazard
Windows	Supervisor	Test	Daily	Report to caretaker
Doors	Supervisor	Test	Daily	School head / Management committee
Outside areas				
Perimeter fence and gates	Assistant 1	Visual	Daily	Remove hazard –
Ground area (for rubbish etc.)	Assistant 1	Visual	Daily	Report to:
Structures/fixed equipment	Health & safety officer – city council	Detailed survey	Monthly	Report to health & safety / Report to repairs section
Equipment				
Play materials out:	Assistant 2	Visual/	Daily	Remove/replace
Tools	Assistant 2	Test	before use	Report to supervisor
Electrical	Whoever uses it	Test before use	Before use	Send for repair / Report to:
Fire prevention				
Procedures displayed	Supervisor	Visual		Report to: management
Fire exits	Supervisor	Visual	Daily	Get advice from fire department
Extinguishers	Supervisor	Visual		
Fire blanket	Supervisor	Visual		
Fire drills	Supervisor	Carry out	3 x a year	Repeat drill
Emergencies				
First-aid box	Named first aider	Visual	Once a week	Replace used items
Procedures displayed		Visual	Daily	Ensure new procedures displayed
Other items				
Storage shed	Assistant 1	Check secure	Daily	Report to management committee
Toilets	Assistant 2	Visual	Daily	
Cleaning materials	Supervisor	check complete & store correctly	Daily	Replace as required
Heating	Supervisor	Check comfortable temperature Fire guards etc.	Daily/as required	

Supervisor: Sarah
Assistant 1: Paul
Assistant 2: Brenda
Named first aider: Paul

Contact for health & safety – Local authority: Gill. Tel. 07777
Fire department: Tel. 006644
Caretaker: Tel 11113
Management rep for safety: Bill. Tel. 36666

Visits, trips and outings

Many play facilities will include outings and visits such as a trip to the park, to the swimming pool, to the nearest bit of woodland or a day trip to the seaside. Off-site activities demand particular attention to health and safety. While you would regularly check your outside play area, you cannot check the whole of your local park for hazards such as discarded syringes. Once again, it is important that you encourage children to take responsibility for their own safety. The ground rules for going off site need to be agreed and clearly understood by workers and children. They include when not to run ahead or cross the road and what to do if a child gets lost. Children should be made aware of any hazards they might come across during the outing such as waste materials, poisonous plants or deep water (see also Chapter 13 on organising and supervising travel).

Children need to become responsible for their own safety

Children do not grow up or live in totally safe environments. Through play, children can learn how to cope with dangers in everyday life, from crossing the road to handling tools, by understanding what can cause harm and learning how to protect themselves. It is not the aim of any play setting to provide a totally accident-proof, sterile setting, different and apart from the world in which the children live. Even if this were possible, it would severely limit the opportunities for play it could offer. Use your knowledge of child development and the needs, interests and abilities of the children in your care to plan appropriate activities. Use your knowledge of health and safety issues to enable children to develop independence in taking responsibility for their own safety. Talk to them about potential hazards and what to do if they encounter one. If children know where things are kept and how to put them away safely when they have finished with them and are involved in making the rules and decisions of the setting, they will be better able and more willing to take on this responsibility.

Children learn through imitation and example. You can provide good role models for safe behaviour and handling materials and equipment in a safe way. You could also plan activities specifically around health and safety topics or invite experts in to give talks or lead activities on topics such as fire, road safety and first aid.

Health and safety law

Health and safety legislation that may have a bearing on your work within the play setting includes:

- Health and Safety at Work Act 1974
- Health and Safety (First Aid) Regulations 1981

Through play children learn to take responsibility for their own safety

- Control of Substances Hazardous to Health Regulations 1988
- Electricity at Work Regulations 1989
- Health and Safety (Information to Employees) Regulations 1989
- Reporting of Injuries, Diseases and Dangerous Occurrences Regulations 1985
- Workplace (Health, Safety and Welfare) Regulations, 1992
- Management of Health and Safety at Work Regulations, 1992.

Health and safety law is enforced by one of two agencies: your nearest health and safety executive or your local authority environmental health department. You should have a Health and Safety at Work Act information poster (published by HMSO and available from large bookstores) displayed where staff can see it. Alternatively, employees can be given leaflets covering the same information. On the poster, there is a space for filling in the address and contact number of your health and safety enforcement office. If there are more than five people employed in your organisation you must, by law, have your own health and safety policy for the setting.

Insurance and transport

All play settings employing staff must be insured against employer's liability and a copy of the employer's liability certificate must be displayed – in the office if you have one (Employer's Liability (Compulsory Insurance) Act 1969). It is a requirement for all play settings to have public liability insurance. Buildings should also be insured, although this will probably be the responsibility of whoever owns the building. Additional insurance may be needed to cover materials and equipment (contents), personal effects and special events such as overnight stays or trips and outings (see Chapter 13 for more on organising and supervising travel).

Playwork and children's health

The role of the playworker regarding children's health

As a playworker you have a responsibility to:

- be aware of what can affect children's health
- get information regarding the individual child's health needs
- act on information regarding individual health needs
- provide an environment within the play setting which promotes healthy development
- encourage children to take responsibility for their own health, in and outside the play setting.

However experienced you are as a playworker, you should not allow yourself to be regarded as a medical expert either by children or parents. Information about the best way to deal with health issues changes frequently. Medical advice should be sought from qualified medical practitioners such as health visitors and GPs. Ensure that any reference material you have in the play setting is up to date.

What affects children's health?

Just about everything! Some diseases are inherited, as are the chances of getting certain diseases later in life. The environment into which we are born and live can affect our health

Disease and incubation period	Period when infectious	Period of exclusion of infected person	Period of exclusion of contacts
Bronchiolitis 5–8 days	During acute stage of illness	Until the person feels well	None
Chickenpox and shingles 13–21 days	1–2 days before to 5 days after spots develop	Until the spots have crusted over *and* the person feels well	If contact is a woman in last 3 weeks of pregnancy, seek advice from GP/obstetrician
Conjunctivitis 12–72 hours	During active infection	Until eye no longer appears infected	None
Diarrhoea and vomiting *(Campylobacter Cryptosporidiosis Dysentery Food poisoning Gastroenteritis Giardiasis Salmonellosis)* Varies, few hours to few days	While having symptoms of diarrhoea and vomiting	Until symptom free for 48 hours and the person feels well. In some circumstances you may need to seek advice from a consultant in communicable disease control (CCDC)	None
Fifth disease *(Erythema infectiosum or 'slapped cheek syndrome')* Variable 4–20 days	Infectious before onset of the rash	Until the person feels well	None
Glandular fever Probably 4–6 weeks	While virus present in saliva	Until the person feels well	None
Hand, foot and mouth disease 3–5 days	During acute stage of illness	Until the person feels well	None
Head and body lice *(Pediculosis)* Eggs hatch in 1 week	As long as eggs or lice remain alive	None if treated	None (household contacts should be treated at same time)
Hepatitis A *(Epidemic jaundice)* 2–6 weeks	Several days before first symptom until 7 days after onset of jaundice	Until 7 days after onset of jaundice *and* the person feels well	None (household contacts should seek advice from their GP)
Hepatitis B 6 weeks–6 months	Not infectious under normal school conditions	Until the person feels well	None
Herpes simplex *(Cold sore)* 2–21 days	During infection	None	None
HIV infection Variable	Not infectious under normal school conditions	None	None

Guide to communicable diseases. Always ask for expert medical advice when you need further information

Disease and incubation period	Period when infectious	Period of exclusion of infected person	Period of exclusion of contacts
Impetigo Commonly 4–10 days	As long as septic spots are discharging pus	Until responding to treatment *and* the spots have dried up	None
Measles 7–14 days	I day before first symptom until 4 days after onset of rash	Until 4 days after onset of rash *and* the person feels well	None
Meningitis 2–10 days depending on cause	Clinical cases are rarely infectious	Until the person feels well	None (household contacts may be given antibiotic treatment)
Mumps 12–25 days, commonly 18 days	7 days before and up to 9 days after onset of swelling	Until the person feels well	None
Ringworm on body *(Tinea corporis)* 4–10 days	As long as rash is present	None once under treatment	None
Rubella *(German measles)* 16–18 days	I week before and at least 4 days after onset of rash	Until the person feels well	None (if contact is pregnant woman, seek advice from GP)
Scabies Few days to 6 weeks	Until mites and eggs are destroyed by treatment	Until day after treatment	None (household contacts should be treated at same time)
Scarlet fever and streptococcal infection I–3 days	Day sore throat starts until 24 hours after antibiotics started	Until the person feels well	None
Threadworms 2–6 weeks for lifecycle to complete	When eggs are shed in the faeces (stools)	None after the treatment has started	None (household contacts should be treated at same time)
Tuberculosis *(TB)* Usually 4–6 weeks	Only when sputum contains bacteria	Until the person feels well	None (close contacts may need screening)
Verrucae *(Plantar warts)* 2–3 months	As long as wart is present	None	None
Whooping cough *(Pertussis)* 7–10 days	2–4 days before until 21 days after start of coughing. If treated with antibiotic, 5 days after starting course	Until the person feels well	None

Note: Treatment offered to household contacts may be extended to other close contacts

in many ways. Babies and children need food, shelter, responsive adults and opportunities to explore and develop skills, knowledge and understanding for healthy all-round development. A lack of any of these, such as poor nourishment, inadequate housing, neglect or abuse by parents or other carers, will have ill effects on healthy development. Other factors that can affect the health of the child include environmental hazards (pollution, constant loud noise), infection, accidents and poor hygiene. Economic and social factors affect the ability to provide a healthy environment. They include where the family lives, type of housing, money, access to healthcare and the awareness of parents and carers of health issues.

The health service places considerable importance on preventive healthcare in the child's early years. Doctors and health visitors give advice and support on issues relating to children's nutrition and general healthcare and have programmes for monitoring children's development.

Health issues within the play setting

Your play setting should have a general policy on health that includes:

- information on child's health required on registration
- information for parents and carers about when not to send a child to the play setting for health reasons
- policy on storing and administering medication
- emergency procedures.

Information about individual children

Ensure that parents or carers have included any important health information on the registration form. This is particularly important if the child needs to take medicines or has a condition that might need prompt medical treatment (allergies to wasp stings or peanuts, for example) or has other allergies or dietary requirements.

Communicable diseases

Communicable diseases are those that can be passed on to another person, including colds and influenza. Children suffering from communicable diseases are usually better off at home and may be a particular risk to other children – for example, to those who have a non-infectious illness such as leukaemia or sickle-cell disease or who need to take medication that makes it harder for them to fight off common infections. Staff should follow the same guidelines with regard to staying away from the play setting if they have a communicable illness. It is helpful if you refer to your health policy in a general information leaflet or prospectus for parents and carers of children who are new to the play setting. This might include: 'A child suffering from a communicable disease, other than HIV or Hepatitis B, should not be brought to the play setting until s/he is no longer infectious.'

Children with human immunodeficiency virus (HIV) or Hepatitis B are not normally excluded as these illnesses are only transmitted through exchange of body fluids and are not a risk if good hygiene practices are observed within the setting. HIV and AIDS have had a lot of scare-story publicity in the press. Contact an expert or attend training for the most up-to-date research findings into the causes and spread of any illness you are concerned about or if you need information. (Your area health authority should be able to give you contacts or try the appendix, at the end of the book.)

Where a child becomes ill within the play setting, playworkers need to reassure and comfort the child, ensure that she has somewhere to rest and contact the parent/carer or emergency contact on the child's registration form to ask them to collect the child.

Non-transmittable diseases

There are many chronic illnesses and conditions that cannot be passed on from one child to another. These include asthma, eczema, sickle-cell disease, cancers, thalassaemia, epilepsy, hay fever and all kinds of allergic reaction. Of these, asthma is the most common, with one in 10 children suffering from it at some time. About one in 400 African Caribbean people in Britain has sickle-cell disease.

A good, up-to-date, healthcare book (see further reading at the end of this chapter) is essential for your play setting and can give you full information about all such illnesses and conditions. Remember, too, that each child can be affected to a different degree. Some may feel ill nearly all the time, while others are affected severely only when they have a crisis in their illness. Talk to the parents and the children about their illness and what you can do to support them. Are there any observable warning signs for the onset of a crisis or attack? What medical intervention or support might be needed? Is the child more susceptible to common infections? Does he need to be kept warm or to avoid specific foods or other substances or conditions? Support children in dealing with their feelings about their illness or condition, and encourage them to take the lead in choosing and pacing their play to meet their needs and wishes. Encourage discussions within the play setting about the nature of different conditions. Give accurate information, in language appropriate to the age and development of the children. Focus on what each child can do rather than what they cannot.

Medication

In most cases, playworkers will not be expected to give medicines to children. If children are admitted who require ongoing medication, playworkers should have written permission and instructions from the child's parent or usual carer as to how and when it should be given to the child. The parent or carer should also demonstrate to the playworker how it should be given. Many older children will take responsibility for their own medication, but you will need to discuss this with the playworkers to agree storage arrangements for medicines and emergency procedures. Medicines must be stored in a secure place, inaccessible to other children. Some medicines need to be stored in the fridge. Check the expiry date of all medicines before use.

Food preparation

Your play setting may provide the children with a drink and a snack or a full-scale meal or the children may bring packed lunches. You may also undertake activities involving food as part of your play provision.

In all cases where food is consumed, aspects of hygiene must be considered. Before handling food, children need to wash their hands and to wear aprons to protect their clothes and to protect the food from fibres, dirt or loose buttons. Adults need to be good role models.

Food for health

Health experts agree that we should cut down on fats and sugars and increase our intake of fibre, fresh fruits and vegetables. Where possible use fresh unprocessed foods that are better for children's health than processed or refined ones.

Catering for different needs

Some children in your group will have specific dietary requirements and information on this should be obtained as part of the initial registration process (see Chapter 13). Many cultures have religious grounds for not eating certain foods. Others avoid certain foods for moral, ethical or health reasons. Respect individual and family beliefs and choices and to cater for specific requirements where possible. Vegetarian dishes are usually acceptable in a greater range of diets than meat dishes, as many diets specify avoidance of certain meat products. Bear this in mind when catering for a large group or in advance for a group whose dietary requirements are not known to you. Children with coordination or mobility difficulties may need their own adaptations to equipment to enable them to feed themselves and join the group for snacks or mealtimes. Such equipment – cutlery with especially thick handles, for example – should be obtained with the advice of parents, carers and specialists such as the child's occupational therapist, physiotherapist or support worker.

Involving children in food activities

Whatever part food plays within your play setting, children should where possible have the opportunity to be involved in the planning, preparation and serving. By joining in these activities children can:

- make their likes and dislikes known
- know that their needs and wishes are listened to
- develop skills, knowledge and understanding
- gain awareness of the needs of others
- learn about healthy eating
- develop hygiene awareness and good hygiene practice.

ACTIVITY   Food for health

1 If you offer snacks or meals can you offer:
   - wholemeal bread and flour rather than white?
   - fresh fruit rather than sweets, crisps or biscuits?
   - water, diluted fruit juice or milk instead of sweetened drinks with additives?
2 Display posters and books about food and healthy diets.
3 Involve the children in planning a week's menu of interesting and healthy snacks.

Involving children in food activities

Food preparation and the law

If you prepare or provide any food in your play setting, whether a snack or a full-scale hot meal, you must comply with the Food Safety Act 1990, the Food Hygiene (General) Regulations 1970 and the Food Hygiene (Amendment) Regulations 1990 and 1991. All people involved in providing food for others need to comply. You should register with the local authority food team. Your local authority environmental health department is responsible for enforcing this legislation. They will be able to give advice and guidance on how this legislation affects your play setting and where to get training in food hygiene and will inspect your facilities.

Employees should be encouraged to get all gastric or vomiting symptoms checked with their doctor. Sufferers should report to their supervisor or manager and should be removed from all food contact. Any illness that might have been caused by consumption of food eaten or prepared within the play setting should be reported to your local environmental health department.

Cleaning

All surfaces need to be cleaned regularly, in particular those used for food preparation, using an appropriate cleaning agent (see COSHH regulations, page 209). Use a food preparation board or plates that can be washed and disinfected. Wash fresh fruit and vegetables thoroughly before consumption. You will need somewhere to do the washing up where there is hot water. This should not be the same washbasin used for washing hands after going to the toilet. Paper towels or hot-air dryers are more hygienic than fabric towels for drying hands.

Storage

Some foods (meat, fish, dairy produce, precooked foods, sauces) need to be kept in the refrigerator at less than 8°C, and preferably less than 5°C. These and some other foods such as eggs, which are not fully cooked until hard, are particularly good breeding grounds for harmful bacteria such as salmonella. They are best avoided in the play setting unless you have access to a refrigerator. Even then, you will need to be rigorous in your hygiene practices (washing hands and cleaning food preparation boards) and methods of storage to avoid contamination passing from one kind of food to another – meat juices dripping in the refrigerator, for example. Other foods (flour, rice, cereal, sugar, biscuits) should be labelled and stored in a container or plastic bag, separately from other materials.

General hygiene matters

Good play opportunities often involve getting dirty. Digging in the mud, rolling on the ground, crawling through undergrowth or piles of dry leaves, getting covered in paint or glue or sloppy wet sand are all common examples of the kind of play you should be facilitating in your play setting. But play settings also need to develop and maintain good hygiene practices.

Poor hygiene is a major factor in the spread of disease. Children might need to be reminded to wash their hands after using the toilet, blowing their nose, touching pets or handling waste. Body fluids – in particular blood and faeces – can carry infection. You cannot catch diseases such as HIV or Hepatitis B by kissing, touching or sharing cups and crockery.

Cleaning of spillages of body fluids needs particular attention to hygiene, to protect the playworkers and the children, even if you believe there is no risk of yourself or anyone in your play setting carrying or becoming infected with these viruses. Where possible cover spillages with paper towels and then clean with an appropriate cleaning fluid (see COSHH regulations in the following Spotlight). Staff dealing with the spillage must wear disposable gloves. Cover any cuts, grazes or spots on your or the children's hands with a waterproof plaster before cleaning spillages. Dispose of all waste materials in a safe, secure manner – double wrap in leak-proof bags and mark as waste materials. Your local authority may supply specially marked bags for the disposal of contaminated waste materials.

ACTIVITY   Improving hygiene

Look at the hygiene practices within your workplace. Can you think of any ways of improving them?

Example: One playworker found that the same cloth was often inadvertently used for different cleaning purposes. She introduced different coloured cloths for cleaning – white for before and after food preparation, blue for art and craft, red for cleaning the floor.

Help with personal hygiene

Some children need help with regard to personal hygiene. Access to toilets and handwashing facilities need to be considered for children with specific mobility needs. For an older child with incontinence, particular washing or changing facilities may be required. Use every opportunity to encourage the children to be independently responsible for their own hygiene requirements. Again, individual children's needs should be assessed involving the child and the child's parents or carers. Specialist help – in making adaptations to equipment, for example – should be sought where required.

Play can be messy

> ### SPOTLIGHT ON · Legislation: COSHH regulations
>
> The COSHH (Control of Substances Hazardous to Health) regulations require employers to assess the use of all hazardous substances in the workplace, from paint to paraffin, from bleach to hair dye. In some cases this may mean that large organisations have a restricted list of cleaning materials allowed. Some prohibit the use of bleach, for example, but must recommend brand-name alternatives. This may be particularly significant if you share a premises (of a school, for example) and some cleaning agents are not allowed. In all cases, the use of substances hazardous to health needs to be assessed and control measures taken:
>
> - replace with less hazardous alternatives
> - store safely
> - follow instructions for use
> - wear protective clothing.
>
> Find out whether your play setting has restrictions on what cleaning materials can be used under COSHH regulations. What is the recommended cleaning agent for dealing with body fluid spillages? (Your local authority health and safety officer should be able to help if you are unsure.)

Promoting healthy living

You may see health education as the responsibility of schools, health service and the local authority. But children of all ages will ask questions about issues relating to health – from smoking, drugs and alcohol to sexual health, illness and disability. They will need honest and informed answers from adults whom they trust. Even a 5 year old may ask 'What is AIDS?' after seeing a television programme or advert.

Playworkers need to consider how to answer these questions appropriately, without breaching the trust of the child and carers. (See Chapter 6 on answering children's questions.) Older children and teenagers will almost certainly know someone who has had personal experience of some of these issues, if they have not had firsthand experience themselves. You need to be informed in order to give accurate information. If you feel unable to answer a question fully or accurately on the spot, you should know where to get the information from or where to refer the child who is doing the asking.

Management and staff should agree on appropriate ways of dealing with these issues when they arise. They may decide on active health promotion within the play setting, including inviting visitors with specialist knowledge. In the case of 5 and 6 year olds, this may be a 'Look after your teeth' campaign, for 14 and 15 year olds it might be 'HIV and AIDS awareness'. Remember that the primary purpose of a play setting is to facilitate children's play and meet their play needs and health promotion activities should not turn the play setting into a classroom. Seek the advice of your health authority or other recognised health advisory agency about any health promotion materials you wish to display or use in the play setting. There may be legal implications if you are perceived to be encouraging illegal acts, such as under-age heterosexual or homosexual sex, through discussion or distribution of materials relating to contraception and safe sex.

Smoking

The effects of smoking and secondary or passive smoking are well documented. Smoking increases the risks of developing a range of diseases including: chronic bronchitis, lung cancer and cardiovascular disease. A 'no smoking' policy should be maintained within the play setting.

ACTIVITY   Resources for health

Make a list of helpful sources of information and advice on health issues in your local area – including names, addresses and telephone numbers. You might include your local health visitor, community health unit, health education and voluntary organisations. Use the local library, telephone book (look under 'regional health authority' and 'local authority' district/city/county council) and the list of national organisations in the appendix. Many national organisations have local contacts. Next to each contact, make a note of when you think you would need the advice or support of that particular organisation.

Discuss your list with the senior worker and colleagues. If they agree, contact two or three people on your list. Ask them what advice and support they can offer your play setting. Can they suggest other useful contacts?

Looking after yourself

As well as looking after the health needs of the children in your care you will need to consider your own health needs. There are many factors that may affect your health outside the play setting. Part of working as a member of a team is giving and receiving support from other team members (see Chapter 10). Examples of conditions within the play setting that could adversely affect your own as well as the children's health include:

- poor light and ventilation
- moving heavy play equipment
- stress.

Lifting

It is very important that you use correct lifting techniques before moving heavy equipment. You can encourage the children to do the same:

- assess the weight of the load
- assess centre of gravity of load
- check for sharp edges
- get help/use a trolley
- follow correct lifting technique.

Stress

Stress can lead to depression and is one of the most common reasons for people taking time off work. If you are experiencing stress at work it may be because you are feeling unsupported – whether in dealing with the behaviour of a child, parent or colleague, having unrealistic demands made on your time, skills or energy or simply feeling put upon or

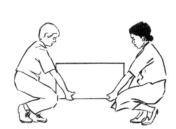
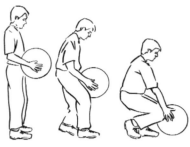

Assess the weight

Use mechanical aids where possible

Get help and work as a team

Lift in stages, taking the load on your knees first and then to the carrying position. The middle of the load should be level with your waist

Use correct lifting technique

unappreciated. It is important to communicate the reasons clearly to colleagues and management as early as possible, so that you and they can take all possible steps to maintain a healthy working environment for all.

Emergency procedures

Dealing with accidents and injuries

Each play setting will need to have its own emergency procedures written down and displayed so that all staff, including temporary staff and volunteers, are aware of them. They should include named first aider, location of first-aid box and local emergency telephone contacts. The following is a sample 'code of practice' for dealing with accidents and injuries. (*Note*: this is a suggested code of practice only. Actions will not necessarily be carried out in this order or by one individual only):

- Keep calm.
- Reassure and comfort injured child.
- Protect the child and others involved from further risk.
- Assess injury without moving the child.
- Diffuse the situation – explain the situation and reassure or distract non-injured children.
- Get cover to supervise children.
- Give clear and accurate information about what has happened to appropriate staff member, named first aider, emergency services or administer first aid as appropriate and according to agreed procedures of your setting.
- Contact injured child's parent or carer.
- If parent not contactable, accompany child to hospital in ambulance if necessary.
- Record accident in accident book.
- Explain accident to parent/carer.
- Report accident to appropriate authority (see later, under 'Legislation: reporting accidents').
- Report any problems encountered with the play setting's emergency procedures to the responsible colleague.

First aid

Knowledge of and training in first aid saves lives in those vital minutes before the emergency services arrive. Ideally, all playworkers should have a working knowledge of first aid. At least one worker should hold a first-aid certificate from a nationally recognised organisation such as the Red Cross or St John Ambulance. These certificates are usually valid for three years, when they need to be updated through further training. As first aid is a skill best developed through such practical training, this book does not cover first aid knowledge and skills; instead practical experience and further reading is recommended. If you are working in playwork or childcare, it is highly recommended that you do a certificated course in first aid. In particular, you will need to know about how to deal with unconsciousness and bleeding. There are several good first-aid manuals on the market and every play setting should have access to one of these.

All play settings require a properly equipped first-aid kit. One person should be responsible for making sure the first-aid kit is always fully stocked. Keep a list of contents within the first-aid kit. The first-aid kit should be stored in a safe place that is easily accessible to staff. The box or cupboard in which it is stored should be marked with the first-aid symbol – a white cross on a green background. The following list is an example of the contents for a first-aid box for 30 children between the ages of 5 and 12:

- card or leaflet giving general guidance
- sterile triangular bandages (4)
- non-allergic adhesive plasters
- sterile eye pad with attachment (2)
- assorted dressings (medium) (12)
- assorted dressings (large) (6)
- assorted dressings (extra large) (3)
- assorted adhesive dressings (plasters) (30)
- safety pins
- paper tissues
- plastic disposable gloves
- disposable bag for soiled material.

Do not keep medicines or antiseptic creams and liquids. Medicines should be given only with proper consent and instructions and should be stored separately. Creams, liquids and sprays can cause allergic reactions. Plasters can also cause reactions, so use hypoallergenic brands and ask a question about allergies, including allergies to plasters, on your enrolment or registration form.

CASE STUDY   First aid saves lives

An adolescent boy was playing 'Sardines' with a group of younger children. He was eventually found in a shed, unconscious and blue having suffered a major heart attack. The two responsible adults gave resuscitation for 25 minutes until the ambulance arrived, keeping him breathing and saving his life.

What would happen if a similar incident occurred in your play setting?

In case of fire

The fire drill procedures should be displayed. They will include what action to take and the assembly point for calling the register. Staff should know who will check the building (including toilets) and who will collect the register and children's records. Your local fire department can give advice. Ideally, alternative premises should be identified locally where children can wait in bad weather while parents are contacted or until the premises are made safe.

There are two main acts on fire safety: the Fire Services Act 1947 and the Fire Precautions Act 1971 as amended by the Fire Safety and Safety of Places of Sport Act 1987. Fire departments are required to give advice free of charge to any person or regulatory authority who requests it. Certain premises require a fire certificate. The main points of concern are:

- the means of escape (easily accessible and kept clear)
- the firefighting equipment (extinguishers and fire blanket)
- means of warning in the event of fire
- heating and fire guards; electrical safety; storage of flammable materials
- staff awareness of procedures and practice of fire drills.

ACTIVITY   Health and safety quiz

1 Does your workplace have a health and safety policy? What does it include?

2 Is your play setting registered by Ofsted (or other regulating body)? If so, where is the registration certificate displayed and are there any special conditions? If not, what are the reasons for this? (For example, does it fall outside registration criteria?)

3 Has the fire officer inspected the premises and made any recommendation?

4 Are emergency procedures and procedures for evacuating the building on display?

5 Do you know where the fire extinguishers and fire blanket are to be found and how and when to use them?

6 When and how often are fire drills carried out?

7 Who is qualified in first aid within the play setting? When do their qualifications need updating?

8 Are there procedures for ensuring the safe arrival and departure of children from the setting?

9 Who has responsibility for checking safety of premises and equipment on a day-to-day basis? Is there a formal process for assessing risks within the setting including for new activities, trips or outings? When and how do they carry this out?

10 Do bought toys and equipment comply to British and/or European health and safety standards?

Summary

As a playworker, you have responsibilities for the health, safety and well-being of the children who come to your play settings. It is important that you are clear about these responsibilities and keep yourself up to date with changes in the law and that you have good links with relevant agencies (fire, police, environmental health) who can advise and support you. It is also important to keep first-aid qualifications up to date. Playworkers need to balance understanding of potential hazards and risks in play with their understanding of the developmental and play needs of children. It is an important function of play to enable children to explore, experiment and push boundaries through creating challenging opportunities for themselves and for each other. Through play, children learn to assess and manage hazards for themselves.

References

Child accident statistics from: www.rospa.com/factsheets/child_accidents.pdf July 05.

Stone, I. (ed.) (1969) *Dear Theo*: *An Autobiography of Vincent Van Gogh*. New Amer Library.

Further reading

Health and Safety Executive CRR (2002) *Playgrounds: Risks, Benefits and Choices –* www.hse.gov.uk/research/.

Lindon, J. (2003) *Too Safe for Their Own Good? Helping Children Learn about Risk and Lifeskills*. National Children's Bureau.

Play Safety Forum (2002) *Managing Risk in Play Provision*. Children's Play Council. Available to download from www.ncb.org.uk.

Playlink (1997) *Risk and Safety in Play: The Law and Practice for Adventure Playgrounds*. Spon Press.

Whiting, M. and Lobstein, T. (1998) *The Nursery Food Book*. Edward Arnold. (Nutritional information, food activities and multicultural recipes easy to adapt for older children.)

www.4children.org.uk for example policy documents and briefing available.

Useful reference books for the play setting

Paterson, G. (2002) *First Aid for Children Fast*. Dorling Kindersley.

Smith, T. (2000) *Complete Family Health Guide*. Dorling Kindersley.

CHAPTER 13
Playwork paperwork

I love being a writer. What I can't stand is the paperwork.

(Peter de Vries, American novelist and satirist)

Many playworkers love being a playworker but can't stand the paperwork. However, it's an essential aspect of the work for many reasons. While it should not get in the way of the primary purpose of playwork – to be in the service of the child at play – a level of accurate and efficient paperwork is necessary to ensure the smooth management of the setting, enabling it to run safely and within the law.

Each play setting will have a different system for administration and record keeping. The kind of information and records you keep in your play setting will depend on its aims, organisation, staffing and legal status. This chapter also looks at aspects of dealing with money, which, particularly in smaller settings, is often part of the job of a playworker. In this chapter, we will consider:

- Access procedures
- Recording and keeping information
- Organising trips and outings
- Working with money

Access procedures

Dealing with enquiries

Who is responsible for responding to enquiries from prospective new children or their parents at your play setting? If you are one of them, you will need to have copies of any written information about the play setting to give to them (see Chapter 6 under 'Welcoming new children'). If you are not responsible for dealing with initial enquiries, you need to know who is so that you can direct interested visitors appropriately. Your manner in dealing with enquiries will affect the parent or child's opinion of your setting. If you are courteous, clear and organised in answering their questions, it will reflect well on the staff and will give them confidence in the setting as a whole. If you are unsure of some of the answers to their questions or you are unable to give the enquiry your full attention, apologise and explain that you (or an appropriate colleague) will be with them (or will call back) in a short while. Then find the appropriate person or the answers to the questions, and respond to the enquiry promptly.

Enquiries about future places

A parent may request a place when your setting has no places currently available. If that is the case, explain the situation to the parent and let them know, to the best of your knowledge, when a place might become available. Be clear if you are unsure about when a place may become free – a parent will appreciate an honest answer, as it will enable them to make alternative arrangements if necessary. Explain to them about your setting's waiting list, if you have one. (You may also have an admissions policy, which gives priority to certain children, for example, siblings of other children who attend or children who are referred to you by social services. If so, let the parent know about the policy. For more on admissions policies see Chapter 6.) If the parent would like to put their child's name on the waiting list, take down the parent's name and contact details, the child's name and any specific needs (so you can make any necessary preparations). As soon as a place is free, contact the person at the top of the waiting list. If the parent cannot wait until a place becomes free, you might direct them to other play settings in the local area.

Initial information

Once a place is agreed, gather all the necessary information about the child on a registration form (see next section). The information should be recorded clearly, as it may need to be read by other people in future. If it is written by a parent, check it is clear and legible. Ask them to rewrite any part which is unclear.

Recording and keeping information

Who is responsible for record keeping?

Discuss and agree with your managers what records you need to keep and how to keep them to ensure that all relevant information is collected and stored appropriately. This includes what forms must be filled in, when they should be filled in and who is responsible for making sure they are satisfactorily completed, updated, maintained and stored. In some voluntary organisations, a member of the management committee will have responsibility for completing and maintaining some of the records. For example, the treasurer may deal with all aspects relating to money and insurance and the secretary or waiting list organiser with admissions. In a large organisation or business, the play setting may have paid administrators. Whatever your situation, as a playworker you need to know what records are kept and who keeps them so that you can pass on, record or retrieve information when you need to.

Registration forms

In any play setting offering childcare, an initial registration form will need to be completed and signed by the child's parent or carer and given to the senior playworker or supervisor before the child can be enrolled. The following information should be collected:

HILLTOP PLAYSCHEME REGISTRATION FORM

Please contact the playscheme coordinator if you have any questions about the form or need help filling it in.

All children who attend must be registered. Please let us know immediately if any information changes.

All records are kept in a secure place and no parent or member of the general public will be given access to records other than those of their own child.

Child's full name: *Steffan Voight*

Name by which the child likes to be known: *Steff*

Address: *20a Green Street, Oldstone, Oxon*

Postcode: *OX28 22P*

Date of Birth: *26.10.96*   Gender: (Female or Male): *Male*

Ethnic origin: (this helps us monitor our equal opportunities policy): *German*

Parents'/guardians' full names: *Ms Bel Voight and Mr Jon Mann*

Telephone numbers: Daytime: *Bel: 33322, Jon: 11666*   Evening: *88800*
(Please give both parents' numbers if appropriate)

Child's dietary requirements: food to be excluded from diet, known food allergies etc.:
Allergies to peanuts and dairy produce

Any known medical problems or needs (including allergies):
Occasional asthma, takes inhaler himself

Any other special needs or information you want to give:
Friends with Tipu Singh

Name and address of person collecting child from playscheme if different from above:
Mrs Halida Singh, 6 Brown Street, Oldstone   Telephone: *44448*

Details of a second contact who may be able to collect the child in an emergency:
Mr Ronald Voigt   Telephone: *22299*

Please note: Any changes to the person/people who are to collect the child must be notified in advance, in writing to the playscheme coordinator. We will only let the child leave with a named person.

Name of child's doctor *Dr Elliot*

Address: *The Surgery, Elm Rise, Oldstone*

Tel. Number: *82828*

I consent to my child being given emergency medical treatment in my absence.

Signature of parent/guardian:

Print name: Date:

Example of a child's registration form

- child's full name and the name they prefer to be called
- home address
- date of birth
- gender and ethnic origin (to help you assess equal opportunities at your setting)
- name(s) of parent(s)/carer(s)
- telephone number(s) of parent(s)/carer(s) – home and work
- emergency contact number(s)
- any specific needs, dietary needs and medical needs
- name, address and telephone number of person who will collect child (if not parent/carer)
- name, address and telephone number of child's GP
- signature of parent/carer
- a note stating that the setting should be notified of any changes to the given information
- a note stating that the parent/carer must tell the setting in advance, in writing, of any changes that are made to the person who will collect the child – and that you will only let the child leave with a named person.

It is helpful if parents give you permission to sign emergency medical treatment consent forms in their absence, if they themselves cannot be contacted and the doctor advises that treatment is urgently required. Asking parents to complete such a form also gives them the opportunity to let you know if they have objections to particular treatments. These can be included on the form or on additional, separate forms.

Some play settings may require different or additional information. For example, the section on who is to collect the child would not be relevant in an open-access or drop-in play setting. Check that you can read all the details on the form and that you understand them fully. Make a particular note of any specific, medical or dietary needs so that all staff can be informed. Forms should be filed alphabetically for ease of retrieval, and kept up to date. Forms should be stored in a secure place that is easily accessible to authorised people. Files of children who no longer attend the play setting should be removed and stored at least until after your next inspection.

Documents to be displayed

For reasons of safety, and to comply with legislation, certain documents need to be displayed during opening times of the play setting. The documents and the issues they raise are dealt with in separate chapters. The following checklist summarises the documents you need to display:

- registration and inspection certificates
- inspection report
- certificate of public liability insurance
- fire/evacuation procedure
- health and safety at work poster.

If you are providing childcare, the following additional statements must be displayed or provided to parents:

- complaints procedure
- child protection policy and procedure
- a statement of the procedure to be followed if a parent fails to collect a child.

Records for health and safety

(For further information on health and safety records, see Chapter 12.)

Who is here?

It's necessary to record the arrival and departure times of all children, staff and visitors.

Daily register

In a setting that offers childcare, a daily register will be maintained for marking children present, including their hours of attendance. The names and full contact details of all staff and volunteers should be kept with the register. If children leave at different times you will also need a system to ensure that you know who is in the building at any time. The register should be keep in a place that is accessible should it be needed for a fire drill or evacuation.

Staff rota

It must always be clear who is working in the play setting on any particular day, and at what times. This may mean creating staff rotas or schedules, a copy of which should be displayed in the office and on the noticeboard. Playworkers', volunteers' and managers' names, addresses and contact numbers should also be kept near the telephone, together with names and contact numbers of anyone who can cover in the event of staff sickness or emergency.

Visitors' book/signing-in and out book

Some settings ask parents and carers collecting their children to use a signing-out book. This is useful for safety reasons, but can also be an interesting way to remember visitors. Get feedback about how they experienced your play setting by including a column for their comments on leaving. In drop-in and open-access settings, such as many adventure playgrounds, daily registration may not be appropriate or even possible as children come and go throughout the session. In these cases, particular attention needs to given to supervision of the premises and how evacuation procedures (fire drills) are carried out.

Overall numbers

All children using the setting need to be monitored. Playworkers need to identify new children quickly and obtain the necessary information for admission – including emergency contacts and any signed parental consent forms required.

The accident book

All accidents and injuries that take place in the play setting should be recorded. In most cases, this will be in an accident book. Once an accident has been fully recorded (including time, date, name of child, nature and location of injury, circumstances and action taken), the staff member (and any witnesses) must sign the record and ask the parent to countersign it when they pick up their child.

Some larger organisations have their own accident report forms. The accident book can be kept together with the first-aid kit.

ACTIVITY The accident book

Marion is the playworker supervising outside one afternoon when two girls collide during a game of 'Stuck in the mud'. Lucy appears to have twisted her left ankle and Min has bumped her head on the concrete. It is bleeding slightly and a lump is appearing, but Min did not lose consciousness. While comforting the children,

Marion sends another child indoors to fetch Aislin, the senior worker, who is also the first aider. Aislin determines that the ankle does not appear to be broken and helps both girls indoors in order to clean Min's head and bandage Lucy's ankle:

1 Decide who should fill in the accident report.

2 Fill in an accident report or entry into an accident book as if you were the responsible playworker in this situation, including all relevant details.

**HILLTOP PLAYSCHEME
ACCIDENT REPORT FORM**

Date and time: 7-7-2005   2.30 pm

Name of injured person: Millicent Stevens (Millie)

How and where the incident occurred:
Fell off bench playing tig in outside area

Nature of the incident/injury sustained: (be specific – r or l limb etc.)
Bumped head (grazed forehead), slight swelling. No signs of concussion
Twisted right arm. No swelling but painful

Witnesses to the incident:
Mari S and Lou G (playworkers)

Action taken by staff: (include name of staff member dealing with incident/administering first aid etc.)

Mari cleaned graze with cold water. Mari monitored situation during afternoon.
Millie continued to complain of painful arm. Mari informed her mother on collection
and suggested she take her to casualty if pain continued

Parent/carer informed: (signature of parent/carer)   *Sarah Stevens*

Example accident report

Incident book

Many settings use an incident book to record details of specific events such as breaches of security, racist comments and behaviour issues. Details of the incident, how it was dealt with and by whom are recorded and can be used to track behaviour or make changes that will be of benefit to the play setting.

Medicines

If a child needs medicine to be given by staff, a consent form, signed by the parent, is required. Keep a record of all medicines that are given to children in the play setting, including the date and the person who administered it. More information on medicines is given in Chapter 12.

Equipment list

Keep an updated list or inventory of equipment, including safety checks and repairs, in the play setting. This is important for insurance purposes and a copy should be held by the person responsible for dealing with insurance matters. Keep separate lists for consumables, such as craft materials, and longer lasting equipment that will be replaced only when it becomes too worn or broken. The inventory is useful for playworkers to keep a record of materials bought and for reordering. Add details of new equipment to the inventory as soon as possible after you receive them, and remove obsolete items.

				Page: 3
Item (equipment)	Supplier	Date ordered	Cost/price	Date received
Music Gato drum	Local music shop	3.8.2005	£58.60	3.8.2005
6 x hand bells	NES Arnold	10.8.2005	£3 each	28.8.2005

				Page: 5
Item (consumables)	Supplier	Date ordered	Cost/price	Date received
Finger paints x 8 pots	Early Learning Centre	29.7.2005	£2 per pot	29.7.2005
Paper (newsprint roll)	Collect from local newspaper printers	1.8.2005	free	1.8.2005

Example equipment inventory

Other records

There are occasions when other records are useful or necessary. Some of them are dealt with in other chapters. Other records kept in your play setting might include:

- notes or minutes of meetings (see under 'Effective team meetings' in Chapter 10)
- health and safety checklists, including risk assessment and fire safety (Chapter 12)
- forms for recording formal complaints (Chapters 6 and 10)
- records of contact with other agencies (for example local authority Children's Services department) with reference to concern about safety or well-being of a child see Chapter 11)
- programme of activities and planning notes (Chapter 5)
- playworker's observations (Chapter 2)
- participation in trips and outings
- signed consent from parents for photos of children to be taken and used by the play setting
- records of financial transactions (see later 'Working with money').

There will also be personnel records relating to staff employment.

You can involve the children in record keeping (Morgan, aged 9)

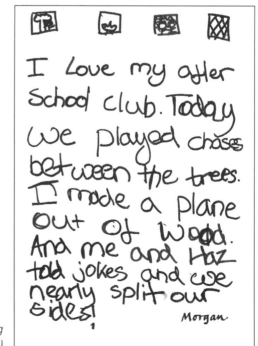

I Love my after School club. Today we played chases between the trees. I made a plane out of wood. And me and Haz told jokes and we nearly split our sides!

Morgan

Written records

1 How do written records contribute to the quality of your play setting?
2 List all the records you think are essential to maintaining high standards in your play setting.

Storing records

As already mentioned, any records you keep should be stored in a secure place that is easily accessible to those who are authorised. Records should be stored on the premises or in another location agreed with your regulating body.

Confidentiality

Children's records must be kept in a safe place, but you must be able to get access to them quickly in the event of an accident or other emergency (including if held by password on a computer). They should not, in normal circumstances, be accessible to anyone who does not have responsibility for the care and well-being of the child. A registration officer or inspector will need to know that you are keeping appropriate records and may ask to see them as part of your setting's inspection. Parents have the right to see records containing information about themselves or their children (but see Chapter 11 for child protection issues). If you store information about individual children on computer, you may need to be registered under the Data Protection Act. There are some circumstances in which you can apply for an exemption. You can find out more from the data protection registrar (see further reading at end of this chapter).

ACTIVITY **Which records and policies?**

Consider the following situations:

1 You and another playworker take 20 children on a trip to the seaside. One child cuts herself badly on a broken glass bottle and needs to go to hospital to have the wound stitched.
2 While involved in a collage activity with a group of children, you use the last of the glue.
3 A father brings a new child to your play setting for the first time.
4 A small fire breaks out in the kitchen and you need to evacuate the building.
5 You arrive at work to find that your play setting has been burgled and all the play materials are strewn around the floor.

In each case, decide:

- What documents or records would need to be completed or referred to in dealing with the situation.
- What action needs to be taken and what records would need to be completed.
- Who would be responsible for completing any such records in a similar situation in your play setting.

Organising trips and outings

Planning ahead

You need parental consent to take children on off-site trips and activities and outings. Some play settings ask parents to complete a consent form giving them permission to take the child on local trips – the park, swimming, to buy cooking ingredients – at any time during the opening hours of the play setting (see also Chapter 12 on off-site activities). This can be included on the initial registration form. A separate consent form is usually required for longer individual trips such as an outing to the seaside or overnight camp, particularly if the trip involves leaving or returning outside the normal opening hours of the session.

Discuss ideas for trips with the children. They may know of interesting places to visit that are unknown to the staff (ensure, of course, that it is cost effective, safe and practical, including for any children with specific needs who attend your setting). Once a venue has been chosen, make sure the children are briefed about where you are going, how you will get there and the things you might see and do. Some children feel rather nervous of going to new places and will be reassured if you prepare them sensitively for the trip. Provide parents and children with full information about the chosen trip, including place, timings, any cost and any items that children might need to bring. A consent form that has to be signed and returned helps to ensure that parents receive and are aware of the necessary information.

Trip safety

Safety points you should consider when planning an off-site activity include:

- *Insurance* – does your insurance cover off-site activities?
- *Consent* – do you have parents'/carers' written consent?
- *Supervision* – what supervision (staff–child ratios) will you need? This will depend on the age and abilities of the children, the type of activity and, in some cases, your insurance policy. It is a good idea to divide children into small groups, each with a responsible adult.
- *Transport* – are you fully licensed, is the vehicle roadworthy (insurance, road tax and MOT) and are seatbelts fitted? Is there safe parking at the venue? If you use a minibus to transport children on trips, you will have to comply with the Transport Act 1985. Your minibus requires a permit, the driver must be over 21 years with full driving licence and insurance and you must carry appropriate fire extinguishers and first-aid equipment. Many insurance policies insist that the driver is over 25 years old. Seatbelts should be fitted in all seats. All passengers must be able to open all door locks from the inside. Contact the Department of Transport or your local traffic commissioner for further information.
- *Children's records* – who will be responsible for taking a register and keeping count of children? It is useful to take a duplicate set of children's registration forms with you on trips. This means you will have all the relevant details and contacts in the event of an accident but a copy will remain in the play setting in case of loss or damage.
- *Contact* – take the number of someone to contact in the event of a delay so that they can inform and reassure parents and carers when they come to collect the children.
- *First aid* – take a first-aid kit, accident book and someone with emergency first-aid training.
- *Timings* – ensure everyone (staff, children and parents) are *very* clear about the time you will leave and the time you will arrive home. Impress on everyone the importance of keeping these timings – for everyone's safety, to avoid delays and, where applicable, to meet parents on time back at the setting.

Contingencies

It is quite a rare occasion when a trip goes fully to plan, without even the smallest of hitches. A seasoned trip organiser knows that there are certain aspects of outings for which you need to have a contingency plan:

- *Weather* – you are unlikely to plan a trip to the seaside in November, but even in summer, you can't ensure that it will not rain. So it's a good idea to choose a venue that has an covered area nearby that can be used by children. If it rained and you needed to entertain the children for 10 minutes, what would you do? Take out your harmonica and do a round of 'Hokey cokey'? Take out a circle of paper called 'The joke spot' and invite the children to take turns standing on the spot and telling a joke to the others? See the CAN DO series of children's activity books for more ideas about resourcefulness. If you are walking or cycling to your venue, ensure everyone brings appropriate clothing!

- *Accidents* – the same resourcefulness also applies if your vehicle broke down, or was in an accident. Keeping children calm and entertained are necessary playworker skills for trips and outings.

- *Staff numbers* – do you have a contingency plan in case a staff member calls in sick on the day of the trip? Perhaps you would have one or two extra adults booked to come along (or as standbys) in case of such an issue arising?

- *Timing* – there may be unforeseen delays during your trip, such as heavy traffic or a child or staff member who is late. Bring with you ideas for entertaining the children – both on and off the vehicle. If there is a delay, explain to the children what is happening.

Working with money

Many tasks within the play setting require dealing with money. These may include:

- collecting fees
- budgeting
- buying day-to-day purchases like fruit for snacks
- buying large equipment and restocking supplies of materials
- keeping accounts and other financial records
- paying bills, rent, salaries, insurance costs
- paying volunteers' expenses
- fundraising – including applying for grants.

Who does what?

Managers will be responsible for overall financial planning. They will set the budget and decide how many staff can be employed and how much can be spent on play materials and other needs. In voluntary organisations, management committee members may also take on many other tasks. Some large organisations or businesses may have a paid member of staff to keep the financial records. Everyone must be clear about who does what. This should be written down, and your responsibilities should form part of your job description. If you need to improve your skills in working with money, there are many simple, easy-to-read books on the subject – see the further reading list for ideas.

Budgeting

Overall budgeting is the responsibility of managers. But you may be involved in setting priorities about what is most needed – deciding whether to use money for paying more volunteers' expenses or buying a large piece of equipment, for example. You may have sole responsibility for a part of the budget such as the money that has been allocated for purchasing play materials and other frequently used goods such as food, cleaning materials and paints. If you have responsibility for all or part of a budget you need to know how much money is in it and for how long it has to last. You will need to plan ahead to work out what should be spent when. It is a good idea not to plan every penny but to set aside a contingency fund for unexpected or spontaneous events. If you find you are running out of money well before time, you need to inform the person responsible for the overall budget as early as possible. This will allow them to assess the reason for this and, if necessary, re-prioritise or fundraise to allocate more to meet continuing needs.

Petty cash

You will probably need a regular amount of cash for small purchases. For this, you will need a lockable petty cash box and a system for recording what you spend and getting the cash you need. The Imprest system for petty cash works by allowing you a weekly float – an agreed sum of £50, for example. Record your receipt of this cash in the petty cash book. Record details of everything you spend and attach the relevant receipts. Each week the float is then topped up to its original amount. So if £50 is put in the cash box on Monday and you spend £48.50 during the week, the £48.50 will be transferred to the petty cash box the following Monday, so you start off with £50 again. Of course, you can operate this system fortnightly or at any other agreed interval. Whenever money is taken out of the petty cash box, a petty cash voucher (available from stationery shops) should be made out recording who has taken the money and what for. Once the purchase has been made the total section should be filled in, recording what has been spent. Pin the receipt of the purchase to this voucher.

Petty cash voucher		Folio	24	
		Date	21/4/2005	
For what required		AMOUNT		
		£	P	
Cooking ingredients		5	00	
Change returned (receipt attached)			26	
Amount spent		4	74	
Signature	Samantha Creaner			
Passed by	J Whistle			

A petty cash voucher should be completed for all money taken from the petty cash box

---

ACTIVITY   Money, money, money

Do you know the financial policies and procedures at your setting – or do you know who does? If you found yourself in the following situations, what would you do?

- Another playworker says she is in a real rush to get home and could you please take today's cash to the bank?
- A parent asks you if there are any subsidised places, or any other help with fees, at the play setting.
- A volunteer asks you for his expenses.

CLIENT

SUBJECT Analysed accounts (petty cash) 2005

		RECEIPTS				EXPENSES					
Date	Descrip.	Amount	Date	Description	Total Payout		Post	Refreshments	Travel	Craft materials	Sundries
4.4. 1	Cash	50 –	4/4	Stamps	5	30	5 30				
2			7/4	Milk	1	75		1 75			
3			10/4	Volunteer bus fares	3	–			3 –		
4			21/4	Food for snacks	17	50		17 50			
5			24/4	Paints	6	20				6 20	
4.5. 6	Cash	33 75		Total	33	75					
7											
8											
9											

Keeping careful record of what money is received and how it is spent is essential for budgeting, planning and accountability

Keeping accounts

For S/NVQ Levels 2 and 3 you are not expected to be responsible for keeping the overall accounts of the play setting. At Level 3, it is assumed you are required to keep accounts of your own budget. The accounts should record details of all payments made (including what for) and all money received (including from whom and what for). This is essential so that the overall accounts of the play setting can be accurately audited (a legal requirement) and so that you can be accountable for any money for which you are responsible. Keeping accurate and up-to-date records also helps in budgeting, forward planning and protects you from any misunderstandings or accusations of mishandling money. Use an analysed account book with lots of columns (available from stationery shops) whether you are keeping records of a petty cash account, a goods and materials budget or casual staff wages and expenses. The example shows you what an analysed petty cash book might look like. If you are required to keep more complicated accounts or need to 'reconcile' or balance accounts with bank statements, you may need to attend a basic bookkeeping course. (See also suggested further reading at the end of this chapter.) Record enough detail so that you or anyone else may clearly see how much was spent by whom and how much was received from whom and what for. Invoice and cheque numbers should be recorded.

Collection of fees

If you are collecting fees, you will need a receipt book to issue a receipt each time you receive any money. The receipt will give the date, amount received, from whom and will have space for your signature. Keep a copy of these receipts for your own records. If you bank the fees yourself, keep a copy of who you have received the money from and the bank counterfoil to give to the treasurer, your manager or accountant. If you do not bank the income from fees yourself, as soon as you hand the money over get a receipt for the full amount from the person (usually the treasurer) who takes the money from you and deposits it in the bank. Make sure you have somewhere secure for keeping cash. Follow the procedures of your workplace with regard to how the fees are collected and the amount of money each family must pay. If you have any difficulty with collecting fees, report this to a senior staff member and the person responsible for banking the fees. Keep all money received from fees separate from petty cash and other income.

Ordering equipment

New equipment may be bought from local shops or suppliers or ordered from specialist or general mail-order companies. If you are the person responsible for ordering and re-ordering play materials and equipment, you need to be clear about the funds for this. Make sure you have checked with the person authorised to make the payments that the money is available, before making a commitment to new purchases.

How are decisions made concerning what to buy? This will depend on play opportunities planned and the resources already available. All involved in planning for play within the setting can help decide what is needed. They must know how much money is available and realise the consequences of particular choices: 'If we buy glitter paints we can't get sequins as well'; or 'If we replace the slide we will not have enough money left to buy more skipping ropes this time.' Get quotes or price lists from more than one supplier so that you can compare and ensure you are getting value for money. You may be able to borrow or lease equipment: some local authorities have equipment they will loan or lease to voluntary organisations. You may have a toy library or play association that you can join and from whom you can borrow equipment. Some areas have resource centres or 'scrapstores' that collect waste materials – from paper, cardboard tubes and wool, to industrial spare parts, nettings, rope and so on – which are safe to use (with some added imagination) in the play setting.

Once you have received the goods, check that your order is complete and that you have received what is written on the receipt (if you have paid) or the invoice (if you have not yet paid). If the order is incorrect, deal with the mistake promptly, in person or in writing. If this is not your responsibility, inform the appropriate person. Ideally, the person responsible for ordering will check the order and invoice and make the payments. If you do not receive an order within the time stated by your supplier, it should be followed up promptly by the person responsible. Where possible all purchases should be paid for by cheque, as carrying a cheque book is safer than carrying large amounts of cash. There is also no chance of being short-changed and you will have an additional record of the amount spent on the cheque book stub. Small items such as biscuits or bus fares will obviously be paid for in cash. Keep a receipt for all these payments and record each transaction in a petty cash book. Keep cash in a safe place at all times.

ACTIVITY   Ordering equipment

1 Make a list of all the play materials and equipment you use or might need in your play setting.

2 Divide the list into:

- things to buy
- things that you can maybe borrow, lease or hire (contact your local authority for advice on what can be loaned or look in the telephone directory).

3 Get price lists and mail-order catalogues. Do you know how to fill in the order forms? If this is not a job you usually do, ask if you can be involved in completing the next order.

4 Find out the procedures for ordering, including paperwork and deposits required for any materials that can be borrowed.

Help with fees

At least one member of staff should know about and be able to help parents understand how they can get help with fees if they need it. Such help might come from local bursaries, subsidised places schemes or through tax credits. For information contact your local children's information service (see the appendix) or your nearest Inland Revenue office.

Summary

Although it can be time consuming, paperwork and administration are vital for the smooth running of a play setting. Playworkers need to know who is responsible for keeping which records and should inform others of any information relating to records under their responsibility. Paperwork works best if you record all transactions as soon as possible and keep all records up to date. Make sure you have a secure place to store records, which can only be accessed by the appropriate people. Using some simple records, such as petty cash books, account books and receipt books makes working with money easier.

Further reading

Davy, A. (ed.) (2002) CAN DO series of play activity books. Thomson Learning.

Hayes, R. and Reason, J. (2004) *Voluntary But Not Amateur: A Guide to the Law for Voluntary Organisations and Community Groups*. London Voluntary Service Council. www.actionlink.org.uk/lvsc.

Hughes, V. and Weller, D. (2003) *Setting up a Business*. Teach Yourself Books.

Piper, A.G. (2003) *Book Keeping*. Teach Yourself Books.

Data protection

For further information about data protection, contact Office of the Data Protection Registrar, Wycliffe House, Water Lane, Wilmslow, Cheshire SK9 5AF (tel: 01625 533 5777).

Websites

Over 30 example policies and procedures framed by the National Standards for Out of School Child Care are available to download from the 4children website: www.4children.org.uk.

CHAPTER 14

Playwork and the wider community

It takes a whole village to raise a child.

(African proverb)

Your playwork setting is likely to touch the lives of more than just the children who come along and play. The services you provide can have a positive impact on their families, other adults and other organisations within the community. An active, buzzing setting can become a community 'hub', where people meet, share information and where new ideas are formed.

Chapter 9 looked at your professional development as a playworker. This chapter focuses on developing the service you provide for others within the community. We also look at making links with other people and organisations and the beneficial effect that can have on your setting. In this chapter, we will consider:

- Play in the community
- Monitoring and reviewing your play setting
- Developing your play setting
- Promoting your play setting
- Creating links with others

Play in the community

Your play setting does not exist in isolation. The children who come to your setting have families, homes and schools and live in a community. Your play setting is part of a network of other facilities catering for children and their families. The people or organisations paying for the service will want to know that they are getting value for money – whether you charge fees or are funded by grants. Your play setting will need to earn its place as a well-used resource that is recognised as valuable both by those who use it and by others who may not fully understand the value of play. They may see play settings as a low priority compared with other services. You should be clear about your aims and objectives within your play setting and translate them into policies that are regularly monitored and evaluated. You need to consult and work with others to ensure that your play setting continues to meet the needs of the children it is intended to serve. If you successfully promote your play setting and the values of playwork, you will be able to draw on many sources of support in your work with individual children and for playwork as a whole.

CASE STUDY   Visitors to the play setting

Hilltop Leisure Centre provides after school and holiday play and care for children aged 5–14. Five people are visiting today:

1 Ms Sheehy, who is looking for childcare for her 10 year old son.

2 Carl Sheehy, who is visiting with his mother.

3 Mrs Akhtar, a teacher from the local school, who wants to know more about the centre, which several of the children from her class attend. She also wants to find out if an Asian girls' youth group that she runs after school twice a week can use any of the leisure facilities.

4 Mr Kirk, a social worker, wants to find day-time respite care for a child whose family is under stress.

5 Ms Broom, a local councillor, wants to see how the grant from the council is being spent.

In the case study, what will each of the visitors be looking for? What information will they need? What might each of these people have to offer the play setting? As the playworker, what might you want to ask them?

What can we offer you – what can you offer us?

In the case study 'Visitors to the play setting', Ms Sheehy and Carl will want to know whether the play opportunities of Hilltop Leisure Centre will interest Carl and meet his needs. How welcoming and friendly is the centre? Carl wants to know whether any other children he knows go there and how strict the rules are. Ms Sheehy wants to know whether the opening hours will fit in with her work. She wants to know that Carl will be safe and happy. Are the staff qualified? Is the centre registered with the local authority? Can she afford the fees? Are there concessions for people on low income or lone parents? Carl and Ms Sheehy are potential customers. They are the people the leisure centre aims to serve. Without them, the leisure centre would not exist.

Mrs Akhtar wants to share some concerns she has about a girl in her class who uses the centre and whose behaviour has recently become withdrawn. How does she behave in the centre? Have the playworkers noticed any changes? Mrs Akhtar wants such communication to continue between the school and the centre. She also wants to see the facilities and to find out who can use them. Do they have an equal opportunities policy? Are the facilities used by the Asian community? Mrs Akhtar can provide playworkers with information and understanding of the some of the children who attend (those who are in her class). She might also help to create closer links with the Asian community and suggest changes or improvements to the services offered that would attract more Asian customers.

Mr Kirk wants to know what kind of play opportunities are on offer. Will they meet the needs of his client? What approach is taken by the playworkers? Are they qualified? Are there any places free? If not, are there any priority places for children in need? How much will it cost? Representing social services, Mr Kirk is a potential customer. He may be able to set up a service contract with the centre that pays for two priority places for use by children referred by social services at all times. He may know about grants or opportunities for staff training (in child protection issues, for example). He may be able to help the centre meet its commitment to equal opportunities with advice or by referring further children in need.

As a councillor, Ms Broom wants to know that the centre is meeting its obligations under the terms of the large grant and service agreement with the local authority. How many children attend? Do they fully represent the local community? Is work carried out in accordance with the local authority's health and safety and equal opportunities policies? If she likes what she sees, Ms Broom can be a very important voice of support – for the leisure centre and for the value of play to the local community – when decisions are made about budgets, grant and cuts. She can put the centre in touch with council officers and others who can support and promote their work and activities. She wants to see last year's accounts and evaluation report. Do the play and care services offered by the leisure centre warrant the money, in the light of resources needed by other services – for building and for roads, for education, for the sick, the elderly and the unemployed?

All the visitors to Hilltop Leisure Centre want to know about the general approach of the staff and management to their work. Is it a safe place to be? Is it an enjoyable place to be? Who does it aim to serve?

These are the sorts of people who will visit your setting. Their questions are those which may be asked by your visitors. Staff at your play setting will be able to give full and clear answers if you have the following:

- clear aims, shared objectives and policies that are regularly reviewed
- a simple information booklet containing essential information for potential customers
- written policies and evaluation reports available on request.

What are your aims?

Your play setting came into being because of a need or a demand. It may have been a group of parents who needed childcare or a head teacher concerned about children going home from school to an empty house who started things moving. It may have been a group of representatives from a local community, including parents, who were concerned about the lack of safe spaces for children to play in their area. Perhaps your play setting was set up by an organisation as a service for its employees and their families, a local authority offering play as part of its recreational services or a leisure company wanting to sell out-of-school care and/or play activities as part of a business.

The reasons behind why it was set up will form the basis of the aims of the setting (see also Chapters 2 and 3). As more people become involved – children, staff, parents – it is important that everyone is aware of the aims and shares them, so that you can work together to meet them.

Once a common aim has been agreed, those involved must consider exactly what they are going to provide to meet it – for example, art and craft, games, food, opportunities for unstructured play and experienced workers. You should develop a shared approach to achieving objectives within resources available and current legislation. This will form the basis of the policies of your play setting.

The aim is to facilitate and support good quality play opportunities

Monitoring and reviewing your play setting

Some things that you, your colleagues or management may take for granted may not actually be happening in practice. The management of your play setting need to know that what actually happens is the same as what the policies say should happen. They must also make sure that the play setting meets the needs it was intended to serve or that it changes or expands to meet new needs. For this, they should have a system for monitoring and reviewing.

Your involvement

You may be involved in various ways such as:

- asking parents and carers to fill in questionnaires
- contributing to discussions at team meetings
- alerting managers to matters that you observe in your work and believe to be contrary to the play setting's policies, such as a safety hazard, a problem with numbers and new admissions, or an example of discriminatory practice
- giving verbal or written reports.

 **ACTIVITY** Any gaps between policy and practice?

Read the following case studies:

Case study A: A play setting is situated in a geographical area with a population of 20 per cent Asian families. No Asian children attend the setting. There is an equal opportunities policy in place.

Case study B: A child with cerebral palsy is refused a place at a play setting on the grounds that they do not have the staff to cope. The written information about the play setting includes a statement that they aim to cater for disabled children.

Case study C: The staff agree with the policy of the play setting that they value and respect other cultures, but the books on the bookshelves and pictures on the wall contain stories and images of only white children and their families in a European context, apart from one poster of a famous black athlete.

Answer the following questions in respect of each case study:

- How might this gap between policy and practice have occurred?
- What action would you take to ensure that the play setting puts its policies into practice?

Monitoring who uses the play setting

If you ask parents and carers to fill in forms that involve monitoring of ethnicity, gender or other criteria of the user group, such information should be sensitively handled. Always explain why you need information. Confidentiality must be guaranteed and the forms should be detached and stored securely (see also Chapter 13 on confidentiality). You can compare this information about the children who use your play setting with publicly available information about the population of particular areas (available from your local authority or library). If there is an imbalance, there are positive steps that can be taken. In a situation such as that in case study A in the activity 'Any gaps between policy and practice?', you could:

- ask why this situation could have occurred
- find out how the information about the play setting can be translated into other languages
- talk to representatives and spokespeople of the local Asian community (such as a community worker or a representative from local temple or mosque)
- consider whether the opening times or activities should be varied, expanded or changed
- ask what other reasons there might be. Perhaps the club is not perceived as catering for the Asian members of the community, that the activities are aimed at the current user group and parents or carers and children would not feel comfortable. If there are no Asian workers or managers and the images and resources of the setting do not reflect different cultures positively, this might also be a barrier. (See Kapasi 1992.)

In case study B of the same activity, it is possible that staff and management are unaware of local sources of support and financial assistance or the possibility of additional staff to support the integration of a child with special needs. Steps should be taken to acquire this knowledge. Contact your local authority, local support groups or national organisations (see the appendix). Training may be needed to give existing staff the skills and confidence to provide for the disabled child or contact could be made with organisations who train and support volunteers who might help (see the case study below, 'From policy to practice – Josh's story').

In case study C of the activity 'Any gaps between policy and practice?', the books and posters may have been chosen (or donated) without very much thought. It is useful to take an overall look at the images represented within your play setting. They should reflect the wider society we live in, with its colourful range of skin tones. Look also at the way men and women from all cultures are portrayed within your resources – are the images stereotypical? If so, there are many sources of more positive images – you could try The Festival Shop or Letterbox Library (see further reading for more information).

CASE STUDY   From policy to practice – Josh's story

A parent approached Julie, a playworker at West Park after-school club, enquiring about the possibility of her son, Josh, attending the club. She was concerned that there may not be enough support for Josh, who has Down's Syndrome. Josh's specific needs include assistance with eating and going to the toilet and he has little awareness of his own personal safety or that of others. Julie said she would check if there was space for the day requested and would look into support for Josh, so that he could be involved fully in the club's activities. They agreed to meet again in three days' time.

Julie discussed support for Josh with the club's coordinator. They agreed that Josh would need support over and above the staff ratio. A list of possible agencies that could help was drawn up. This included the play development team at the local council, PARASOL (a local grant-funded charity that enables disabled children to attend mainstream play settings) and the local play association.

After a few phone calls, the coordinator rang PARASOL. They told her that they had funding for just such a situation. They would be able to provide a playworker to enable Josh to join in all the fun. They suggested a date for their playworker to meet Josh, his mother, the other staff and to be shown around the club. They agreed to keep in regular contact to review progress.

Josh started the following week. He showed everyone his photograph in the PARASOL newsletter. His mother has asked about the possibility of him coming for an extra day a week. Josh says he wants to come every day!

External monitoring

Monitoring can take many forms. If your play setting is registered, your registration and inspection officer will want to see that your policies are within the framework of the law and will also look for evidence of how they are put into practice. If you are funded by a local authority, council officers will need to monitor that you are providing the service intended and that the authority's money is properly spent. They may ask for questionnaires to be completed and reports submitted and may examine your accounts.

Reports

You may be asked to give reports on different aspects of your work. Depending on the kind of play setting you work in and your level of responsibility, this could range from reporting to your team members on a conference or training event you have attended to giving a verbal or short written report to your management committee on the summer playscheme. You might also be responsible for giving a written annual report to your local authority department on how your play setting has met its aims over the previous year. Whatever kind of report you have to give there are four main things to remember:

1 What is the purpose of the report?

2 Who is it for?

3 What are the main points you should make?

4 What are your conclusions or recommendations – that is, what should happen as a result of your report?

If you are giving a verbal report, make notes under each of these headings. A more formal written report should be laid out under the following headings:

- title of report
- contents list (for a long report with appendices)
- introduction (aims and objectives or purpose and scope of report)
- main body of report (current situation, what happened, your research advantages, disadvantages)
- conclusions and recommendations (summarise main points and give an opinion).

A written report should have your name, job title and organisation and the date – day, month and year. If you have statistics, results of questionnaires or additional relevant information you should attach them as numbered appendices. Keep the body of your report to the point.

Developing your play setting

Evaluating the service you provide

Once you know your aims and objectives, it makes it much easier to evaluate the service you are providing. If you take the time to think about every aspect of your play setting, you are likely to come up with many strengths and positive features that you provide for the children and others in your local area. If you are really honest and thorough, you will probably find areas that could be developed, changed, renewed or adapted so that your play setting can be improved for its users – and may even attract new users. The activity 'Evaluating your play setting' provides a framework from which to start your evaluation. You might choose different, fewer, or more headings, but the process is very simple. The important thing is giving yourself the time to reflect on each of your chosen headings. If all the staff do this activity together, an energy can be created that will kick-start the process of making improvements to your play setting.

Other ways to evaluate the services you provide are:

- Create a questionnaire for users – ask the users of your setting (and their parents) for their comments and feedback on what you offer.

- Create a questionnaire for non-users – ask people in the wider community what they think of the service you provide and if they have any particular positives or criticisms to share. You could ask local shops, libraries, doctors' surgeries and community centres to stock your questionnaires.

- Interviewing – you could approach users and non-users with the questionnaires and ask them for their views directly.

- Hold a 'focus group' meeting – ask a few people (perhaps a mixture of children, parents and staff) to attend a meeting to focus on improvements to your service.

- Hold an open meeting – advertise it widely and ask users, non-users, people who share the building, local businesses and organisations to attend. This will give you an idea of how you impact on people outside your setting.

Choose which method of evaluation will work best for your play setting. Keep a record off all the feedback and comments you receive. If you have been thorough in your evaluation, the advice for changes and improvements will be useful for creating a more effective, user-friendly and fun play space. The next step is, of course, making the changes.

How would this child describe the value of this activity?

ACTIVITY Evaluating your play setting

You can do this activity on your own or with other colleagues, perhaps at a staff meeting. Take a pen and paper (or flipchart), and write the headings shown on the following table. Think about every aspect of each heading that relates to your setting and make notes about areas that could be developed.

Area to evaluate	Things to think about	Things to develop
1 Meeting play needs	• Do the children have the chance to engage in the full range of play types? • Are children engaged in sustained play for long periods of time? • What factors limit or inhibit children's play?	For example, you might: • Develop children's opportunities for risk and challenge in their play to promote 'deep play' • Provide more 'loose parts' – things that children can move and adapt within their play
2 Engagement with children	• Is the setting well used every day? • Does the range of children reflect the range of children who live in the community? Does any particular group *not* use the setting? • Are the children contented? Are there any issues that need dealing with (such as bullying or other negative behaviour)? • Are the children involved in the running of the play setting?	For example, you might: • Need to advertise that we have vacancies on a Monday, Thursday and Friday • Promote services to local traveller families • Discuss recent vandalism of the playground with the young people's committee
3 Staff	• Enough staff employed? • Equal opportunities applied? • What qualifications held? • Access to training courses for professional development?	For example, you might: • Need more volunteers • Find out about locally run playwork qualifications at levels 2 and 3
4 Building we use	• Easy access for all users (and potential users)? • Still suitable for our needs? • Good relationship with others who use the building? • Meets all safety requirements?	For example, you might: • Attend building users' meeting next month – ask about improving access
5 Equipment	• Enough equipment to meet the needs of all the children? • Good range of equipment? • In good safety order?	For example, you might: • Look in books and on internet for ideas on new, more exciting activities and equipment for children
6 Information to others	• Is a summary of the information available, plus more in-depth info for those who wish it? • Is it up to date, informative, attractive? • Is it provided in different formats (e.g. the main community languages, large print?)	For example, you might: • Bring information leaflet to next staff meeting for revision • Ask Nilofer if she can translate the info into Urdu
Other areas to evaluate: Activities provided; child protection; staff teamwork and morale; the play environment; health and safety, including all children; administration; links with the local community			

Making improvements

Making changes can be daunting, or it can be stimulating, depending on the approach and the support given! It is important that agreed changes are manageable – too many can be overwhelming. Decide with the children, the manager and staff which of the recommended changes and improvements will be made. If you agree to make all the changes, decide on an order for implementing them. Agree a timescale for each of the changes or improvements. Make sure there is enough funding and people to make the changes. Be realistic about which changes to make – is the outcome going to be worth the time and effort?

There may be some small changes agreed, which might take only minimal effort, such as:

- change the activities and/or equipment
- update the information leaflets
- keep the noticeboard up to date.

Other changes may make more demands on your time and may require help from others. You might agree to improve the services you provide, such as:

- employing volunteers
- increasing the opening hours of the setting – for example, running a breakfast club or holiday playscheme
- increasing the numbers of children you can take and, therefore, the number of staff.

Major changes in particular will require the agreement of the manager or the play committee. Each major change will require a project plan, detailing what needs to be done, who will do it, by when and resources needed. Don't try to make too many changes too quickly! Focus on the quality of the core play services you provide.

Promoting your play setting

Why might you want to promote your play setting? You might need to advertise your services in order to increase the number of users. You might want to attract a specific group of potential new users. You might be offering a new service, such as extended hours or a revamped outdoor area. You might want to make links with local businesses and organisations. Or you might want to simply promote the benefits of play for children's well-being.

How can play settings benefit people in the community?

- They are places where children can be children.
- They can provide paid and voluntary work.
- Play settings can be one of the focal points of communities, a place to meet people you know and people you don't. It is a place that is accessible and welcoming to people from all cultures and of all abilities – a community within the community.
- They are places where children can have fun with their friends in a safe but challenging environment. They learn useful social skills, such as sharing, discussing, listening, understanding others, compromising – skills which will help them become positively valued members of the community.
- Knowing their children are in an exciting and safe place, parents are free to work, study, relax or look after other children.
- Play spaces promote the value of play and give parents ideas for play at home.

- Children learn how to entertain themselves, and are then more able to create positive play opportunities for themselves outside the play setting.

You may be able to think of other ways your setting benefits the people in your particular area.

Marketing your play setting

It's worth spending a bit of time thinking about how to get your message across. Discuss the 'message' with the staff and management to make sure you all agree. The first thing to do is to think about who your target audience is and how best to inspire them into action. Your local area children's information service can help to promote and market your setting to a wide audience.

Effective communication

If your target audience is local families with children, you are likely to use different language than if you are promoting yourself to local businesses. Think about your message – what are the key pieces of information that will get your message across?

For example, you want to advertise a new breakfast club at your setting. The target audience is parents and children in the local area. The main features of your message might be:

- who might need the breakfast club? (Parents who need to get to work?)
- why the breakfast club is fun (and nutritional) for children.
- when it will run (days and times).
- where it will run.
- who will run it.
- who to contact for further info.

The language you use will probably be accessible and fun, but with a reasonably 'professional' feel. Don't try to give *too* much information – just enough for people to want to find out more.

How will you get this message across? How can you reach the people in your target audience? An advert in a national newspaper is obviously casting your net too wide and an hour of handing out leaflets in one street may not be casting it wide enough. You need to think about the range of promotional tools available and choose the one that suits your message and the resources you have (such as staffing, time and money).

Publicity

How to get good publicity is a specialist area in itself. The identity of the play setting can be helped by having a catchy name that relates to what the play setting is about and a good logo for use on posters, newsletters, notices and letter headings. You could use one or more of the following types of promotion.

Your noticeboard

This is a very useful way of sharing information and presenting what you do. Make sure your noticeboard is located where people will pass by and read it – daily, if possible. Don't let it become a sad affair with out-of-date information, tatty notices and faded posters or pictures. One person should be responsible for maintaining the noticeboard and changing displays. Include names and photographs of staff, at least one thing done by the children and ways in which people can get more involved. You might have a table or leaflet holder nearby to display your information leaflets and policies.

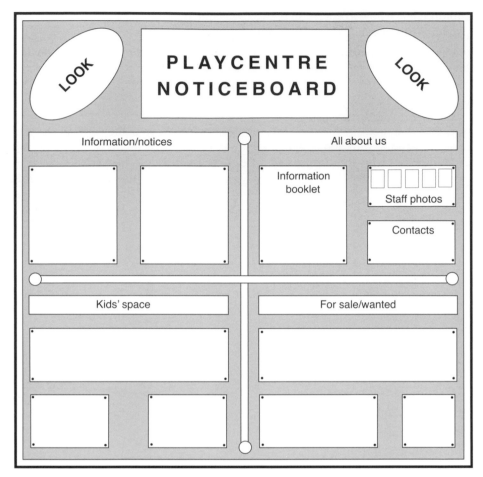

Your noticeboard can say a lot about your play setting. It should be well positioned (easily and often seen), well presented (clear and simple) and well maintained (frequently updated)

Leaflets and flyers

If your play setting has the resources it is well worth having an attractive leaflet or poster printed, preferably in colour and on reasonably good paper. This could be the general information leaflet you give to children and parents or it could be a simpler, bright promotional leaflet. You could advertise any free spaces you have or other services you provide. Is there a need to print it in more than one language?

Displays

Many libraries will allow groups to advertise their services on a week-by-week basis, providing a display stand free of charge. You just need to create your own display with posters and leaflets and ensure a plentiful supply of leaflets is available. You might also buy a display stand, which could be used at exhibitions or which another business might display for you (perhaps on a reciprocal basis).

Promotional give-aways

You can advertise your setting by standing in a prominent place, such as a shopping centre (always get permission first) and giving out leaflets – you can attract extra attention by giving away items such as helium balloons or by face painting. When people come over, you can tell them about your setting.

Open days

If you want people to come and see your setting (such as children who may want to use your setting or local organisations with whom you would like to work), an open day gives them hands-on experience and you can show off the setting in all its glory. You will need to make sure you have extra staff employed to talk to the people who attend and also to maintain normal supervision levels.

Local media

This is a very useful medium for reaching many people in your local area. If you want to advertise for more children or new staff members, you can pay for an advert in the local newspaper or on the local radio. The local media are always very interested to promote stories of local interest and this will publicise your setting without your having to pay. If you can think of an interesting 'angle' for the story, the media are more likely to highlight it – for example, 'Local play centre needs playful staff!' or 'Children enjoy their brand new play equipment!'

Other businesses and groups

You might agree with another organisation to promote each other – perhaps you each stock the other's leaflets or you each display the other's poster. This can be a good way of making initial links and relationships with other businesses.

Children's information service

Most local authority areas now have a Children's Information Service (CIS), which provide local childcare information. They can help to market your play setting to prospective customers in your area. Go to the national CIS website at www.childcarelink.gov.uk or freephone 08000 960296.

Creating links with others

Children and their families may have contact with many people outside the play setting who contribute to their education, well-being and support. There may be teachers, doctors and other healthcare workers, police, social workers, religious leaders and advice centre or ethnic minority and community organisations. Your play setting is part of the network of community services in your local area. If all the members of that network know about each other – what each service provides, how to make contact or be referred, what is on offer and who can benefit – they will be in a good position to meet the needs of the children with whom they come into contact. For example:

- a teacher might identify a health problem and refer the child and family to the doctor
- a community police officer might identify a care or play need and refer to a play setting
- a playworker might hear about a problem a family is having in receiving the right welfare benefits and can refer them to an advice centre.

Networking – what are the advantages?

By networking, you can find out about mutual benefits from working together with other local organisations and create new friends and allies for your play setting. You might be given special offers on the products supplied from some groups. You might be able to promote each other's businesses and services. You might find out information that helps you to do a better job or provide an improved service.

Benefits for other organisations

You can help other groups, businesses and organisations to see the benefits of working with you by having a clear idea yourself of what networking will offer the other party.

Benefits might include:

- a chance to build relationships with children and young people in the local area
- the chance to give funding to a positive cause
- an opportunity to consult with children
- a creative opportunity to change the dynamic of the local area by developing play opportunities and environments for children
- different knowledge and skills, and perhaps a new way of approaching work.

ACTIVITY   Making local links

1 Choose three groups or organisations in your local area (could be a school, Woodcraft Folk, Brownies or a local shop, for example).
2 Think of one way in which working together could benefit your play setting.
3 Think of one way in which working with you could benefit the other organisation.

For example: Making links with your local fruit shop. You and the children might benefit from reduced price healthy fruit and vegetables for your snacks and cooking activities. The shop, in return, might be able to display some promotional leaflets at your noticeboard.

Methods of working cooperatively

Methods range from the simple:

- telephone calls now and again
- visits now and again
- attending meetings now and again

to the more involved:

- joining each other's management committees
- holding networking meetings.

Identifying organisations and individuals for networking

You may have already identified a group with whom you would like to make contact. Or you may have decided that networking would benefit the setting and you now need to choose a group (or some groups) with whom to network. The list of possibilities is just about endless, but could include:

- local schools
- local shops
- doctor's surgery

- community centre
- cultural centre
- other play organisations
- playwork training providers
- other business with related (or unrelated) services
- local authority (such as fire service, parks department, childcare development team, road safety department, police, social services, play development and so on)
- children's centres.

CASE STUDY | Play exchange!

Our manager, Nishma, suggested at a team meeting that we could have an 'exchange' with another after school club. She thought it would be a good way of bringing new ideas into the club (and, of course taking some of our good ideas to the other club!) She called Fields Kids' Club, which is about three miles away. At first, they were a bit unsure, but after a week or so, they came back and said 'Yes'. Nishma arranged the swap for the following week – with me being the first guinea pig!

It was a bit nerve-racking when I first walked in, but the children and staff were very friendly and soon had me playing 'Dodge ball', making masks and helping the children make fruit kebabs. And that was just in the first hour! We then played 'Hide and seek' (or '40 40 in' as they called it) and 'Silly musical statues' where you had to be in a 'silly' position when the music stopped! It was hard to keep still for laughing!

So I had all these new ideas to bring back to our club. I also had the chance to show a new game to some children who were keen for me to play with them (it was actually an old game from my childhood – but it was new to them). I also brought back an excellent idea for emphasising the ground rules – a member of staff asked an older child to read a younger child (who had sworn at another child) the rules and especially the one about, 'speak nicely to each other'.

I got the chance to tell our staff about the new ideas at the next staff meeting. We added some of the ideas into our timetable. In fact, making fruit kebabs turned into a whole fortnight's focus on 'fun food for health'. A member of staff from the other club came to ours and he was really funny, and the children loved him. We have an arrangement to swap every fortnight (different staff) and it has really worked – there is a new buzzy vibe to our club, the children love the new ideas and the staff are more inspired. And we have all made new friends. The children meet each other during the holiday playschemes – we arrange joint trips to places like the icerink and the seaside. And both staff groups meet in the park on Saturdays for a picnic and a game of frisbee! I would recommend a play exchange to any playwork setting.

Making contact

If you and your colleagues or management agree to make contact with a local group or business, think carefully about what you are going to say. Be clear what the benefits are for both parties and the level of involvement you are suggesting. Is it a friendly chat to discuss possible ways of working together? Is it a business proposal, which may need to be put in writing and sent to a named person? Whichever it is, a clear, friendly approach is more likely to get positive results. Outline your organisation's main aims and ethos. Discuss initial ideas for joint working. It is useful to arrange a meeting, so that issues can be discussed further.

If another group makes the first contact with you, you might not yet feel prepared to discuss joint working. If that is the case, have a friendly chat, tell the other person when you are likely to reply and bring it up at the next team meeting. Discuss with the team what the benefits could be, if any, of working with that particular group. You might agree that it is a good opportunity to network. Or you may decide that the amount of time or effort needed would be excessive. Whatever your decision, even if you have not yet decided, do get back in contact within the stated time.

ACTIVITY   **Play links**

Find out about any other play organisations in your local area. Can you get together to share ideas, resources, social events or perhaps celebrate National Play Day? Do you have a local play association or umbrella group with shared aims and interests? Which of your local authority departments is responsible for supporting or promoting play? Does your local authority have a play policy?

Pros and cons of networking

Although there are many advantages to joint working (see earlier), some potential pitfalls may arise. It is worth thinking about these in advance, so that you can attempt to avoid the problems and so smooth the way for a good working relationship. Difficulties that may arise and some ways of working them out, are shown in the following table.

Difficulties of joint working	Possible ways of working them out
Disagreements about the direction the joint work is taking	• Agree the aims and parameters for the work, put in writing and copy to key people • Key people meet regularly to ensure everyone is happy with the direction
Key people do not work well together	• Have a joint working agreement in writing • Make attempts to improve the relationship – try to notice and comment on the positive, rather than the negative • If necessary, change the link person
People not doing what they said they would do One organisation doing more work than the other	• State clearly the roles and responsibilities within the joint working agreement • Write minutes or notes for every meeting and call and send to all key people • Discuss the project regularly to ensure other people's commitment

Maintaining contact

If you become involved in a joint initiative, the other people need to know that you are committed to it. You can reassure them by keeping in contact by phone or email. You could agree to contact one another within an agreed period, such as once a week, fortnight or month. Good working relationships can also be developed through:

- good, clear communication (including listening, assertiveness and keeping in touch)
- an open, honest approach
- a willingness to try out new ideas
- a flexible approach
- being reliable (doing what you say you will do, on time, and timely arrival at meetings)
- showing trust for your networking partner.

Summary

Developing your play setting helps you to adapt and improve according to the needs of the users and potential new users. Making changes can also be stimulating for the staff and helps avoid stagnation of your service. You can promote your setting in order to create new business or to promote the value of play for the children in your area. Another way of promoting your service is to create links with other local organisations or groups – with a bit of creative thinking, and a little effort, you can work with others in a way that will benefit both groups.

Reference

Kapasi, H. (1992) *Asian Children Play*. PLAY-TRAIN.

Further reading

Brown, F. (ed.) (2003) *Playwork Theory and Practice*. Open University Press. (See Chapter 10 'It's not what you know, it's who you know!' by Jackie Martin.)

Community Matters, (2004) *Getting Your Message Across*. www.communitymatters.org.uk or call 020 7837 7887. Also produces many useful community documents and runs an advice line for community groups.

Petrie, P. (1994) *Play and Care*. HMSO. (See Chapter 3 on clients, customers and users and Chapter 6 on evaluation.)

Surestart, *Marketing your Childcare Business*, available at www.surestart.gov.uk.

Websites

For information on positive, non-stereotypical resources:
The Festival Shop: www.festivalshop.co.uk or tel: 0121 444 0444.
Letterbox Library: www.letterboxlibrary.com or tel: 0207 503 4801.

Glossary

admissions policy printed and published guidelines that a play setting devises to decide who gets priority if the setting is full and there is a waiting list

adolescence the physical, social, emotional and psychological changes that take place during puberty

adulteration inappropriate intervention into children's play by an adult for reasons other than facilitating or supporting play

assertiveness the confidence to express opinions clearly while mindful of the feelings and expectations of others

behaviour management monitoring and intervention designed to produce positive behaviour

body language *see* 'non-verbal communication'

Braille written language for the blind using raised symbols and characters

bullying frightening, threatening or hurting someone through verbal, physical, emotional, sexual, racist or discriminatory behaviour

child-centred environment a place where children are respected as individuals with rights and opinions and where their needs are the starting point for planning and provision of services.

cognition the ability to acquire knowledge by thinking, understanding and solving problems

confidential information information which must be kept secure and only shared with people who possess the right to access it

conservation the stage of a child's development when they are no longer dependent on visual and sensory perception and begin to use rational thinking

COSHH Control of Substances Hazardous to Health – regulation of a range of materials which could be harmful – including cleaning materials and some paints and varnish

disabled the perceived result of an impairment

discrimination any sort of behaviour that is more or less favourable to a person or group of people based on their group identity, such as their skin colour, religion, gender, etc.

emotional abuse the malicious withholding of love, attention and stimulation as well as associated physical care from a child

equal opportunities providing people with the same chances regardless of their background

ethos the values, spirit and approach of a setting

hazard something that could cause harm to someone

hygiene the theory and application of health and cleanliness

latency period a term used by Freud to describe middle childhood as being a period when strong sexual feelings experienced in preschool years are repressed until puberty

LSCB Local Safeguarding Children Board

medical model of disability the view that a disabled person's impairments can be 'fixed' with medical procedures

named (key) worker someone who takes special responsibility for the welfare of a newly arrived child and forms a primary relationship with that child on an ongoing professional basis

national childcare standards a list of things that must be in place in every registered childcare setting that inspectors will check when they visit

nature the element of a child's development influenced by inherited genes

neglect the denial of a child's right to food, warmth, medical care or other aspects of care including supervision to ensure that they are not exposed to danger

non-transmittable diseases illnesses and conditions that cannot be passed on from one child to another

non-verbal communication any communication not conveyed by speaking (often called 'body language')

NSPCC National Society for the Prevention of Cruelty to Children

nurture the element of a child's development influenced by social and environmental factors

observation a key playwork skill involving the monitoring (and sometimes recording) of a child's play behaviour or development

open-access setting play setting where children can come and go independently and can choose to stay as long or short a time as they please

peer group people with one or more similar factors that draw them together as a group, such as age, interests, or social status

physical abuse any form of actual injury inflicted (or knowingly not prevented) by a person having care of the child

play a broad term open to a variety of interpretations that are discussed in Chapter 1

play cue a signal from a child indicating a desire to play

play cycle a description of the play process devised by Gordon Sturrock and Perry Else

play drive children's natural impulse to play

play frame a physical (for example, a fence) or imaginary (for example, rules of a game) boundary that contains play

play return a response to a play cue

play space the physical environment (building, park, yard), as well as the mood and appeal of a place where play occurs

playwork the provision of environments and opportunities for children's play and an approach to working with children that puts children's play at the centre of the work

playworker someone whose job it is to be first and foremost of service to children at play. Playworkers often have other responsibilities such as childcare responsibilities in after-school clubs or holiday playschemes

prejudice a negative judgement or opinion formed without reason or experience

puberty the physical changes necessary for a child to become a biologically mature adult

punitive imposing punishment

quality assurance scheme a rigorous process of assessment against a set of quality standards

racism behaviour, usually an abuse of power, based on racial distinctions

reward the provision of a positive response or incentive to a child displaying positive behaviour

RIDDOR Reporting of Injuries, Diseases and Dangerous Occurrences Regulations

senses how the body recognises its external environment (through sight, sound, touch, taste, smell and movement)

sexual abuse the exploitation of children to meet the sexual demands of adults

SMART a format for focusing on and achieving priorities (**S**pecific, **M**easurable, **A**chievable, **R**ealistic, **T**ime bound)

social model of disability the view that society (not an individual impairment) disables a person

Spieltrieb Friedrich Schiller's 18th-century term for 'play drive'

zone of proximal development the area between a child's existing abilities and what they could achieve (particularly with external stimulation)

Appendix: Useful contacts

Some organisations supporting play and playwork

4Children (formerly Kids' Clubs Network)
City Reach, 5 Greenwich View Place, London E14 9NN
Tel: 020 7512 2112
Website: www.4children.org.uk
Provides ideas, support and advice on aspects of play and childcare.

Children's Play Council
Tel: 020 7843 6016
Email: cpc@ncb.org.uk
Website: www.ncb.org.uk.cpc
Aims to raise awareness of the importance of play and to stimulate better play opportunities and services.

Children's Play Information Service
National Children's Bureau, 8 Wakley Street, London EC1V 7QE
Tel: 020 7843 6303 Fax: 020 7843 6007
Website: www.ncb.org.uk/library/cpis
Information service for all matters relating to play, playwork and playwork training, including a comprehensive library and resource centre.

Fair Play for Children
35 Lyon Street, Bognor Regis PO21 1YZ
Tel: 0845 330 7635
Email: fairplay@arunet.co.uk
Website: www.arunet.co.uk/fairplay/home.htm
Fair Play for Children campaigns for children's right to play and provides information, advice and resources for those working with children in a play setting.

Free Play Network
66 York Road, New Barnet, Hertfordshire EN5 1LJ
Tel/Fax: 020 8440 9276
Website: www.freeplaynetwork.org.uk
Promotes the need for better play opportunities for children.

International Association for the Child's Right to Play (IPA)
Website: www.ipaworld.org/home.html
International association promoting the child's right to play, with members in over 50 countries.

Kids (formerly Kidsactive)
6 Aztec Row, Berners Road, London N1 0PW
Tel: 020 7359 3635
Website: www.kids.org.uk
Promotes and supports inclusive play, childcare and education for disabled children – including managing adventure playgrounds.

London Play

Units F6–F7 89/93 Fonthill Road, London N4 3JH
Tel/Textphone: 020 7272 2464
Fax: 020 7272 7670
Website: www.londonplay.org.uk
Comprehensive newsletter, website with links and contacts, quality assurance scheme
– very useful contact, not just for Londoners!

National Association of Toy and Leisure Libraries

London Office: 68 Churchway, London NW1 1LT
Tel: 020 7255 4600 Fax: 020 7255 4602
Website: www.natll.org.uk

National Playbus Association

Brunswick Court, Brunswick Square, Bristol BS2 8PE
Tel: 0117 916 6580 Fax: 0117 916 6588
Email: playbus@playbus.org.uk
Promotes the use of mobile community resources around the UK.

National Playing Fields Association

Stanley House, St Chad's Place, London WC1X 9HH
Tel: 020 7833 5360 Fax: 020 7833 5365
Website: www.npfa.org.uk
Aims to preserve and develop recreational and play facilities.

Play Scotland

Midlothian Innovation Centre, Pentlandfield, Roslin, Midlothian EH25 9RE
Tel: 0131 440 9070 Fax: 0131 440 9071
Website: www.playscotland.org
Works at a strategic level to promote the child's right to play throughout Scotland.

Play Wales

Baltic House, Mount Stuart Square, Cardiff CF10 5FH
Tel: 029 2048 6050
Website: www.playwales.org.uk
The national organisation for children's play in Wales. Useful website.

PlayBoard

59–65 York Street, Belfast BT15 1AA
Tel: 028 9080 3380 Fax: 028 9080 3381
Website: www.playboard.org
The lead agency for children's play in Northern Ireland.

Playlink

72 Albert Palace Mansions, Lurline Gardens, London SW11 4DQ
Tel: 020 7720 2452
Website: www.playlink.org.uk
Supports local authorities, organisations and groups that want to create the best
possible play opportunities for children and young people.

Useful contact for all those working with children

Children's Information Service
Every local authority area now has a Children's Information Service (CIS)
Website: www.childcarelink.gov.uk
Freephone: 08000 96 02 96

Council for Disabled Children
8 Wakley Street, London EC1V 7QE
Tel: 020 7843 1900 Fax: 020 7843 6313
Website: www.ncb.org.uk/cdc
Forum for the discussion, development and dissemination of policy and practice issues
for disabled children and young people and those with special educational needs.

Daycare Trust
21 St George's Road, London SE1 6ES
Tel: 020 7840 3350 Fax: 020 7840 3355
Website: www.daycaretrust.org.uk
Promotes affordable and quality childcare. On hand to advise parents, providers,
employers and policy makers.

National Children's Bureau
8 Wakley Street, London EC1V 7QE
Tel: 020 7843 6000 Fax: 020 7278 9512
Website: www.ncb.org.uk

OFSTED
OFSTED, Alexandra House, 33 Kingsway, London WC2B 6SE
Tel: 020 7421 6800
Website: www.ofsted.gov.uk

Save the Children
Tel: 020 7012 6400 Fax: 020 7012 6963
Website: www.savethechildren.org.uk
Save the Children fights for children in the UK and around the world who suffer from
poverty, disease, injustice and violence.

SCOPE
Tel: 020 7619 7100
Cerebral Palsy Helpline (freephone): 0808 800 3333
Website: www.scope.org.uk
Works with and supports people with cerebral palsy and related disabilities.

Scottish Out of School Care Network
Level 2, 100 Wellington Street, Glasgow G2 6DH
Tel: 0141 564 1284 Fax: 0141 564 1286
Supports school-aged play, care and learning in Scotland. Promotes, supports and
develops good-quality, sustainable out-of-school care.

Playwork training and education

There are now many different kinds of playwork training and education on offer from entry level through to degree courses and beyond. Here are some of the useful organisations and contacts that might be able to help point you in the right direction.

Common Threads Training Ltd
Tel: 07000 785215 Fax: 07000 780625
Email: info@commonthreads.co.uk
Training and publications for playworkers.

DYNAMIX
Dynamix Ltd, Unit 4d, Cwm Road, Hafod, Swansea SA1 2AY
Tel: 01792 466231
Website: www.seriousfun.demon.co.uk
Provides support and training in creative play, cooperation, circus skills and carnivals, environmental play, teamwork and communication.

Joint National Council for Training in Playwork (JNCTP)
Email: contact@jnctp.org.uk
Website: www.jnctp.org.uk
Exists to promote and support playwork education, training and qualifications that reflect the values of playwork.

National Network of Playwork Education and Training
There are nine national centres. To find out more about playwork education and training in your region, go to SkillsActive Playwork Unit's website for more information.
Tel: 020 7632 2000
Website: www.playwork.org.uk

PlayEducation
Email: played@dial.pipex.com
Website: www.playeducation.com
An independent playwork organisation set up to provide training, seminars and conferences covering practical playwork knowledge and scientific expertise.

PLAY-TRAIN
149–153 Alcester Road, Moseley, Birmingham B13 8JW
Tel: 0121 449 6665 Fax: 0121 449 8221
Website: www.playtrain.org.uk
Consultancy promoting both quantity and quality of creative play opportunities and offering a range of playwork training courses tailored to meet needs of the client.

Playwork Unit in SkillsActive
Castlewood House, 77–91 New Oxford Street, London WC1A 1PX
Tel: 020 7632 2000 Fax: 020 7632 2001
Website: www.playwork.org.uk
Supports playwork and playworkers in a range of ways. Extremely useful website.

UKplayworkers
Web-based discussion forum for everyone involved in or interested in play and playwork. To join UKplayworkers, log on to www.groups.yahoo.com/group/UKplayworkers and select 'Join group'.

Equalities

Commission for Racial Equality

St Dunstan's House 201–211 Borough High Street, London SE1 1GZ
Tel: 020 7939 0000 Fax: 020 7939 0004
In Scotland: Tel: 0131 524 2000 Fax: 0131 524 2001
In Wales: Tel: 02920 729 200 Fax: 02920 729 220
Website: www.cre.gov.uk
Tackles racial discrimination and promotes racial equality.

Disability Discrimination Act

Website: www.disability.gov.uk
Information and ideas for providing equal opportunities for children and staff who
are disabled.

Equal Opportunities Commission

Arndale House, Arndale Centre, Manchester M4 3EQ
Tel: 0845 601 5901 Fax: 0161 838 8312
Website: www.eoc.org.uk
Working to eliminate sex discrimination in Britain.

Health, safety and well-being

Child Accident Prevention Trust

4th Floor, Cloister Court, 22–26 Farringdon Lane, London EC1R 3AJ
Tel: 020 7608 3828 Fax: 020 7608 3674
Website: www.capt.org.uk
National UK charity committed to reducing the number of children and young people
killed, disabled and seriously injured as a result of accidents.

ChildLine

Tel: 020 7650 3200
Fax: 020 7650 3201
Children and young people call: 0800 1111 Textphone: 0800 400 222
Website: www.childline.org.uk

Health and Safety Executive

Tel: 0845 345 0055
Website: www.hse.gov.uk
Ensures risks to people's health and safety at work are properly controlled.
Information on all aspects of health and safety, including risk assessment. COSHH
and RIDDOR. Many free leaflets.

KIDSCAPE

2 Grosvenor Gardens, London SW1W 0DH
Tel: 020 7730 3300 Fax: 020 7730 7081
Helpline for parents, guardians or concerned relatives and friends of bullied children:
0845 205 204 (A child with bullying problems should call ChildLine on 0800 1111.)
Website: www.kidscape.org.uk
Proactive in the prevention of bullying. Publish anti-bullying booklets.

NSPCC

Helpline: 0808 800 5000

Textphone helpline: 0800 056 0566 (English only)

Welsh helpline: 0808 100 2524 – Open Monday–Friday 10am–6pm

Asian helpline:

- Bengali: 0800 096 7714
- Gujarati: 0800 096 7715
- Hindi: 0800 096 7716
- Punjabi: 0800 096 7717
- Urdu: 0800 096 7718

Asian helpline in English: 0800 096 7719

All of these lines are open Monday–Friday 11am–7pm

Website: www.nspcc.org.uk

Royal Society for the Prevention of Accidents (RoSPA)

RoSPA House, Edgbaston Park, 353 Bristol Road, Edgbaston, Birmingham B5 7ST

Tel: 0121 248 2000 Fax: 0121 248 2001

Website: www.rospa.org.uk

Information, resources, materials and equipment

The following organisations are just a few of those offering non-discriminatory play materials, books and guidance. Many larger manufacturers and distributors of toys and equipment such as Galt and NES Arnold also supply a good range.

Child's Play

Ashworth Road, Bridgemead, Swindon, Wiltshire SN5 7YD

Tel: 01793 616286

Website: www.childs-play.com

Multicultural books, toys and games, available through mail order.

Community Insight

The Pembroke Centre, Cheney Manor, Swindon SN2 2PQ

Tel: 01793 512 612 Fax: 01793 431 773

Website: www.communityinsight.co.uk

Books for trainers and practitioners in childcare and play issues.

Development Education Centre

998 Bristol Road, Selly Oak, Birmingham B29 6LE

Tel: 0121 472 3255

Email: info@tidec.org

Website: www.tidec.org

The Festival Shop

53 Poplar Road, King's Heath, Birmingham B14 7AG

Tel: 0121 440 0444

Website: www.festivalshopco.uk

Multi-faith books, posters and educational resources, including the multi-faith calendar. Call or visit website for free catalogue of resources.

Scrap Store Network

Website: www.home-education.org.uk/scrap.htm

A list of children's scrapstores in the UK, with contact details.

SHAP Working Party on World Religion in Education
PO Box 38580, London SW1P
Tel: 020 7898 1494
Website: www.shap.org
Produces the famous SHAP Calendar of Religious Festivals and other publications.

Woodcraft Folk
13 Ritherdon Road, London SW17 8QE
Tel: 020 8672 6031 Fax: 020 8767 2457
Website: www.woodcraft.org.uk
A registered educational charity. Publishes books and other resources.

Working Group Against Racism in Children's Resources (WGARCR)
Unit 34, Eurolink Business Centre, 49 Effra Road, London SW2 1BZ
Tel/Fax: 020 7501 9992
Website: www.wgarcr.org.uk

Additional sources of information and advice

Children in Scotland (Clann An Alba)
Princes House, 5 Shandwick Place, Edinburgh EH2 4RG
Tel: 0131 228 8484 Fax: 0131 228 8585 Textphone: 0131 22 22 439
Website: www.childreninscotland.org.uk
The national agency for voluntary, statutory and professional organisations and
individuals working with children and their families in Scotland.

Children in Wales (Plant yng Nghymru)
Children in Wales, 25 Windsor Place, Cardiff CF10 3BZ
Tel: 029 2034 2434 Fax: 029 2034 3134
Website: www.childreninwales.org.uk
The national umbrella children's organisation in Wales.

Children's Legal Centre
University of Essex, Wivenhoe Park, Colchester, Essex CO4 3SQ
Tel: 01206 872 644 Fax: 01206 874 026
Education Law Advice Line: 0845 456 6811
Website: www.childrenslegalcentre.com
National charity concerned with law and policy affecting children and young people.

Department for Education and Skills (DfES) Childcare Unit
Caxton House, Tothill Street, London SW1H 9NA
Tel: 0870 000 2288
Website: www.dfes.gov.uk

Index